Tattooed In The Cradle

The SEARCH Foundation
July 1993

Published in the United States by:

The SEARCH Foundation,
1631 Fort Washington Avenue
Maple Glen, Pennsylvania 19002

Cover Design & Book Layout:

Karl A. Benner
Gottshall & Associates, Inc.
Hatfield, PA 19440

Library of Congress Cataloging in Publication Data:
ISBN 0-9636686-0-9

Satterly, Lamont
Tattooed in the Cradle

TATTOOED IN THE CRADLE

The Healing Journey from Family
to Spiritual Wholeness

LAMONT R. SATTERLY

The SEARCH Foundation
1631 Fort Washington Avenue
Maple Glen, Pa. 19002

TABLE OF CONTENTS

Introduction

A Personal Word

SECTION I

SECTION II

SECTION III

References

Tattooed in the Cradle is a book written for everyone.

A bold statement of this type could only be made about two significant subjects—family and religion. This book speaks of both as it discusses the powerful impact of the family legacy on the many and diverse ways in which individuals experience God. In this sense, *Tattooed in the Cradle* addresses both therapeutic and spiritual issues.

Everyone, regardless of birth or upbringing, has a family legacy. Handed down from generation to generation, the legacy reflects the teachings and values of the family system. It is a powerful force, designed to model the young in a fashion which will accurately and positively point to the beliefs of the preceding generations. The styles of holiday celebrations and the wisdom of saving money are mirrored in the legacy. Choosing to further one's education or remain in the family business are legacy issues. The practice of a religious faith or the manner of disciplining children both reveal the teachings of the legacy.

Children are the most susceptible to the teachings of their parents and grandparents; they are also the most vulnerable. Well-meaning and loving parents are charged with the responsibility of raising their children to demonstrate the pride in their own legacy. "Your grandmother would turn over in her grave if she knew about your behavior" is not some ridiculous statement made by a disappointed parent to a naughty child. Rather, feeling that he or she has let down the legacy teachings on raising children, it is an announcement of relief by an adult child.

The theme of this book focuses on two distinct issues:

(1) The impact of the family legacy on personal identity; and, *(2) The many ways in which that identity confuses and blocks loving or joyful relationships with God.*

As children listen with great respect and trust to the voices of the previous generations, they are daily shaping their own sense of self-worth and identity. Unfortunately, human behavior and frustration being all that it is leads to harsh criticisms and shaming of children. In turn, the children internalize many of the legacy teachings, leading to a multitude of problems such as guilt, self-condemnation, and inadequacy.

Since parents are viewed as gods by their children, the belief system put in place during childhood is all powerful, becoming virtually deified. This being the case, there is little that can be said to counter the early teachings of parents, even when those beliefs lead to problems in relationships or life's choices.

Tattooed in the Cradle discusses the enormous religious and spiritual pain which occurs when adult children are unable to harmonize legacy teachings of identity with loving and grace-filled messages from their religion and spirituality. Self-condemnation and judgment, learned through inter-generational teachings, always holds more power than any words of peace and promise from scripture or prayer.

The first part of this book defines the family legacy in detail. The fact that families seem to divide themselves into legacy types is discussed in the second section. Discussing the power of the legacy on religion and spirituality is the focus of Section Three, accompanied with some thoughts and direction for finding a path from spiritual pain toward spiritual healing.

Tattooed in the Cradle, then, is a book which focuses on the journey from spiritual pain toward spiritual wholeness. In order to understand how people find themselves in such a religious or spiritual dilemma, it is critical to understand the concepts and power of the family legacy. This is a book of connections: a joining of the therapeutic and the spiritual. It speaks to people in a language they can understand, a voice of common experience. No one can read of the legacy and not relate to it. Equally, those who read this book with an open mind will quickly find their own universal experience of spiritual pain.

To move from points of "stuckness" in life to avenues of healing is a lifelong journey. This book has been written to help those who wish to understand their past, and at the same time, discover new ways for healing in their relationship with God and others. It is, indeed, a pilgrimage offered to all on the path toward wholeness.

A PERSONAL WORD

Writing a book is hard work.

I discovered this shortly after I typed the first ten pages of the manuscript. It calls for discipline and a highly structured mind. I tend to have neither. It also asks for an unusual amount of skill with vocabulary and grammar. Unfortunately, those subjects were not my best in school.

Nevertheless, I have written *Tattooed in the Cradle* because I have something to say that I truly believe in. I have already learned that I am not going to make a lot of money writing a book. In truth, I could probably make more hourly selling milkshakes at McDonald's. Therefore, this book is written not for the money, but for the sheer need I have to share what I have learned from listening to people for the past quarter of a century.

A book about family legacy is nothing new. There are probably hundreds written about systems and family theory by now. But a book about the relationship between family legacy and spirituality is a different breed. It has grown out of years of working with the dying—those persons who are taking the greatest journey of their lives and who no longer need to lie about anything. Dying people are honest; they have little to lose.

Working as a hospice chaplain has given me entry into the lives of hundreds of dying patients and their families. It was sitting bedside with whispering patients which opened the door for my understanding of spiritual pain, the primary concept presented in this book. I marveled at good and generous people, who in the last days of their lives, talked of their "badness." There were times when I walked to my car with my head filled with the self-condemning words I had just heard from a patient who had spent over seventy years as a church leader. The privilege of working with the dying has taught me an enormous amount about living. As Stephen Levine says, "work with the dying is always work on the self."

Not only have I learned of spiritual pain from dying people, I have wallowed in it myself. Therefore, I suppose this book has been written more for myself than for others. My life has twisted down a series of footpaths and trails that I never could have predicted in the early years of my childhood. It has, however, led to life changing discoveries and lessons for which I am eternally grateful.

A PERSONAL WORD

As you read *Tattooed in the Cradle,* I hope that you will recognize parts of yourself. The case studies are all well disguised, keeping in mind the incredible fragileness of each one of us. Nevertheless, we all live within each other and you may find yourself on several different pages of the book. When you do, smile and give thanks that others are as you are, and perhaps together we can create a more joyful world.

This book is not a scholarly journal; it is rather a sharing of discoveries in a simple and straight-forward method of writing. It is my deep hope that while you may not agree with what I have written, you will clearly understand it. I write as I speak and make no apologies for my simple style. First and foremost, I am a teacher and that will come through in some of the ways in which I have repeated myself. Secondly, I have tried to write with great clarity so that anyone who reads this book will have no doubts as to what I am trying to say.

Ultimately, it is my hope that people will be helped by this book. I believe that we are here for one another, to try to lighten each other's load, and to find ways to bring peace to a hurting and frightened world. This book is my way to share what I have learned with you. I have tried to write very personally, as though you are on the receiving end of a rather lengthy letter. Don't be disturbed by my references to my own family; I know them best and have their permission.

It is critical to close this personal word with some expressions of deep thanks. In reading countless other books, I never knew before how important this paragraph is. Let me give my deepest thanks to my wife, Sue, who read every chapter with a loving and helpful eye, taking great care not to offend me with her gentle remarks and suggestions, and who made this book possible. Thanks also to Doris Kettells, a friend and scholar who kept after my grammar, and whose expressions of integrity I have always admired. And to Luanne Fisher, one of the busiest and most capable friends I have, for her time and suggestions in reading the early manuscript. Finally, to my mother and father who encouraged me to write for years; thank you for believing in me.

Lamont R. Satterly
July 1, 1993

To Sue,
my mate and my finest teacher.

THE FAMILY LEGACY

*"We are all tattooed in our cradles
with the beliefs of our tribe;
the record may seem superficial,
but it is indelible.*

*You cannot educate a man
wholly out of the superstitious fears
which were implanted in his imagination,
no matter how utterly his reason may reject them."*

**Oliver Wendell Holmes
1872**

CHAPTER I

THE LEGACY

*"And speaking of horns that are just a bit queer,
I'll bring back a very odd family deer;*

*A father, a mother, two sisters, a brother
Whose horns are connected, from one to the other,*

*Whose horns are so mixed they can't tell them apart,
Can't tell where they end and can't tell where they start!*

*Each deer's mighty puzzled. He's never yet found,
if his horns are hers, or the other way 'round."*

Dr. Seuss

*"If you want to know what that girl's gonna be like,
look at her mother."*

Dad

*"I can't help detesting my relatives.
I suppose it comes from the fact
that none of us can stand other people
having the same faults as ourselves."*

Oscar Wilde

THE LEGACY

A BOY AND HIS POT

Once upon a time there was a husband and wife who loved each other very much. The one sad place in both of their hearts was an empty spot that could only be filled with a child. They had a longing for a child, someone to love and to be with them in their older years. Each night they prayed to the gods for a child, promising to give a part of all they owned in gratitude should the gods see fit to answer their prayer.

Months passed into years while the husband went to work each day, cutting down small trees in the forest. Using a small saw, he would cut the trees into logs and then take them to a nearby lumber mill in exchange for coins. His wife kept a tidy house, trying to make each evening a cozy invitation to her husband as he wearily came home from the forest. Even though they were both very tired, they still remembered their nightly prayers to the gods. Their longing for a small child remained.

And then one day the wife gave birth to a son.

When the child was born, the husband and wife were overcome with thanksgiving. They named their son John, and keeping their promise, they gave a part of all their possessions to the gods.

Within a few months, however, their joy turned to sorrow as John's head began to change shape. Bit by bit, it began to sink in from the top and spread out at the sides, until it looked like a rather large pot. Although his parents were very upset, John didn't seem to mind at all since he didn't understand he should look differently than he did.

As time passed, people in the village grew accustomed to John's "pot-head," and walked by with scarcely a glance. In fact, some people even dropped small items in the top of his head, as if it were a type of wastebasket.

At first John didn't even mind people littering in the top of his head, until more important people in his life started to do the same thing. First, it was his grandmother, who dropped in a handkerchief and said to him, "John, this is my present to you so that you can keep all your tears inside, and no one will know when you want to cry. Every time you feel like crying, this hankie will dry away all your tears. Isn't that wonderful?"

John wasn't sure since he didn't know what was wrong with crying on the outside. It had seemed so natural to him to cry when he was sad, and he had cried since he was very small. But now, he wouldn't have to do that anymore.

One day, his father walked by and dropped in a very small handful of carrots. "Eat one of these every day, my son, and every day you will grow stronger so that people will know you're a real man."

"But you already said I am a man, father," protested John.

That's right, son, but it's very important that others think so, too. A real man lets other people KNOW that he is a real man. So be sure to eat a carrot every day."

John walked away, carrots swishing in the top of his head. He began to wonder to himself if something was wrong with him, just the way he was. After all, he now knew that he shouldn't cry if he was sad, and apparently he didn't look like a real man, whatever a real man looks like.

A few days later, his grandfather wandered by him when he was sitting under his favorite tree. As he dropped several small seeds into the top of his head, John looked up at him, puzzled. "There are just a very few seeds I have been saving for you. They are special because they will make you think like a real man. It's very important, you know, to think like a man. Everyone will know, then, that you are a real man."

"What do real men think like?" asked the boy.

"Oh, you know, common sense, logic, and stuff like that. You've probably watched your father think through his problems so carefully. That's how a real man thinks." His grandfather smiled and patted John on the back.

John shook his head and felt the carrots, seeds, and handkerchief rattle around inside. "I always thought my thinking was all right," he said to himself. And then he began to wonder if he was not a real man in his thinking, too. "Perhaps something really is wrong with me," he thought as he touched the top of his head.

It was only two days later when his mother came into his room while he was reading one of his favorite books. There was a very sad part in the middle of the book, and he had always cried as he read about the little dog getting lost. However, since he had his grandmother's handkerchief in his head, he didn't seem to be able to cry at the sad part anymore. He felt as if he wanted to, but the tears just wouldn't come.

"I have something special for you, John," his mother said to him as she reached into the pocket of her apron. She pulled out a small bag that had a very sweet smell to it. John looked at it as she put it over his head, dropping it in with the carrots, seeds, and handkerchief. *"This is a very important present from me to you,"* she smiled at him, *"It will help you to truly feel, deep down inside."*

"But, mother," he said, *"I already know how to truly feel."*

"Well, I know you do," she looked at him warmly, *"but this will help you feel things the way I do."*

"But, what's wrong with the way I feel things, Mother?" he asked her. *"I didn't know I was feeling things wrong."*

"It's not exactly that you feel things wrong," she told him, *"It's just that you are a man; and men don't know how to feel things deep inside. So, I'm giving you this special powder that ladies love to smell, to help you feel deep inside, like a woman. Women feel things so much better than men do, you know."*

As his mother left his room, John wondered again about himself. *"There surely must be something wrong with me,"* he told himself, *"I don't know how to cry like a man, think like a man, or look like a man; and now I'm supposed to feel deep inside like a woman."*

As John was thinking these thoughts to himself, the strangest thing began to happen. His head suddenly closed at the top, grew more narrow at the sides, and became perfectly normal. He stood up and looked in the mirror, feeling his head with its new shape.

Walking out of his room, everyone stared at him, first with surprise and then with delight. *"Are you all right?"* asked his father.

John shook his head and felt the carrots, seeds, handkerchief, and powder safely closed inside. Now he knew how to hide his tears, think like a man, look like a man, and feel deeply like a woman. Looking around the room, he took a deep breath, squared his shoulders like a real man, and said, *"I'm fine."*

Everyone in the family applauded.

The End

THE FUEL FOR THE FAMILY

Every family, regardless of the size, level of education, or culture, has a legacy. Somewhat like a fancy roadster, passed down from generation to generation, the family motors into current times, fueled by the legacy. It is impossible to escape, powerful in its grip, and constantly present. In many ways, the family legacy is an invisible presence, prepared to drive through every decade and avenue of life.

For those of you who like definitions, the legacy is the "values and traditions that pass down from generation to generation." It is the teaching of the parent to the child about the *stuff* of life—the important *stuff*. But who has taught the parent if not the grandparent? And who taught grandfather if not great-grandfather, and so on, ad nauseam? And then there is the question of who decides *the important stuff?* Well, no one really knows, but if it is contained in the legacy, it must be important.

The legacy is not any deep, psychological mystery. As you read about it, you will realize that you already know the legacy. Your legacy *grew* you; it sits on your shoulders as you read this book. For those who are interested in computers, it is your *programming*, a sort of software for life.

TAUGHT AND CAUGHT!

If you are somewhat suspicious of your parents and their motives, rest assured that most family members haven't the slightest idea what they're doing as they pass on the legacy. It is called simply "raising children." The legacy can be taught as a mother tucks her little one into bed at night. It can be caught at the supper table, or it can be modeled when guests come for an evening. Very few families, if any, carefully plan to teach the legacy.

When I was growing up, I remember my father coming home from work with stories from town about various happenings. We really never needed a weekly Gazette; we had my father. As I listened to these stories, and, in particular, my parent's conversation, I was learning their legacy. I never realized what was happening at the time, and, I suspect, neither did they. All in all, I still *caught* the legacy, almost every evening.

THE LEGACY

"Did you hear about Fred Wilson?" my father asked my mother one evening as we were eating supper.

"What about Fred Wilson?" My mother would always put her fork down when dad asked a "town" question.

"Lost his job," Dad would keep right on chewing. "Factory didn't get the contract."

"That's terrible," mother responded. "What are they going to do? Christmas is only a few weeks away." Christmas was a big event in our house, so it was natural my mother's thoughts would go there. But that's another legacy story.

"I don't know," he said, "but when you work in a factory, these things can happen. You know," he looked at me, "no contract, no work. No work, no pay." He chewed some more.

My mother was troubled. "Well, is the church going to do anything, you know, to help out? Christmas is an awful time to be out of work."

"I don't know," Dad answered, "all I know is that factory work is unpredictable. You never know what you can count on."

"Maybe some of us can help? Do you think we could do something?" My mother looked at my father, and then my sister and me.

"Well, I'm sure we can take up a collection. At least they won't have to starve. " My father looked at me since starving was one of my fears. "It's too bad, but when you don't have an education and end up in a factory, these things can happen."

If my father could reappear today and sit down to dinner with me, he would swear that he NEVER told me that I couldn't work in a factory. Nevertheless, I'm not totally stupid, nor was I as a young boy. I CAUGHT the legacy about vocation. Without saying so in a definitive teaching, my father taught me about the permissible jobs that would be available to me.

In most families, the legacy *is* caught more than taught. Often times, parents and grandparents give little thought to what they are saying and how it may be perceived by the children. Casual comments about the neighbors, the spending of money, or the town citizen discovered with his hand in the cash drawer all get caught by children. Remarks about the latest Hollywood scandal, or the school board member who had a bit too much wine, are heard and digested at the dinner table, right along with the chicken and potatoes.

Sometimes the legacy is taught as in the case of a father sitting down with his son to talk about "a real man," as happened to John in the beginning story, or as I found out when I was working as a pastor in a small, urban Baptist Church and discovered the accuracy of an old saying: Whenever three Baptists are together in a meeting, there are four opinions. This, by the way, is a true statement.

Baptists have an issue with baptism; for some it's theological, and for others, it's legacy. Somewhere along the way between the pilgrims and the Civil War, Baptists decided to immerse people as the proper, correct and only form of baptism. In an unfortunate sense, for many of those early Baptists, if you weren't immersed, you weren't "cleaned off" by God. In fact, you were downright in danger of the fires of hell.

While this teaching worked somewhat well in the rural 1800's, as time marched into the 1950's, suburbia was born. Along with this birth, Protestants began being less fussy about which church they attended, and more concerned with convenience. If the Methodist church was close, why not attend there? If the closest church was Presbyterian, what difference would it make? After all, "They're pretty much all the same." This created a major problem for the Baptists since a lot of visitors from the neighborhood, looking for a convenient place to worship, had not been immersed. Most Baptist church constitutions required immersion for church membership.

Not only did this cause difficulty for the church, it created some conflict of its own for those visitors who felt their own "sprinkled" baptism was acceptable to God, thank you.

As the pastor, it was my feeling that this small church needed more members. "Why not open our doors in a more inclusive way?" seemed like a good question to me. Therefore, I asked the church to consider a constitutional change to an "open" form of membership, accepting people as members who had not been immersed. Without realizing it, probably because my grandfather had taught me his legacy of openness in areas of theology, I had grabbed a tiger by the tail.

The church, in its attempt to grapple with this issue, started to divide. Unfortunately, it was not theology that split people; it was legacy. While I didn't realize it at the time, I learned that theology is seldom the dividing point in religion; instead it is legacy.

One man stood in my office screaming in my face that he would leave the church if this constitutional change occurred; and that furthermore, he would see to it that I never work in another Baptist Church!

"I'm going to tell you something my grandfather told me when I was only 11 years old," he pointed his finger at me. "We had gone down to the lake to chop the ice so that I could be baptized, by IMMERSION," his voice rose when he said the word. "After I was baptized, my grandfather wrapped a blanket around me and told me how proud he was of me that I was a true Baptist. I told him I was also a true Believer, repeating the words the preacher had said to me. I tell you, I never had seen my grandfather so mad. He whipped that blanket off me, grabbed an old umbrella from the back seat of his car, and beat the tar out of me. I don't know whether I was shivering from the cold or the beating, but he got his point across. When he was done hitting me, he threw the blanket back at me and said these words," the parishioner looked at me with great seriousness, "and I never forgot them: 'Son, it's more important that you're a Baptist than that you're a Christian. Never forget that! Jesus was probably a Baptist and so was John the Baptist. Why do you think he was named that? Don't you ever give me any of that Believer shit. You're a Baptist, and that's that!'"

By now, the man's face was beet red, and I wondered if I had a potential heart attack victim screaming in my office. As he finished his story, he wheeled on his heels and walked out of my study. I remember relating the story to my wife, shaking my head over his theological ignorance. Today I realize that he was simply being loyal to his grandfather, a loyalty that transcends logic, reason, and thought. He was being a true son to his family tradition and his legacy.

In this instance, and many others, parents take the time to *teach* the legacy. Sometimes it is something as simple as an issue of safety; "Don't go into the city at night. Bad things happen there." Other times, it is a direction for the future; "You *will* go to college; everyone in our family does." It can be very positive and affirming, "You're going to be a success and make our family proud." On the other hand, it can be abusive and defeating; "You will never amount to anything. You're just like your Uncle Bill; I don't know what we're going to do with you." Prejudice is also taught in the legacy; "Those people are dangerous; they'll steal you blind if you let them." Skin color, religious preferences, and geographical heritage can be an important part of legacy teachings, especially when ancestors have heard stories or experienced negative events that confirm suspicions.

Caught or *taught*, it doesn't really matter, because by the time children arrive at their middle teens they know clearly their own system's legacy. It is impossible to reach the age of adulthood without acquiring a legacy; the only question is, how does it play its way out in my life?

GEOGRAPHY, HOLIDAYS, AND MONEY

Legacy teachings surround us from our earliest years. They focus on virtually every important area of life from marriage to money. They explore religion and traditions, usually teaching us the "right" thoughts about life and values. Spoon-feeding of various teachings begins at a very young age and continues through adolescence. After a decade or so of family curriculum, children become young adults with a head full of the correct and proper way to do things.

The following situation seems to illustrate the power and magnitude of the family legacy in a variety of ways:

I first met Ken and Cindy several years ago when they called and asked for an appointment. An attractive couple in their late twenties, they were both quite articulate in expressing themselves regarding their needs and wants in the relationship. At the time we first talked, they had been engaged about four years. Both had good jobs, and Ken was working on his master's degree.

They had decided to enter therapy because Cindy was "tired of waiting" for a wedding. "It's been long enough," she said, "and I'm getting older. If he doesn't want to marry me, then he should say so. At least I can get on with my life."

"You know it's not that I don't want to marry you," Ken said as he took her hand. "It's just that we had decided we wanted to have some money set aside so we could buy a house, and you know I need to finish my master's classes."

Cindy yanked her hand away from Ken, "You mean YOU had decided we needed to do all these things before we get married. We don't need to have enough money for a house and a complete education before we get married. I don't mind living in an apartment and waiting for a house. Other couples do it all the time." She looked at me, "How many couples start out life with their own house?"

Learning a long time ago not to get caught in those questions, I looked at Ken. "My sister did," he answered her, "and so did my mom and dad. And look at how far ahead they are, just because they were willing to wait."

"That's the whole problem, right there," she said to me, "HIS family, and the way THEY do it, like it's the only way." She looked at Ken, "You know, maybe there are other ways to do things that are just as good as the way your family does things."

"But this has been our plan." He held up his fingers and began counting one by one, "First, we both graduate from college; second, a good job; third, my master's degree; fourth, a new house; fifth, we get married; and finally," he smiled at her, "you have little babies."

"I'm tired of your counting and I'm tired of waiting," Cindy hung her head as a few tears started trickling down the side of her cheek, "and I'm tired of hearing how your family does it."

Some families are very clear about their legacy. When it came to courtship and marriage, Ken had no problem whatsoever knowing exactly the right way to do things. It had been spelled out throughout his childhood, and, giving it more credence, he had watched it work in his family—it made sense to him. If your legacy makes intellectual sense to you, normally you will own it and carry it into adulthood. Why wouldn't Ken try to put his family's legacy into action since he had observed its wisdom and success? As he saw it, the only problem was convincing Cindy of that wisdom; no small task, I might add.

There are few areas in your life that have not been touched, at some level, by legacy. Even those unexplored pieces of your life probably have some family legacy stuffed into them. One of the most incredible discoveries for me has been how long we can wander through life without any awareness of the legacy and its power. For most of us, it's not until we bump into someone whose legacy is quite different that we really become aware of our own, or, when we find ourselves on the sunny-side-up part of a problem—as our life sizzles in the hot pan—that we even begin to examine our family legacy.

While your legacy may be poking its head into several areas of your life, there are a few places that seem common to most of us. Ken and Cindy have illustrated the manner in which a "life plan" can be an integral part of one's legacy. While some legacies have such a plan—very goal-oriented and spelled out with clarity—others do not.

I have found, however, that most legacies contain some fairly strong teachings about holidays, religion, money, geography, marriage, men, women, and education. In thinking of the computer concept of legacy, these subjects are each a software program of their own. When you find yourself in a situation, for example, where the value of a college education is discussed, you will simply insert the software disc marked education. Once inserted, you will be able to speak your opinion, which, of course, is probably a somewhat filtered opinion of the one you heard expressed by your parents and grandparents. The fascinating part of this is that we may not be aware that we are speaking legacy-talk at all. In fact, we are easily insulted if someone suggests we might be reflecting our family's values in a discussion. After all, you know, we all like to have our own individual opinions on subjects. Who wants to sound like a parrot?

GEOGRAPHY

A brief examination of cultural history shows a fascinating fact: it has only been in very recent times that children have moved away from their parents. Like many of us, I imagine that you thought your parents raised you to move away from home and support yourself. While that may have been indicated to you by various lectures and expectations, there is another part of parents which cannot bear to accept the departure of their children.

It was not that long ago, in the history of developed civilization, that our entire culture was rural. Children were born and raised on the farm with a powerful legacy regarding geography. Once raised and married, they would move onto the south forty acres, build a house, and stay put. They would live and work there, have children, and be an active part of the larger, extended family. When Mom and Dad got sick, or died, they would move into the big house. At that time, the cycle would begin all over again with their children. For generations, this was the legacy implant regarding geography.

One time I was attending a meeting with a group of elementary school teachers. One by one, they were sharing the stories of their childhood, explaining their own legacies as they understood them. A kindergarten teacher told a remarkable story about her family and the lack of permission for her to move away from home as she reached the age of adulthood. She was, she said, "an only child of parents, who themselves were only children." Claiming that she had felt responsible for her parents since she had been very small, she told the group, "They had no one else, you know. My father and mother needed me at home and, I guess, like the princess in the fairy stories, I needed to feel it was all right to marry and leave them." With tears streaming down her cheeks, she told the story of how, on her fiftieth birthday, she had moved into her own apartment. "I remember backing out of the driveway, my cat curled up beside me on the front seat, and my parents crying as they stood waving to me from the front porch. I felt so guilty."

This teacher's story is a powerful example of the legacy's strength. Geographic disloyalty, for this woman, was simply a move across town.

For most people, however, with the formation of the industrial society and the metropolitan scene, many of the rural attitudes have vanished. Nevertheless, the legacy of old regarding geography has maintained a certain hold—almost at a cellular level—as though children feel it in their bodies beginning at birth.

A young student of mine, age twenty-three, shared the following story with a class on Marriage and The Family:

"I live up the road in Frenchtown; that's about twenty minutes from here, up Route 72. And I'm the oldest in my family. I have three younger sisters and a brother. We live on my grandfather's farm, but my dad owns it now. He doesn't farm it anymore, but it's kind of neat living there.

"Anyway, a few weeks ago, my girlfriend and I saw this

really great apartment for rent over in Marsh Valley. We went to look at it and liked it a lot. I mean, it was something we could afford. So I told my Mom and Dad I was ready to move into my own place. After all, Marsh Valley is only about twenty-five minutes from home, you know.

"It was real crazy, though, because Mom and Dad sort of freaked out. I couldn't believe it, you know, because it's not like Marsh Valley is the end of the world, or something.

"So the weirdest thing happened. On Sunday afternoon, everybody came over to the farm. My Dad's two brothers, you know, my uncles, they came. My Mom's whole family was there, even my cousins. And dad called, like a family meeting, to discuss my moving out. Then, (can you believe this?) they took a vote which said they forbid me to move to Marsh Valley. Instead—and I didn't even know this—my Dad had found a place for me to live just down the road; it wasn't even a half mile away from the farm. My Mom said it was on the condition that I would come home every night for supper and I had to go to church with them on Sunday—same as always."

Some of you may shudder at reading this young woman's story, but it serves as a powerful example of the strength and direction of the legacy. In most families today, an attempt at control such as in this girl's life, would fail miserably. Nevertheless, there are always hidden "family meetings" with the aim at directing children into honoring the legacy. With all of our sophisticated, metropolitan ways, most of us are less than three generations from the farm. There is still power is the Geography Legacy.

HOLIDAYS

The most obvious legacy of all lies in the celebrations of our holidays. Virtually every family has developed certain traditions, ongoing in nature, which rise to the surface at holiday time. From the time most of us were very small, we were learning our family's way of *doing things* around each separate holiday. We were taught what foods belonged with the Fourth of July and what pies followed Thanksgiving dinner. Watching which relatives marched through the front door told us something about the holiday being celebrated. Grandparents arrived for Christmas dinner; cousins, for the Labor Day picnic. Sometimes your family traveled to your uncle's house for Easter while everyone stayed home on New Year's Day.

For many, the holidays never change. Now and then a relative dies, an aunt moves into a new house, or someone shows up with the same old food made with a slightly different recipe. The routine of each day might vary by fifteen minutes, but only with a very good reason. Ask any of your friends to describe Thanksgiving Day for you, beginning at 9:00 A.M., and you will discover the day is already pre-determined, including the time for dinner and which football game will be watched.

I grew up in a home where Thanksgiving dinner featured ham. Because it was an annual family event, I never knew there was anything out of the ordinary about it. I liked ham; it smelled good in the oven, and cold sandwiches are great with a glass of milk. Because it never came up in conversation, my childhood friends and I didn't compare Thanksgiving Day menus. As I look back on it now, I suppose they all ate turkey. Certainly we drew enough turkeys and pilgrims in school for me to be suspicious. Nevertheless, I thought ham was normal.

My first Thanksgiving as a married man, however, created some difficulty. Pushing the shopping cart through the aisle the week before Thanksgiving, my wife and I found that when ham meets turkey, there's a problem. Because of my own personality, we had turkey that first Thanksgiving together, but only I knew that it wasn't *really* Thanksgiving dinner we ate. Instead, it was simply a turkey dinner.

It is probably because holidays carry either cultural or religious packaging that they are such a powerful legacy issue. Between Madison Avenue, Santa Claus, and "Oh, Little Town of Bethlehem," Christmas conveys a strength of its very own. Even non-Christian traditions struggle, and many unsuccessfully, to avoid developing a Christmas legacy.

Holiday legacies are neither right nor wrong. As is the case in all legacies, they simply exist. The difficulties, as you will see in Chapter 3, occur when two family legacies come together with a loud bang.

MONEY

Sam was a 52 year old executive, highly motivated and rapidly rising to the top of his company. His income had recently topped the six figure amount, and life seemed only rosy and sweet. With his three children and wife, Sam lived in an executive development, about twenty minutes from his place of work. Sandy, his wife, worked as a teacher, allowing her the summer to enjoy their tennis courts and nearby golf course.

One night Sam called for an appointment to announce that he was resigning from his job. He had a "hunch," he told me, that his company might go under in the next several months.

"Just getting ahead in the game," he smiled at me. "I can devote myself full-time to finding some new work. It shouldn't be any problem."

Sam talked for a while about his concern for Sandy, who apparently wasn't taking this action lightly. "She's been totally unreasonable," Sam said, "and I told her that it doesn't show much faith in me. But then, she's always been overly worried about money and security. I tried to tell her that I can always support us, but that doesn't seem to give her any comfort. Any suggestions?"

During the next several months, Sam went from interview to interview with little success. There were many "possibilities," but in reality, his income level would have to drop drastically in order to make him an employable commodity in the job market. Soon he was into his savings, borrowing from the funds set aside for the children's college education.

Then an opportunity hopped up into Sam's lap—a soft ice cream franchise. With an up-front price of $25,000, it was a hefty leap; nevertheless, Sam jumped. Regardless of Sandy's hesitation and reluctance, Sam entered the ice cream business. It failed miserably.

Apparently Sam "forgot" to check the traffic pattern at the location of the ice cream stand. Cars could only turn one way at the intersection, making it difficult for the business to offer access to the entire highway. The parking lot was inadequate for traffic to turn around; and behind the stand was an unattractive, weedy lot that smelled suspiciously like a cesspool. Two blocks further down the road was another ice cream stand with a drive-through lane. Behind that stand was a community swimming pool, with the stand offering a special daily treat to the kids. Sam's business floundered and went under—so did Sam's

$25,000, along with most of the kids' college money.

After several months passed, with little success and no firm offers, Sam had exhausted the family savings. Sandy was now supporting the family, with mounting debts and expenses continuing at home. Tensions grew between Sam and Sandy; her anger at his "mistakes" was at the boiling point most of the time.

One day the telephone rang in my study with some good news from Sam. He had found a job in a nearby community. Of course, they would have to sell the house, but that didn't matter. He had already found a nice, modest home in an old neighborhood, one like they "used to live in." Sandy was going for a teaching interview next week, and it looked as if their problems were over. Sam shared his distress that it looked as if the kids would have to go to state school. "But then," he said to me, "I went to state school and I guess it didn't hurt me. After all, graduate school is really what's important."

Sam continued, then, with a fascinating monologue that went something like this: "I suppose, all in all, this is a good thing. Actually, it's probably not good at all to get so far ahead in life that you forget your roots—you know, where you came from. It wasn't so long ago, just a couple of months before I quit my job, that my Dad was visiting with us. I think I told you that. Well, anyway, he and I were sitting beside the tennis courts and he said to me, 'Sam, why in the world would you ever think you need all of this to make you happy? I don't know what you're making, but I'll bet it's a hell of a lot.' I couldn't resist, you know, because I was proud of my income, and I wanted him to be proud of it too, so I told him. You should have seen his mouth drop open.

"Anyway, we kept talking for awhile, but I don't think he felt too happy for me. He kept shaking his head and saying, 'It's nice, but I don't believe a man needs all of this to be happy.' By the time we left the courts, I wasn't at all sure if maybe I had blown it, you know, put my emphasis in the wrong place. I had felt real good about my salary back then, but I really started to wonder about it after that.

"So, I guess life is strange because we're right back where I started from. And the darndest thing, it's almost as if my Dad is more proud of me now than he was back then. Oh well, wish me well. It's a new ball game." Sam hung up the phone and I began to puzzle about his story.

Cash is never the problem; instead it is the family's attitude toward money that forms the legacy. You cannot grow up without a legacy on money. Do you spend it or save it? Should you worry about it, stew over it, give it away, put it in your mattress, or gamble with it? How much is enough? How much is too little? What are you worth, money-wise? What about those who are rich? Do they deserve it? Do you deserve it? If you marry into money, is that acceptable?

Most of us watch and listen to our parents. Little eyes and ears see and hear a great deal. You arrive at adulthood knowing full well what is permissible and what is not, as it concerns finances. Some families borrow to take vacations; others would never consider a vacation if they didn't have the cash. A father may hoard his money all year, only to spend it foolishly and extravagantly at holiday time.

When examining legacies, it is important to remember a crucial fact: children always seek the approval of their parents. In spending money, this is constantly a concern. With the ever increasing push on credit financing and the use of plastic, more and more young people are able to acquire as much as their parents. For some parents who feel it's wonderful that their children can have so many nice things at such a young age, there are other parents who feel jealous and angry over their own sense of deprivation from childhood. Adult children have to deal with both types.

While it is somewhat unusual to find a father like Sam's, all children need permission to surpass their parents when it comes to financial matters. Sam, obviously, did not have his father's permission to continue on the road to financial and vocational success. It cost Sam too much to do so; therefore, he found his way back to the familiar and comfortable—the old neighborhood.

The Money Legacy is probably more taught than caught, since most parents are talking about finances almost daily. The purchase of an automobile, buying a new home, discussing insurance premiums, or questioning the price of a doll or baseball takes place in most families. The children experience these conversations, filing them away in their program as a part of the legacy-implant. Again, there is no right or wrong legacy of money; it simply exists. All of us have, however, a responsibility to understand our legacy as a part of becoming our own person in thought and decisions.

CHAPTER II

FAMILY LESSONS

"Hysteria is a natural phenomenon,
the common denominator of the female nature
It's the big female weapon,
and the test of a man
is his ability to cope with it."

Tennessee Williams

"I refuse to consign the whole male sex to the nursery;
I insist on believing that some men are my equals."

Brigid Brophy

In my position as a therapist and teacher, I find myself traveling around to many different audiences. To me, it is continually fascinating to listen to people as they connect with the concept of the family legacy. Invariably, heads will shake as I explain parts of the legacy. Sometimes people will smile openly as they remember the way it was when they were growing up. In virtually every place I go, I listen to stories about "Mom and Dad" and the ways they taught the legacy. Many people will comment about the "common sense" approach to the legacy and that it is not just "shrink" talk.

In the last chapter, I wrote about the ways in which legacy lessons are learned. Because no one escapes childhood teachings, every person, in a true sense, could write his or her own book on the family legacy. It is one of those subjects, just like eating, where everyone is an expert. Every person learned about money, religion, and holidays. All adult family members, even those without diplomas, taught the kids about life; and most children are willing students, particularly during their early years.

Even though there is a thread of commonality that winds its way through all family legacy issues, I usually talk about my own family since it is there I am truly an expert. Hopefully, as you think about your own childhood experiences and the "teachers" in your history, you will examine the impact the legacy has had on your own life and relationships. To the degree that you examine your own legacy, you are opening yourself to the possibility of change.

Since legacy issues are difficult to measure in order of importance, prioritizing is virtually impossible. Each family has its own *stuff*, pushed by the older generations and quickly learned by the younger as *vital*. Some families list religion as the number one legacy issue, doing everything in their power to be sure the children understand it as such. God becomes a priority. Other families worry constantly about the neighbors and what they think. Children from that type of system quickly learn that *shame* is one issue this system avoids.

As I have written before, and will again before the end of this book, there is no right or wrong with the legacy; it just is. Obviously some parts of the legacy are more helpful than others; which is the most important is up to you. However, in my work as a therapist, as well as in my own personal journey, the question of "What is a man?" and "What is a woman?" seems to carry important weight in all family systems. While going undisclosed in many families, and disguised in others, the concepts of womanhood and manhood are considered critical.

WHAT IS A MAN?

In my own family system, men were charged with taking care of women, who, on the other hand, obviously needed to be cared for. Silently implied in the charge was that women were fragile and held together with something several strengths less than Elmer's glue. My father, very carefully, on many occasions, saw to it that I heard the legacy implications regarding the sexes. More than once, I was taken aside and taught that women needed to be treated with kid-gloves. "When you're playing with girls, make sure you use your left-hand and don't try as hard. You don't want to hurt them, you know." Little did my father realize that most of the girls in my neighborhood, especially in their tomboy years, could run faster and fight harder than I ever could.

Most families have certain stories, which, if examined, point out a number of legacy lessons. In our family, it was the famous, or infamous, "Stove Story." To tell this with any kind of meaning, I need to recall a time in my childhood when my parents did something they called "taking care of the money." Each Saturday, when my father was paid, he brought the money home in cash. Sometime during the afternoon, my mother and father would sit together at the kitchen table with a worn budget book filled with tattered and yellow envelopes, each marked with a certain budget item. I remember watching my parents place $10 in an envelope marked mortgage, and $2 in one marked insurance. Each envelope would receive its portioned amount until all the money was gone. My father would then place the budget book in the freezer portion of the refrigerator, and there it would stay.

In those days, the insurance man came to the house to collect the premium. When he arrived, usually during the day, my mother would go to the freezer, pull out the budget book, and hand him his $2.00 in cold cash, literally. Each week, for years, I watched my parents carefully tend to their money; budgeting was their way of life.

While my father worked outside of the home, my mother's job was to be a full-time wife and mother. She took her work seriously and tried to do it well. As I look back on those days, I realize how difficult it must have been for her having to depend on my father for her only source of money. I learned long ago that money sometimes equals power; my mother had neither. What she did have, however, was the satisfaction of a job well done. This meant that the house was clean and cozy, the children equally so; although to be honest, my dirty elbows caused her more than her share of grief. Supper was supposed to be prepared on time and tasty, probably a legacy learning from my grandmother.

The problem for my mother was that the stove was unpredictable. Havoc was sometimes wreaked on a casserole or cake because the oven door would not stay closed properly. In fact, it seldom closed the way oven doors are meant to close. To solve this problem, my mother would take a piece of cardboard and jam it in the door as she slammed it shut. Sometimes this worked, and other times it didn't. This meant, of course, that the thermostat was totally unreliable, leading to the same potential for the casserole. For my mother, this raised the possibility that the food could be undercooked or overcooked. It was, truly, pot luck.

On several occasions when my mother felt unhappy with her food preparation, the dinner table grew quiet. While both my sister and I knew something was up, we weren't sure what that meant. I never understood until decades later that my mother's sense of value came from her "job"—housekeeper, cook, and child-raiser. An undercooked casserole became a reflection on her sense of being—her value as a person. I suspect my father never understood this.

During these quiet times, I watched my mother carefully. Since in our family I was the family "alert," it was important for me to know what was happening at all times. It seems as though each family has at least one alert, charged with keeping track of everything, and if possible, making all problems go away. When the first tear trickled down my mother's cheek, I saw it. Sometimes I saw it a full two minutes before my father was aware that she was upset. Shortly after the first tear, it was not unusual for my mother to push her chair back from the table and head for the bedroom at the top of the stairs. Without a word, within a short time after my mother left, my father would push his chair back, give a sigh, and head for the stairs. My sister and I would quietly finish our dinner.

When my parents came back downstairs, apparently there was some resolution of the conflict; a conclusion I had reached since my mother had stopped crying. Upon reflection, I always found it interesting that neither my sister nor I ever asked my parents the simple question, "Where did you go?" I suppose it was our part in the conspiracy to avoid airing family differences. We kept quiet about what happened "up there," and so did they. I often joke about the fact that conflict resolution, in my system, seemed to be connected with "going upstairs." When I married and we moved into a ranch house, we had nowhere to go to resolve issues; so we never did.

It is important, at this time, to remind you that all that has happened in the "Stove Story," from taking care of the money to heading upstairs to resolve issues, is a part of the legacy lessons for both my sister and me. This is how family members learn about life, values, and behavior. Neither my mother nor father ever said anything about resolution of conflict, nor of what to do in relationships when things break down; instead, I just watched and went to school on their behavior, methods and words.

A little later in the evening, while I sat doing my homework, my parents would return to the issue of the undercooked casserole and an oven door that wouldn't close. Since, as Robert Bly says, my father had "hired" my mother to be angry for him, in her frustration she became a good employee. Sitting around the corner with my notebook in hand, I listened to my mother's tirade about the oven door and the need for a new stove. It would have been impossible to call this exchange between my mother and father a dialogue, since my father simply sat silently. He did what he did best when my mother was enraged—he said nothing. While I suspect he never knew it, his silence always seemed to fuel my mother's anger. It is important to understanding the legacy to remember that I was going to school on "being a man," and I was learning lessons "extra-ordinaire" at those times.

My mother's anger would spill over throughout the kitchen for a lengthy period of time as she ranted and raved about the need for a new stove. In reality, she was simply expressing her feelings of helplessness and powerlessness.

Unfortunately, no one knew this then, not even she. However, gradually, my mother would begin to wind down, like some type of wind-up toy that was running out of unraveling spring. Repeating her message and frustration in many different ways, she finally would grow silent.

When the silence had filled the room for a period of time, I would realize that I was holding my breath, waiting for whatever might happen next. It was then my father taught me the next lesson in "being a man." He would take a deep breath, with an audible sigh, and say, "Now, Lillian." There always was a pause between the word "Now" and my mother's name. Perhaps it was for effect, but my sense was it was to give my mother a message as to how exasperated he was with her "ridiculous" outburst.

"Now, Lillian," he would repeat, "let me ask you a question." I listened carefully, around the corner, learning with every word. "How much does a new stove cost?"

My mother would sit quietly and then say, "About a hundred dollars."

"That's right," my father would say, and I would nod my head in agreement.

He would continue, "And how much do we have saved for the new stove in our budget envelopes?"

"Sixty dollars," my mother's voice was now nearly a whisper. I nodded my head again because I had watched them put money in the envelope marked "Stove" only last Saturday.

"And," and here my father would pause, "how much is $60 from $100?"

"Forty," my mother answered, totally subdued, emotionally exhausted, and defeated by now. I nodded my agreement at the subtraction.

"Well...?" my father would say, and although I couldn't see him around the corner, I imagined him spreading his hands in a gesture of victorious anticipation.

At this point, everything would grind to a halt. There would be no more "dialogue." My mother would go to the sink and finish the dishes, my father would gather up his bowling shoes and bag, and I would take my books and head for my bedroom.

Can you see how many legacy lessons were presented in this one episode? During the course of several years, children in all families experience similar events. Every family has a "Stove Story" that serves to illustrate legacy issues and teach children the important values of the system. In this instance, my father was teaching me that men have an important task, namely: to point out to women—who, by the way, are irrational, emotional, and unreasonable—the errors in their thinking. The "Stove Story" taught both my sister and me a whole host of lessons about men, women, communication, money, logic, and conflict. It goes without saying that what we learned wasn't the most helpful way of growing a relationship. Ask any of the women with whom I have been in relationship, and they will gladly point out to you how well I learned my lessons.

It is vital to see that legacy issues are taught in every instance of daily living and family exchange. What is correct seldom matters; instead the continuation of the legacy values appears to be what counts. The "proof in the pudding" lies in how well the children carry out the legacy in their own adult lives.

What is a man? If I were to list the lessons I learned in my legacy, it would be astounding. Men are "logical, responsible, wise, silent during conflict, quick to point out errors, and in charge of the money and decisions within the family. Women 'need taking care of' and men are charged to do just that—to save the ladies from themselves and their irrational behavior, which if not checked could lead a family into bankruptcy." Is it any wonder that it took me years of therapy and education to understand why my relationships with women steered into both familiar, and unworkable highways? And I don't believe that my family is any different from the millions of others out there who daily teach the kids about the stuff of life, and the meaning of womanhood or manhood.

WHAT IS A WOMAN?

My sister, on the other hand, had the same legacy teaching but experienced it from the female point of view. In my opinion, she had the tougher road. Consider the fact that she was extremely bright, athletically gifted, and a natural leader being raised in a family legacy that saw women as "less than." In defense of my father, I am sure that he would never own up to a second class view of females; nevertheless, it was a part of his own legacy upbringing. Undoubtedly he would claim that women were *equal* with men. What that meant, however, was that no one was better than anyone else in the eyes of the Almighty.

It was into this system that my sister entered the world, screaming and kicking, four years after my debut. Named Gail, but behaving more closely to the "gale" of the weather forecasters, she found herself living with a father who saw women as needing special care, and a mother unable to express her own power and position.

I certainly do not feel qualified to answer many questions regarding womanhood. I do, however, feel able to speak to the ways in which a legacy of female subservience was taught. We all paid a price for this lesson, nevertheless; all family members pay for unworked stuff being passed through the decades from generation to generation. It is important to remind ourselves that family legacy issues were never taught as a way of being cruel or unkind; instead they were simply presented as the ongoing way things were. In most cases, parents saw legacy values as critical for children to understand, in order to know their place in life and to be successful in what they do, both vocationally and relationally. Parents do not pass on legacy beliefs that they believe to be harmful or detrimental to their children.

For my sister, this created an incredible conflict of expectations and values. On one hand, she could—and should—receive good grades in school. She could star on the swimming or gymnastic team and sing in the school choir. Her boy friends needed to reflect values of work and sports. "Well-roundedness is a good motto for life," was echoed from both parents. Gail needed to find summer jobs that paid well, and which gave her a chance to be responsible and dependable—all positive attributes of the legacy.

The dilemma occurred for her when she left the office place, the school room or the swimming pool. This capable and talented young woman now entered the home where she was to be an irrational and emotional female with little power to get things done. As a teenager, she did her homework perfectly, and then lost it. Because of her ability at the workplace, she was given the responsibility of opening and closing. Each morning, however, there was great confusion in the home while all family members searched in every nook and cranny for the key to the office. Eventually it was put on a key ring the size of a small baseball bat so that she would not lose it.

Today, she holds an extremely responsible position for one of the largest corporations in the country. She manages a multi-million dollar budget but cannot balance her checkbook. For years, long after she had married, my father spent several days every quarter helping her re-work her bankbook. She manages equipment at work with incredible skill and speed, but breaks her garage door opener on the average of three times a year—when she can find it.

Attending business meetings all over the country, she finds hotels, airports, meeting rooms and restaurants in cities where she has never visited, but leaves her purse at the car rental booth as she prepares to go home. "You're just like Rachel," my father would say, shaking his head. This was a reference to his sister, whom—on more than one occasion—he called "crazy." Apparently, in my father's system women didn't think things through. They couldn't keep track of simple things around the house, so, of course, how could my sister find her curling iron?

My father's mind was so incredible, and his logic so impenetrable, that few people could stand over against his position. My mother, with her own female legacy of second class citizenship, only served to enforce my father's sense of being right all the time. Watching all of this, just as I held to a position of male superiority, my sister was thrust into a place of female inferiority, but only at home. Today, therefore, she finds herself in the remarkable position of responsible and wise leadership within the corporate structure, and chaotic non-sense within the home.

Again, it is important to state that no one sets out to discredit females and idolize males within my legacy. Parents were teaching what they had been taught, and most of the time doing so without any sense of harming anyone. Certainly, they did not deliberately set my sister up to lock herself out of the house or carry around feelings of inadequacy because she is a female.

Expanding this concept in another direction, consider Nancy, a woman in her early twenties and recently married. She came to talk with me about her feelings toward her husband's apparent inability to make a decision. "He upsets me all the time," she said, "because he's afraid to decide about anything, even which restaurants we should eat in. It's almost as though he is afraid I'll get mad at him if he makes a different choice from the one I might make."

In describing her legacy, Nancy told me about Anna, her grandmother, a well-educated woman from an upper class family. Anna's mother had died when she was only 14, leaving Anna and her two younger sisters to be raised by a grief-stricken father. When she was 18, Anna's father married a woman whom she could not stand. In an act of defiance, Anna ran away and married a young and unsophisticated farm boy. Moving in with his parents, Anna adapted to a new way of life, experiencing both an economic and cultural shock. Very quickly she began to realize that she had made a mistake; nevertheless, and with pride, Anna decided to stick it out and make the best of it.

It was not long before Anna began to understand that she was beyond her young husband. Using both her anger and education, she started to manipulate and control him. As he responded to her anger with his own fear, Anna started to lose respect for him, just as she had lost respect for her father. Eventually they divorced.

Over a number of years, several children were born. The girls were taught a legacy of power and control. They were raised to be "take charge" women, setting out to find "weaker" men who needed to be led and guided. One of these women was Nancy's mother; the "weaker" man, her father. By now, Nancy's family legacy was in place. What is a woman? In her system, the answer was very clear. A woman is one who is responsible and capable, the necessary ingredients to care for a man who is unable to care for himself. By way of verification, Nancy watched her mother boss and bully her father. On one hand, she hated seeing her father treated in a mean way, resulting in some conflict with her mother. On the other, however, she had little respect for her father, and his apparent inability to stand up for himself against the unfair tirades of her mother.

Nancy decided she would find a man different from her father—a man who could be responsible—one who could take care of himself. Instead she found a "pleaser," mistaking his niceness for love. Because he could not stand to upset her,

Nancy's husband became more and more like her father, and she became more and more like her mother. As her husband experienced his fear of upsetting her, he fled from decisions. "After all," he said to her, "you might not like the restaurant I pick." This, in turn, confirmed Nancy's legacy about female superiority and male inferiority. "He's such a wimp!" she shouted in the therapy session. "All I ever wanted was a real man."

The amazing thing about the legacy is that it quickly turns into a self-fulfilling prophecy. "Mother was right after all," is the conclusion Nancy reaches. Even more fascinating is the way in which two people find and marry each other as a confirmation of their own individual family legacies. In all probability, her husband's legacy of female dominance and anger led him directly to Nancy.

All systems teach manhood and womanhood from the cradle through graduation. By then, most kids will have gotten the message. For many, it will take the rest of their lives to sort out the truth from the fiction. It is critically important, for the sake of self-growth and relational well-being, to examine your legacies regarding men and women. You may be walking a road paved by the good intentions of parents, but headed for a dead-end drop-off. If you're not sure what your beliefs are about males and females, ask your mate, or friends, or significant others. And if you really want to take a risk and they are available, ask your parents. You'll find it a fascinating conversation.

CHAPTER III

MARRIAGE AND THE LEGACY

*"The first part of our marriage was happy.
But then, on the way back from the ceremony..."*

Henny Youngman

"Marriage is not a walk in an open meadow."

Anon.(Russian)

MARRIAGE AND THE LEGACY

Standing in the back of the sanctuary, I watched the wedding guests arrive. With less than ten minutes left before the ceremony started, many were entering, laughing and talking, waiting for the usher's guiding arm. Last evening, at the rehearsal dinner, both the bride and the groom had given explicit directions to the ushers that guests were not to be seated on "sides." "It's old fashioned," explained the Bride, "just seat the guests anyplace."

The guests, however, had other ideas. "Friends of the bride," whispered one young woman as she took the usher's arm. Obliging, the man escorted the woman to the left side of the sanctuary, seating her several rows behind the bride's grandmother. Walking back up the aisle, the usher met the groom's cousin being steered to a pew on the right side.

Ten minutes later, I stood in front of an extremely nervous bride and groom. She clutched her father's arm while he lovingly patted her hand. The groom rocked back and forth, grinning in a silly sort of way. Looking over the bride's shoulder, I could see her mother dabbing her eyes with a tissue. Behind the mother sat the grandmother of the bride, her face radiant with a smile of delight. And, behind her, sat the great-grandmother of the bride, her head nodding and swaying from side to side.

I glanced in the direction of the groom's parents. Both mother and father sat nervously in their seat. They were from the Roman Catholic tradition, but today their son was being married in a Protestant sanctuary. Their uneasiness showed. The father was from a large family of eight children; six were seated behind him. One brother and one sister refused to attend because the ceremony was being held in the "wrong" place. Behind the groom's parents sat a large number of aunts, uncles, cousins, and friends.

Standing there, at that moment, looking over the shoulder of these two young people who were about to become husband and wife, I remember saying to myself, "This is not a wedding of two individuals. Rather, it's a bringing together of two tribes!"

It was three years later when the same bride and groom sat with me in my office, both bitterly expressing their feelings of disappointment. Only the Sunday before, they had presented their first born daughter for christening. Her parents had been present, filled with smiles and pride. His parents were "unable" to attend.

"He wants Jennifer to be baptized over at the Catholic church," the bride was crying. "But, I told him she's already baptized. Isn't that right? Why should we have her baptized again?"

"Because it would mean a lot to my parents," he answered her. "You know how important this is to my mother; she's worried about Jennifer," he looked at me, "you know, her soul and all."

"She's just a baby," wailed the bride. "If something happened to her, God would love her. What kind of a god would send a little baby to hell? Besides, we had an agreement. Jennifer would go to church here."

"I know we did," he said, "I'm not asking you to raise her Catholic, just get her baptized over there. What can it hurt?"

"We had a deal." The bride walked out of the office leaving the groom sitting alone, twisting the ring on his finger back and forth. A few seconds later, he followed her into the hall.

These two young people were caught in the middle of a very difficult trap called a legacy conflict. Their family backgrounds and beliefs were painfully bumping into each other. The teachings of their "tribes" took on a powerful meaning at the birth of their daughter.

Already, their marriage was in trouble.

—

No matter how old they grow, adult children still feel a sense of loyalty to their family legacies. It seems as though children, from their earliest years, develop a sense of commitment to the teachings and values of their parents. Even those ideas that are so severely rejected during adolescence can be the source of enormous arguments later on in life. A husband who, ten years earlier, fiercely fought with his mother over the "ridiculous" notion of cleaning the hair out of the bathtub can find himself criticizing his young wife for not keeping the tub spotless.

A young girl who questions her parents over the importance of having both pumpkin and mince pie for

Thanksgiving suddenly turns on her husband in anger when he suggests that it's not necessary to have two different pies for the holiday. Her loyalty to her legacy seems almost like a mother lioness protecting her young. Unfortunately, issues as casual as the two above can be the beginning of enormous marital conflict and fighting. If a couple is not careful, legacy conflicts can spill over into the bedroom, affect the spending of money, and might eventually lead to in-law difficulties, leaving both husband and wife feeling alone and isolated. Intimacy can seldom occur when these legacy conflicts are kicking and breathing at the heart of the marriage.

A young couple came to see me over what appeared to be a "silly" problem of when to open their Christmas gifts. As a child, he had been raised in a small town where his father told him that Santa Claus appeared in the smaller towns and villages on Christmas eve. Since Santa, apparently, had to handle all of the big cities during the night, it only made sense for the jolly fellow to get the small towns finished first. The man said that it was years before he understood that his father was trying to create a story that would fit his grandparents' schedule of holiday visits. They needed to be elsewhere on Christmas morning; hence, the Christmas eve story. "As a child it made sense to me," the young man said.

On the other hand, the young woman had been raised by parents who were from the city. They always opened their gifts on Christmas morning. Furthermore, she had never heard of opening gifts on Christmas eve, feeling that it spoiled the excitement of waking up in the morning with the anticipation of opening "all those gifts." "I never heard of anything so silly," she told me.

Like most young couples, they felt the best way to handle this problem was to ignore it. Although they knew the holiday was creeping closer, they found that trying to talk about it caused a fair amount of tension—more than either one wanted to face. Things came to a head one evening when the telephone rang. His parents were calling to see how things were going with the holiday rush and all. Toward the end of the conversation, they casually asked when the newly-marrieds were going to open their gifts.

With his wife on the other phone, the young man hemmed and hawed until he finally blurted out, "We're going to open half of our gifts on Christmas eve, and the other half on Christmas morning." The solution was sort of a loyalty compromise, a deal with the legacy.

Sadly, the family legacy doesn't make deals; there is always a cost. In this case, the young man felt guilty to his parents as well as to his wife. He did not know how to please everyone, so the best he could offer was a compromise. And, because he was looking for it, he felt he heard disappointment in the voices of his parents. Since he felt he had not supported his wife in front of his parents, he anticipated her punishment. When it was not forthcoming, he verbally pushed at her until she attacked back, giving him the punishment he felt he deserved for being a disloyal son.

Disloyalty to the legacy is always costly. It simply depends on the power and importance of the issue to determine what the cost is.

When I moved away from home, which translated into a geographic disloyalty, my father said to me, "You know where we live, and you know when the holidays are," implying that I would be the one traveling. It was simply the price to be paid for moving away; it was not allowed in my family system. In this case, the disloyalty cost was not severe; other issues would be much more expensive.

A 27 year-old, single woman came for an appointment, bringing her mother and father along for the session. During the hour, she told them that she was a lesbian in relationship with a woman back in the community where she now lived and worked. She asked her parents to understand, pleading with them for their support, telling them that she had "tried" to make it with men, but she felt nothing.

Many tears were shed by both this woman and her mother. Her father said nothing but eventually stood, and taking his wife's hand, spoke to her, "We're leaving now because we no longer have a daughter."

While this father's attitude may anger some people, it simply reflected the power of his legacy. Sexuality is a legacy issue; there was no space in his for a lesbian daughter.

For his daughter, the price of being a disloyal child was the ultimate one—the dismissal from the family.

MARRIAGE AND THE LEGACY

Disloyalty is always a perceived action against the legacy. While it is expected in adolescence, it is never acceptable in adulthood without a price. The cost can range from a minor slap on the wrist, as in the case of my moving away, to the enormous price of dismissal, as in the situation described above.

OPEN AND CLOSED LEGACIES

Some family systems are more open than others. In these systems, children are often encouraged to explore the legacy. Parents may model the exploring by questioning their own legacy. For instance, at the dinner table, children may hear parents dialogue with each other about childhood experiences, areas of family growth, or even stories from their own adolescent rebellion. When children hear their parents questioning the intergenerational legacy, they begin to feel permission to examine issues from their own family of origin. Parents who are able to open the legacy for evaluation give their children a wonderful gift.

Closed systems, on the other hand, are very rigid and tight. Children are seldom given permission to explore the legacy. Many times they are told "this is the way we do it, and that's that!" Questioning the legacy is equated with disloyalty. Since children are fast learners, they soon keep a closed mouth when it comes to important legacy issues. The loyalty in closed systems is often encouraged and sometimes rewarded with parental praise and gifts.

Closed systems often use guilt as a way of assuring the continuation of the legacy. "What would your grandfather think if he knew about this?" is not an unusual statement in the closed system. Children begin to experience an uneasiness any time they find themselves questioning the legacy, and flooded with guilt if any action is taken in opposition to it. By the time these children reach adulthood, it seems as though the legacy is etched in concrete; change appears to be impossible.

If God has a sense of humor, the marriage of two people from opposing systems seems to be the best place it's displayed. When a woman from an open system marries a man from a system that is closed, fireworks are sure to follow. Even though she was raised in an open system, she will not understand his need to "please" his parents at every turn, and he will not understand her inability to support him in his loyalty to his system. The holidays will be spent, for the most part, at his parents since they will seem to be the more unreasonable in considering scheduling difficulties, eating arrangements, and other traveling dilemmas. Her parents, on the other hand, being open to different legacies, will appear more tolerant and understanding. When this occurs, the woman's family will appear to be shortchanged in the man's attempt to please his closed system. He, although unable to understand her parents' open attitude, will, nevertheless, be most grateful for it.

One couple I spoke with several years ago presented the holiday struggle in incredible fashion: "His parents said to us, 'You can spend Christmas, New Year's Eve and Day, Easter, Memorial Day, the Fourth of July, Labor Day, and Thanksgiving with us; and you can be over at her parents on Valentines' Day and Arbor Day.'" While this can sound funny, there was little humor in it for these two. How much clearer can a message be to a person from a closed system?

While attending a banquet one evening, a professional speaker told me of his knotty problem with a closed system. He was driving to Scranton, Pennsylvania, the next morning to speak at a luncheon; his wife would accompany him. Since she was born and raised in Scranton, with her parents still living there, she wondered about stopping by for a visit. Her parents told them, "If you can drop in while you're here, we'd love it. If you can stay for dinner, it would be wonderful. If not, that's O.K., too. We'll catch up with you the next time." "And they meant it!" this man said to me incredulously. He was obviously from a closed system. If his parents had lived anywhere close to Scranton, within one or two hours, he would be expected to visit, convenient or not.

While there are not many studies in this area, a general rule appears to be: the more rural the system, the more likely it is to be closed; likewise, the more ethnic the family, the greater the chance for a closed system. Open systems tend to be more educated as well as more metropolitan in nature. This, of course, does not mean that the exact reverse cannot be true. Normally, however, the differences between closed and open systems are rooted in geography, education, and ethnicity.

MARRIAGE AND THE LEGACY

THE DILEMMA

For several reasons, marriage is never an easy road. It calls for great insights, patience, and devotion to bring a marriage to intimacy and joy. Two people coming together from different legacies have enormous work to do in order not to complicate the marriage with unresolved issues of childhood. Because it takes great courage to face one's intergenerational legacy, most people end up muddying the waters of their marriage. It sometimes seems safer to be angry at one's mate than at one's parents. Often, stuff that belongs to history gets resurrected into the present and blamed on a spouse.

In recent years, many books have been written on communication styles, the management of conflict, money problems and the like, to guide married couples on the road to marital bliss. Entire movements have been formed to escort parents into the correct and proper methods of raising children. While all well and good, if the intergenerational legacy is not considered, with all of its conflicts and power, little help will be forthcoming from one more book.

Unfortunately, beyond the husband and wife, the ones to pay the ultimate price of unresolved legacy issues are the children. They can be innocently and severely wounded by well-meaning parents who are desperately plodding through life, yet trying to be loyal to their own histories. At the same time, these parents find themselves avoiding legacy issues, since they produce too much guilt and fear. When this occurs, blame and anger generally rise to the surface and, if not careful, children may suffer greatly.

It is in this dilemma that children learn about life, themselves, and the family. Self-esteem can be profoundly impacted at this time, ultimately piloting a child into the future with little sense of self and a great deal of shame. It is also during these times when confused children, receiving blame and guilt-producing messages from parents, begin to form concepts of God. These thoughts and conclusions can shape spiritual experiences for decades to come. This will be an important issue to be discussed in later chapters.

CHAPTER IV

THE LEGACY AND OUR BELIEF SYSTEM

*"'Tis education forms the common mind;
Just as the twig is bent, the tree's inclined."*

Alexander Pope

*"Here I am, fifty-eight,
and I still don't know what I want to be
when I grow up."*

Peter Drucker

"Garbage in, Garbage out."

Computer Graffiti

THE LEGACY AND OUR BELIEF SYSTEM

We live in a world of constant change, a time in which typewriters are obsolete and computers are carted around in notebooks. Recently I purchased a telephone that had to be programmed before I could use it, but then again, so did the power seat on the driver's side of my van. The new television set in my bedroom can be programmed for day, week, hour, and minute, while my travel alarm requires programming skills just to wake me up in the morning.

Programming seems to be a necessary skill if a person is going to walk into the twenty-first century and still be able to u   s   e the appliances in the home. It's a rather frightening obstacle for many people raised on simplicity. I remember visiting my grandmother one day, a few months after she purchased her first television set. She was watching a sports show— obviously not her style. When I asked her about it, she responded by saying that she was afraid to try to change the channel button since she wasn't sure how to do it. She simply watched one channel all the time, taking pot-luck with whatever program appeared.

By now, however, most of us have at least learned the elementary skills of programming. We arrange to manipulate our VCR's to record movies, we set the buttons on our car radio to our favorite stations, and we have even managed to operate the critically important automatic teller machines supplied for easy cash by our friendly, community bank.

We've come a long way in developing a new skill.

Machines and electronic equipment, however, are not the sole users of programming. As mentioned briefly in Chapter I, another word for the legacy is "programming." I've been talking about ways in which the legacy is the fuel that runs the family; it powers the engine of your life. It steers you into relationships, vocations, and lifestyles, many times on automatic pilot. In a real sense, you have been programmed yourself by well-meaning parents, teachers, and relatives. In all probability, you now find yourself in the unique position of programming others around you, namely your children, employees, friends and neighbors. This happens every time you express a belief, or silently support one.

For those of you comfortable with the computer, the terms "hardware" and "software" are very familiar. Hardware is literally just that. When you walk into Sears and see the machine sitting there with all the colored graphs, words, etc., on the screen, that's the hardware. The software, on the other hand, is the stuff you put into the hardware to make it work. Similarly, the pages of a book along with the cover, glue, and binding could be considered hardware. The story that gets printed on the paper is the software.

A computer is only an empty lot waiting to be seeded with software. This software is simply information that is programmed into the computer (the hardware). When you turn on a certain "program," the information programmed into the machine appears on the screen. I haven't the slightest idea how it works—it's just nice that it does.

In many ways, the brain is like a computer. It's filled with cells, electrodes, and memory banks which "talk" to each other. Working with a speed beyond light, the brain amazes us with its ability and reliability. Step on a bee in your bare feet, and the speed with which the brain tells your body to respond is phenomenal. Bump into an old high school classmate and watch your brain do a "search for a name" into the memory banks, as well as any other "old data" you may have placed away. The brain is a miracle, and aptly named so in Judith Hooper and Dick Teresi's recent book entitled **The Three Pound Universe.** Indeed, the brain is a universe unto itself.

It is this "universe" that is our own personal "hardware." Like a computer, the brain is that place which houses the information it receives. We all are born with this fascinating storehouse, just waiting to receive any and all harvests brought to it. My brain is my own hardware that I carry with me wherever I go; in fact, I turned it on sometime ago in my mother's womb.

On the other hand, the "software" of life is your mind. Like an empty chalkboard, the mind waits for information from parents, teachers, and relatives. It eagerly receives each teaching, belief, and lesson, writing it on the board like an overanxious school child. Day by day, lessons are taught and caught into the mind. This chalkboard, filling up with information, is a developing software package for each of us. A day never passes in which new information is not written on the walls of the mind.

By the time you are five years old, all sorts of information has been written on the mind. "Don't pull the cat's tail" and "Be kind to older people" is part of your software package, as well as, "You really can't trust men" or "Women are out to get you." These messages and thousands of others are written on the pages of the mind. All that is needed then, is to place the software into the hardware. When certain situations occur in life, the mind enters the brain and imparts its learned information onto the memory circuits of the brain. Doing its job well, the brain instructs you to behave in a certain way.

For all of us, our minds are filled with whatever the important people in our lives feel we need to know. My grandmother's views about the "neighbors" soon belong to my mind. Seeing a certain neighbor, my mind informs my brain that I need to cross the street and not walk in front of his house. With these instructions, my feet simply obey without question.

My teacher tells me that uneducated people never get good jobs and often go hungry. When the guidance counselor calls me in to talk about my choices for junior high school curriculum, my mind tells my brain to choose academic. My mouth does the rest while my hand signs the application.

My grandfather told my father that women needed to be "looked after," implying they could not "look after" themselves. A lifetime of mind-building led my father to explain to me that it was my sister he worried about, not me. "After all," he said, "you're the man." I got the message (the mind usually does) and quickly converted it into programming. In turn, the brain received this important software without question and sent me looking for women who needed to be looked after. Fortunately, or unfortunately, I found a lot of females out there whose teachers had entered similar data on their minds.

As we develop and grow through childhood, the mind receives more and more information. Most of the lessons are given by well-meaning people who love us and want us to have the best. By the time we reach our early twenties, the mind is crammed with an enormous *belief system* created from our family legacy, the legacies of our school teachers, and the unspecified, but clear messages from the culture and television.

For most of us, our software package is never complete as we analyze, add to, and delete from our minds. An interesting fact, however, is the VETO button most of us had installed at a very early age. "Don't mess with certain parts of your software package" is the message from childhood. Stated another way, "When someone wants you to question those critical lessons and teachings, be polite, listen, and then push the VETO button."

To question a childhood belief written on the mind is not only threatening, it opens the mind for the possibility that other beliefs might be mistaken or need examination. This thought is so frightening to the mind that some people actually try NOT to think about things, for fear the entire belief system might surface for a new look. Such a thought is totally unacceptable to the mind, striking terror at its core. To the mind, questioning beliefs is a survival issue potentially leading to the death of the self.

THE BELIEF SYSTEM SEES THE WORLD

Several years ago I visited a school for the blind. Several young people were talking about colors in an attempt to understand a red and blue flag that was being passed around the room. Each person felt very carefully of the materials, but all admitted they could not tell which part of the flag was red and which part was blue. The teacher did a lot of talking about pigment, trying to explain what red and blue looked like. To those persons who had some slight vision, this was easy to understand. To the others, they had no concept of the teacher's explanation.

For those students with minimal vision, the teacher had designed several pairs of glasses, each with different colored lenses. Some were red, some blue, others green and so on. The students put them on and looked at a green-colored world or a red-colored world, getting a sense of those colors.

Can you imagine looking at life through a special pair of filtered glasses so that everything you saw came into your vision through that filter? In a sense, that's exactly what happens to all of us as we look at life through our highly developed belief systems. In virtually every arena of life, we see through our beliefs. Whether we are listening to a lecture at the local school board or fussing over the poor service in a restaurant, we are operating from our highly sophisticated belief system—our software.

If a waitress is not doing her job, as we feel "she's paid to do," our beliefs are showing. When the politician makes a promise and we immediately "know" he or she is untrustworthy, our beliefs are reaching conclusions. The driver in front of you asking directions at the toll booth and holding up the line "should have known better" according to your belief system. When your husband behaves "just like a man" or your wife "just like a woman," where do you think you learned what men and women are all about, if not in the installation of your belief systems?

Until a belief system is examined, it simply operates without question in the world. A belief, for example, that rural people are ignorant and unsophisticated will never be challenged unless that section of software is opened in the mind. Unfortunately, the mind seldom opens for anything except confirmation of the belief system. Even if you have a wonderful relationship with a "rural" person, it may take years before there is any true and lasting change in a belief.

SOME SOFTWARE *PACKAGES*

It only takes a little logic to understand the impact of your belief system on how you view the world. In the wonderful film, *The Accidental Tourist,* John, the main character and a writer of books for "safe" travel, clearly views the world as a place of danger and fear. He writes for travelers who wish to travel but not necessarily engage the world. Offering advice on colors of clothing to wear so travelers blend into the background, John suggests that "hiding" is the only way to travel. His view of life is one of safety and blandness. Operating on a belief system which says that unpredictability is dangerous, John struggles to build a predictable life in every arena of his existence.

I watched this movie with my mouth open as John's sister came home from the grocery store and put the food away in the pantry in alphabetical order. "Everything in its place" is a wonderful belief if safety is the order of the day. No one in John's family answered the telephone because it might be bad news.

When parents teach children about an unsafe world, how can they expect those same children to engage life with any degree of boldness? A software of fear has been created. Looking through a belief system filter of fear, children will only see danger and threat at every turn. Opportunities will be missed because the timing is "just not right," another way of saying the risk is too great. A trip to the city will be discouraged because "you never know what's going to happen there."

If you are raised with the software of fear, there is little chance you will see anything but an unsafe world. Your watchword will be "caution" blended in with liberal sprinklings of prevention. "Be prepared" is not just the Scout motto, it is the cry of the fear-based family which shouts of a hurtful and dangerous world.

In contrast to the programming of fear is the case of Ginny, whose mother was an archaeologist dashing here and there around the world. Well-known for her findings in the Middle East, she found herself away from home and her daughter for months at a time. Since this was an unacceptable lifestyle for her, being caught between career and daughter, she decided to make arrangements for Ginny to travel with her.

"Some of my earliest memories are from the digs," Ginny comments when talking about her family history. "I remember sleeping in tents, going to the bathroom in just about anyplace I could find, and having a whole group of different strangers sort of looking after me. My world was totally unpredictable."

Laughing, Ginny recalls places and events where she would never allow her own daughter to travel today. "My mother saw the world as a safe place and let me know she wanted me to see it like that, too." After a pause she added, "I suppose that all in all, I do see the world that way. Certainly I wouldn't want to spend my life hiding indoors like some of my friends. How far out can we keep moving to escape danger before there's no place else to go?"

Ginny's life experiences profoundly shaped her belief system about the world. When she looked at the city, she did not see crime, filth, and danger; instead, she was more likely to see culture and opportunity. Oftentimes she would argue with her husband, whom she felt was overly cautious about his approach to "city opportunities." Clashing over trips to the city or vacations to remote areas, Ginny and her husband found their belief systems in total disagreement. Like most of us, they took it personally, allowing it to tear away much of the foundation of their marriage.

THE LEGACY AND OUR BELIEF SYSTEM

Contrasting belief systems are built on legacy issues. Most of our earliest teachings from our parents are legacy-based, forming the center of our "mind software." For all of us, what we believe at our deepest level about the core issues of life will be amazingly close to the belief system of our parents. All of our protests notwithstanding, we echo mom and dad.

Ginny's legacy built a belief system in which she saw the world as a safe place. Looking through that filter, she developed a world view of exploration and adventure. In contrast to those who see the world as a fearful spot, Ginny moved toward risk and challenge in her search for growth. Because of her beliefs, Ginny was one of those individuals who operate on the cutting edge of life. It's important to notice that it is not because Ginny is more courageous or intelligent than others that she is continually out there challenging the rapids; it is because of her early leanings leading to the development of her belief system. In contrast is the fact that the more limited our belief system, the more stuck and stagnated we can, and probably will, become. For the most part, the more frightened we perceive our parents to be, the greater the likelihood our own life will be rooted in fear.

GIVERS OR TAKERS?

"What do you mean you traded away your comic books? To that Calhoun boy? My God, they could buy and sell us ten times over and you gave him your comic books?" My mother was incredulous and I knew a speech was on the way. "Don't you know if you're not careful that you'll end up losing everything to people like that? We can't afford to buy your comic books and then have you trade them away for God knows what?" She stood silently looking at me; I stood looking at the floor. "Well, what did you get for them?"

I showed her the sticker book of baseball memorabilia, knowing at the same time that I was dead in the water. "You traded away those comics for this sticker book?" Her voice was rising now and I knew I had made a mistake. "How many books?"

"Seven," I whispered, "but two of them were really old—a Tom and Jerry and Woody Woodpecker."

"Seven books cost seventy cents," she glared at me "and

that stupid sticker book was only 39 cents. Look there," she pointed at the upper corner of the book, "You got taken. What's the matter with you? Are you stupid or something?"

While this conversation was going on, my software was being created. Regardless of whether I agreed with my mother or not, the lesson kept coming while the tape continued playing. Sometimes we tend to believe that because we may disagree with our parents, the mind then will not develop software in that area of disagreement. However, in most cases, that is simply not true; the mind absorbs it, creating more software for daily living.

It is true that as I grow up and have children of my own, I may give them the freedom to own their own things and do with them what they will. If they choose to trade them away, give them away, or horde them, because of my own history, I may back away and allow them total freedom in this area. The tricky spot, however, is to notice that owning and trading your own stuff is not the belief that was entered on my mind when my mother corrected me because of negotiating a poor trade. Instead, the belief had to do with other people as takers, as well as the development of a life view of "rich" people. It also had to do with the belief about myself as inadequate, or stupid. We'll talk about this later on. To examine your beliefs means to get beyond the events that occurred to the *teaching* beneath those events.

As an adult, I have to struggle all the time with my world view of people as takers. It's not that I don't know better; it is that my belief system—my software—continually reminds me to watch out for others. They may be "out to get me." This can go as far as my judgments of the guy who cuts me off in traffic, to my mechanic who might "rip me off" if I don't watch him closely. It can penetrate my insights into politicians, neighbors, and co-workers.

"Rich people got rich by taking from the little guy," is written on my software. My minister added to that belief by thumping from the pulpit about rich folks being in more trouble than fat camels. He called to our attention the unwillingness of the rich to help the widows and the orphans—instead they built bigger barns. This added to my uncle's pronouncements that the "rich get richer and the poor get poorer." I knew we weren't rich so that left only one way for us to go.

THE LEGACY AND OUR BELIEF SYSTEM

By now, you can see how insidious is the development of your software. The mind has been created so cleverly with layer upon layer of beliefs, that it becomes almost impossible to truly get to the level of an honest examination of your belief system. Fortunately, there is an easier way which we will talk about later on.

It is very important to understand that it is not what is *truth* here that counts, it is simply what you believe. If you see people as takers, you will treat them as such, taking great care to protect yourself at all times. This can spill over from the world into the workplace, and eventually into your own home in relationships with your spouse and children.

For those of you who may be thinking about this for the first time, be very careful not to judge yourself for your own belief system and legacy. You were born into your family system and circumstances. In a real sense, you were quite programmable; most children are. Your software is your software. What remains to be done is to examine it, let go of the beliefs that are not helpful to you, and replace those beliefs with ones which you choose to make your own life more joyful and meaningful. To judge yourself will only send you deeper into guilt and shame, neither of which will help you in the slightest.

Perhaps you were fortunate enough to be one of the rare children who grew up with teachings about the "goodness" of others. If so, you will view the world as an opportunity to give and will see others as being as you are. This is a wonderful philosophy—the only danger being one of naiveté. Even that is not necessarily a negative, since viewing others as givers means that you will see them through a giving filter. If others betray you, since you do not see others as takers, you will more likely be understanding and accepting of their "mistakes."

VICTIMS OR VILLAINS

Joe was a forty-five year old clergyman recently turned down for a major post in his denomination. "Nothing good ever happens to me," he moaned, "It was true when I was seven years old and it's still true today. I don't want to spend another month, to say nothing of another year, in this church full of wretched people."

"What happened when you were seven?" I asked him.

"My father started drinking and my sister moved out," he shook his head, "It seemed that my world came crashing down then. I remember asking my Sunday School teacher about it and she said something about Jesus requiring a cross for all of us, and that maybe this was to be my cross. She said I should try to help my mom and forget about myself."

"That sounds like a lot for a little kid," I offered.

His eyes welled up with tears as though this happened yesterday. In some sense, to Joe, yesterday was but another cross, when the denomination turned him down for the position in which he had placed so much hope. "It was a lot," he sounded as though he was whining, "I mean, whoever paid any attention to me, anyway? And now I was supposed to look after my Mom? She was so needy, you know, that I couldn't really turn to her for support." He looked at me for confirmation.

The longer Joe talked about his seventh year, blending it in with yesterday and today, the more his voice became childlike and whining. At times, he sounded like a helpless seven-year-old. Joe's life experiences had taught him to see life through a filter of victimization. His software could be labeled: You are a Victim. Therefore, when Joe looked at the world, he saw his place in it, always, as a potential victim. Many times he rationalized his victimization through the scriptures. When he didn't get a salary increase equal to the church organist, he quoted the Bible about sacrificial living. At the same time, he added one more explanation point to his victim software package. On another occasion, Joe had to return from his vacation early due to the death of one of the "pillars" of the church. Again he talked religious talk, justifying a ruined vacation as the role of the suffering servant. As you can imagine, his software package was running all the time.

Joe saw himself as a victim in nearly all of his work life. Unfortunately, in that we are rather consistent creatures, Joe took the same view into his marriage. Feeling that his wife used him and took advantage of his good nature, Joe filled his software package with resentment as his victim role continued at home. His view of life was powerfully filtered through his glasses of victimization.

It is important here to say that it doesn't really matter if Joe was actually victimized by his congregation and family or not. It is only a matter of whether Joe truly believes he was a victim. If he sees himself victimized at every turn, he will trust that it is actually happening, and store away whatever memories and resentments he can to protect himself in the future. Unfortunately, at this point, there is little his wife or supportive, caring congregants can do. Joe's filter is stuck in the victim color while his software runs in the same program.

The other side of Joe's struggle occurs when an individual feels that, instead of being victimized, he or she ends up hurting others. Believing you cause others pain is as difficult to live with, if not more so, than feeling victimized. Victims tend to feel the world has ganged up on them, leading to feelings of self-pity and persecution. Self-pronounced villains, on the other hand, struggle with guilt and shame for the pain their very presence in the world can bring to the people they love.

Candy was the youngest of three children and the only girl. Not realizing the pain her mother felt because her husband was lost in a gambling addiction, Candy felt a sense of enormous responsibility when she saw her mother weeping alone. After a particular vicious fight with her older brothers, in desperation Candy's mother said, "You kids are always causing me grief. I don't know why we had to have so many of you." Looking at Candy she added, "I certainly never wanted any more kids; your father was the one who wanted a girl."

A quarter of a century later, Candy was still struggling with the pain she felt she caused her mother and other people. Believing that everything she did was wrong, Candy carried her feelings of being a bad person into her intimate relationships as well as into the work place. Relationship followed relationship, and job followed job, as she played out her belief system of pain and shame.

It doesn't matter that Candy was only six at the time her mother spoke out in desperation—the mind got the message. Each time she sensed her mother's disapproval, the imprint of her software grew deeper. In reality, Candy was a good person whose software told her something quite different. Unfortunately, when it comes to making a choice as to what messages we believe, the mind usually wins. Friends can try hard to convince us that we are lovable—the mind knows better.

HELPLESS OR CAPABLE?

As the belief system spills into all of life, one other area is critically important in helping us to better understand ourselves. Do you see yourself as helpless or capable? On the surface, the answer may seem simple; however, even a shallow digging underneath can reveal surprising results. Many apparently talented and capable people run on fear; they anxiously look around for approval and applause. Are they as capable as they seem?

Other less skilled or less sophisticated people may show enormous confidence and peace in their daily work and relationships. They may not have many people surrounding them with praise or approval; nevertheless, a quiet strength seems to be present.

What makes the difference? How do capable people manage to not accept or to not appreciate their own talents and abilities, while less-gifted persons find ways to a sense of strong self-worth?

Raised on a small farm in a remote country setting, Margaret was the youngest of two children. Her parents were loving, active people involved in various church and community functions. Margaret loved to go to any social event held within miles, explaining that she was just a "people person."

Her older brother, Bill, was quiet and shy, often moving into the background whenever possible. He detested Margaret's "showy" ways, sometimes calling her the family "show and tell" doll. Calling him jealous, Margaret only intensified her efforts to surround herself with people, not always an easy task in a rural environment.

From her earliest days, Margaret exhibited an enormous musical talent, singing in Christmas programs at church and school when she was only seven years old. Everyone praised her for her lovely voice, and obviously gifted acting ability. Each time she performed, her face would light up as though energized by some external magical spotlight. It seemed apparent that she would go far in the performing arts field.

For Margaret, the only drawback in this exciting journey, where she was a big fish in a little pond, was her weight. As young as five her grandmother was pointing her finger at Margaret and pinching her "baby fat." "Not from our side of the family," her grandmother would sniff to Margaret's mother.

Margaret's teenage years became a series of diets, interwoven with weeks of bingeing, during which time she would stuff herself with enormous amounts of country cooking. As a particular concert approached, she would switch to a near starvation diet, sometimes eating so little that she would faint in gym class.

"You have such a pretty face" became words of terror for Margaret. Interpreting the compliment to mean her face was acceptable but the rest of her was not, she would go without food for days at a time. "I hate myself," she would say, even as she drank in the applause from a cheering audience.

Margaret won several scholarships for college, accepting one in a metropolitan area saying that she needed to be "tested." During her college years she rose to the top of the class in performance and dramatics. She managed to find herself in nearly every college production, often in the leading role. Margaret became a star.

Her attempted suicide at age 23 came as a shock to her friends and family. "After all," her brother said, "she has the world in her hand; what more can she want?"

"I hate myself," Margaret told me, "I hate my body, my hair, and everything about me. I'm nothing."

Margaret sat in my office, in her size four dress, a purse full of letters from admiring well-wishers, and wished herself away. "I don't belong in this world," she cried softly, "because I'm faulty merchandise. Maybe God does make mistakes... he sure made one when He made me."

In our conversations, Margaret began to talk about her belief that people never really liked her—they only liked her performances. "No one invites me to parties because I'm Margaret," she said, "They invite me because I'm the star of the show. Take away my star and see how many friends come out of the woodwork."

In anger, Margaret related her young teenage experiences in which sitting around the dinner table, her father would poke her breast with his fork, asking her if she was "done yet." Everyone would laugh at his humor except for Margaret, who, humiliated, would dash from the table to her bedroom. "My voice, my breasts, and my 'pretty face,' screw them all!"

Margaret screamed at the world from the four walls of the therapy room.

Looking at Margaret's "successful life," her friends and family could only see her as capable. To view her as helpless would be laughable to them. Margaret, however, did not judge herself as adequate or capable based on a childhood of humiliation and shame. No matter what the size of her dress, her internal critic only knew one word, "Fat!" Her body was "ugly" and her breasts were objects of scorn.

It is important for all of us to recognize that no matter how many standing ovations the "Margarets" of the world receive, it cannot replace their own personal assessment of themselves. External applause is nice; it brings people into the theater and sells tickets. It does not, however, silence the internal, unmerciful judge, trained in childhood, when court is called into session. To Margaret, she is only a tonsillitis case or a bad review away from oblivion. Success has no working relationship with being capable; it is a matter of the judgment of the self. For many, unfortunately, there is a powerful correlation between being successful and being lovable.

Capability and helplessness are more often internal judgments and feelings than they are actualities. That there are degrees of talents and abilities cannot be argued; however, seldom are these the criteria for self-acceptance and worth. To an employer or observer, to be capable means that one is able to perform a task with some degree of skill and accomplishment. To an individual, on the other hand, capability—or lack of it—is connected with feelings that are rooted in self-judgment. Educational degrees and professionalism have little to do with *feeling* capable. Even accomplishments and monetary status, which many might feel would lead to a sense of capability, only serve to sugarcoat a lack of adequacy.

To be capable is to believe in one's own sense of power. Literally, it is the capacity *to be able*, not in the sense of accomplishment and performance, but rather in the strength to meet life with all of its surprises and curves. When you are capable, you simply believe in your capacity to face life; it is your way of saying that you trust in yourself, and, as we will discuss later, the result of this belief is inner peace.

Being capable means that you acknowledge life has certain

unavoidable clashes that you will meet, trusting your capacity to be able in them. It is not in the doing of things that you prove your capability, but rather in your *meeting life* with an underlying trust that you will be able to continue. Helplessness is not a condition of failure or weakness—it is a fact of life. At some time or another, all of us will be helpless; it is "the fear" spoken about by those who work in the field of death and dying. The fact is that even in that helplessness, you can be capable simply by meeting the inevitable. In the "choiceless," you do have a choice.

CHAPTER V

THE LEGACY AND PERCEPTIONS

"Raise a child in the way he should walk, and he will not depart from it."

Proverbs

"The tree doesn't grow far from the root."

"The problem with THAT boy is he's from THAT family."

Aunt Clara

THE LEGACY AND PERCEPTIONS

In some ways, the legacy is like a theme park. While it may have one or two unique rides, it belongs in a section of the park that features similar attractions. Disneyland has Space Mountain—a rushing, whirling drop down the inside of a mountain, as well the People Mover—a gentle, flowing, almost floating experience; both, however, are found in Tomorrowland.

No two rides are exactly alike; nor are any two legacies. The uniqueness in family belief systems is incredible. On any given small town or city block, a host of differing beliefs and lessons will be taught at the dinner table. However, this does not mean that many of these nightly classes do not fall under the same page in the "Family Curriculum Manual." There are similarities and themes that get presented in various forms. In later chapters, for example, we will examine families that circle the wagons of guilt for the children. While each system may have differing names for the wagons, the kids all get the message: "Kid, you always mess-up."

However, before looking at the various themes presented in family legacies, it is important to uncover the part that *perception* plays in all of this. As strange as it may seem to many of you, the "truth" of what happens in a family system is not as important as how the various family members see it. My sister had an inordinate amount of fear of the dark when she was small. Bedtime, therefore, became a frightening and dreaded experience for her as she climbed the stairs 3by herself. In her fear and loneliness, she fussed and cried, a problem my parents solved by suggesting that I, her older and braver brother, go to bed, too. Assuming that protesting would be a useless expenditure of energy, I usually took an apple and a handful of crackers and headed for my bedroom. Being an avid reader, I munched and read until I fell asleep, most times long before my sister finally closed her eyes for the night.

There were times, when I was in my early teens, that I felt it was unfair to go to bed at the same time as my younger sister. Nevertheless, since I was a "good" boy, with a sister who was terrified of creatures in the night, I ate fruit and read. To protest seemed fruitless, no pun intended. Nevertheless, I believed an injustice was occurring, that I was being treated unfairly simply because I happened to live with a frightened sister. The obvious conclusion: my parents valued her needs above mine.

THE LEGACY AND PERCEPTIONS

Decades later, during my "discovery" years, I raised this issue with my parents. They were retired and spending their winters in Florida, so this conversation took place over morning grapefruit on the patio. In hindsight, as I look over that dialogue, I suppose my parents were doing what all of us do: explaining our reasons so that others don't blame us for any unhappiness. That morning, my mother told her story, "Well, Gail was afraid and you loved to read. You took your apple and your book and went up to bed, happy as a lark. Certainly, you never said anything."

Digging into my grapefruit, I realized that I absolutely believed her. It was true—I never said anything; there was no protest. At that moment a great truth swept over me: my parents didn't treat me unfairly, I treated me unfairly, and blamed them. What is critical in this story, however, is that because I *felt* treated unfairly, I behaved and reacted as though it was the truth.

In the family legacy, there are at least two parts to every experience, the actual event AND the way children (and parents) see and evaluate that event. Children do not have to be treated unfairly; they only need to FEEL they have been treated that way. Feelings, within the child, become the springboard to decisions about beliefs, behavior, and life. Some parents reading this might be led to feelings of powerlessness since children will "see what they see," and will "feel what they feel." This is absolutely true, and as a matter of fact, ALL of us are exactly the same; what we perceive to be true, we believe IS true.

Most of the psychology experts claim that perception is "the result of receiving and organizing data from an external experience." In simple language, this says that YOU decide what every event means based on YOUR beliefs and conclusions. In the last chapter we talked about software, the mind-programming of your brain. In perception, a truly remarkable experience takes place. Something may happen to us, or we may observe a certain event, and we immediately draw on our software-programming to interpret what's going on. Conclusions are arrived at, which in turn, are inserted into the software package as confirmation of previous software.

A forty-three-year old college instructor told me a story about his sad and unmet needs with his parents. He was one of three children, the youngest of whom was a physically handicapped sister. Much of his life, he claimed, was spent in stepping into the background because his sister's needs were obviously so much greater than his own. While this angered him, he immediately felt guilty, since he was—in his mother's terms—"so much better off than your sister." He told me that he had tried very hard to never ask his parents for anything. "I'd rather struggle and do it myself than place myself in the position of hearing them tell me 'no.' I don't think I could bear it."

The previous spring he had struggled through a painful and difficult divorce. Placing his furniture in storage, he had lived from "flat to flat" for the first year after leaving his wife. "Then, I found the neatest small house, close to school and affordable," he told me. "But I needed help moving and I also needed some emotional support, so I decided to take the plunge and ask my parents. One night I called them on the phone and asked them what they were doing next month." He paused in the story a moment. "I suppose I should have told them immediately what I wanted, but I guess I was trying to feel them out. Anyway, they told me that my sister had found a new apartment and they were going down to Houston to help her move.

"When my dad asked me 'why do you want to know what's going on next month?' I lied and said I was thinking of coming down, but I would make it another time." He started to softly cry, "I couldn't bring myself to ask them to choose between my sister and me. I guess I couldn't stand to lose again." He brought his fist down on the arm of the chair, "I always lose!"

In this instance, this man's perceptions began in childhood with the *felt*, and, perhaps, taught belief, that his sister's needs were more important than his. This, of course, denied his emotional needs in favor of his sister's physical needs. It provided him with one of his family's legacy truths: your emotional needs are not important. In reality, his parents would never have felt his emotional needs were unimportant. They simply had an enormous amount of their own *stuff* to deal with in their handicapped daughter. Their own sense of *guilt* over birthing a child with physical problems, rooted in a fundamentalist teaching of God's punishment, carried great power. Equally, a fear for their daughter's future, after they could no longer help her, was a topic of daily conversation. They saw their two sons as very capable, and indeed, praised them to their friends and neighbors. "We don't have to worry about our boys," his mother would say, "They never gave us a speck of trouble."

Several years ago I read a book in which the writer made a statement that has stuck with me: "I am the center of my own universe." I'm not sure where that quote came from, but I am sure of its truth. My client was the center of his world. He saw, as we all see, life from his world. Therefore, his perceptions were filtered through his own sun, namely, his beliefs, software, and legacy, as HE interpreted them. The perceptions that his emotional needs were not important, although NOT true, nevertheless became true for him. In turn, he approached each new event with this belief: "My emotional needs are not important." Understandably, it would be virtually impossible for him to see life except through that filtered belief. Looking at life from the center of his universe, he looks *through* his beliefs for confirmation of their truth. His parents going to Houston to help his sister move was one more explanation point in his confirmation search. Unfortunately, going unexplored and unquestioned, he will carry this legacy belief to his death. Even more tragic, his belief is just that—only a belief; it is not truth.

Your beliefs carry so much power that it soon becomes impossible to look at life without them. If you are taught through your legacy that other people are "out to get you," you will not be able to enter even the most innocent of relationships without looking through the "out to get me" filter. The teller at the bank who takes too much time with a customer, particularly if you are in a hurry, is "one of them." The grade school principal who places your child in the class taught by one of the more unpopular teachers is "just like all the rest." When the County Handicapped Fund Drive takes place and you are solicited for funds, you wonder if the money "ever gets there at all," or does it "line the pockets of the solicitors?" It only takes a newspaper story from any place in the country, spelling out a mismanagement of funds, to confirm what you already know: "you can't trust anybody."

Legacy beliefs have a mind of their own. They are always seeking out experiences and events that confirm their truth. Unfortunately, seldom is anyone aware this is occurring. You would never stop to think, for example, that your views on abortion, inner city crime, or political corruption are rooted in your family legacy. Even when it appears that you are abandoning the legacy and moving to another position, it is very difficult to truly do so. Many times the other position is simply a reaction to your original legacy. A child who is forced to attend church every Sunday, regardless of his wants, will take that experience into adulthood. As an adult, he has a choice: to attend church or not. Sometimes his reasoning will go like this: "I had to attend church every single Sunday when I was growing up, and by God, now that I'm an adult, I've had it and I'm not going." So he doesn't—ever.

While it may seem that the young man has abandoned his family legacy in favor of his own choices, in reality he has merely reacted to it. Free choice is just that, free choice. It is not a reaction OR a loyalty; it is a decision based on YOUR wants, needs, and thoughts, not a direction chosen out of anger, powerlessness, or reaction to unhappy childhood circumstances.

On the surface, it may seem that you are making lots of free choices, separate from your legacy, every day. The reality may be quite different. A decision made IN REACTION to your legacy is still a legacy issue, nonetheless. It is only the other side of the same coin. Free choice is picking up another coin and engraving on it your own mottoes.

While I was never fond of math, a sort of helpful formula emerges here.

FAMILY LEGACY + YOUR PERCEPTIONS = YOUR BELIEFS
YOUR BELIEFS + YOUR PERCEPTIONS (LEGACY
EXPERIENCES) = YOUR TRUTH
YOUR TRUTH + CONFIRMATION EXPERIENCES = *THE TRUTH*

Unfortunately, THE TRUTH is really *Your Truth,* arrived at by what you *see* in the world. Of course, what you see is what you are looking for based on your beliefs, which are rooted in your family legacy. "And the green grass grows all around, all around, all around..." as the old song says.

Fred was one of two sons, born just before the Second World War. His father was one of the first men to die in the attack on Pearl Harbor. While his mother, Betty, struggled to provide for Fred and his brother, her own beliefs regarding her inadequacy surfaced. She doubted her ability to keep the children since she felt that she was not capable enough to even care for herself, much less two sons. The first man she met, therefore, became her rescuer and she gladly agreed to his terms that she "give" the boys to her sister to raise, allowing Betty and her new husband to have a "clean start."

Recalling those early childhood days, Fred shudders. "Every day I was beaten for some reason, sometimes just because I was close by. All the other kids had a mom and dad; it made it real hard for me. I talked a lot about my dad being a war hero and pretended that I would grow up to be just like him. My aunt, I guess, had other ideas." Fred described a very difficult childhood in which he, more than his brother, was systematically "cut to shreds" by his well-meaning, but frustrated aunt. Fred's world became very frightening, and his concepts of himself, limited. His aunt told his teachers that he was a "problem" and a "slow learner." It only took this little hint for two or three of his early teachers to focus on his mistakes. Soon Fred was a squirrel, moved to the bottom of the class, away from the more speedy learners, like the chipmunks, rabbits, and foxes. Weeping in my office, Fred cried, "I always wanted to be a chipmunk, but I guess I was just too stupid."

By the time he was twelve years old, Fred's family legacy had led him to his own beliefs. "I'm slower than other people and not as smart," he said. "Besides that, there must be something wrong with me because no mother would give her kid away if he was normal." Once a family legacy issue becomes a belief, the rest seems to go on automatic pilot. Fred failed in everything he tried. Dropping out of school at age 16, he joined the service, hoping to be the hero he believed his father to be. A poor reader and limited at math, Fred soon found himself in the motor pool, washing and waxing cars for the "smarter" officers. It was a bad experience for him, relieved only by periodic and intense bouts of drinking.

After his service time was up, Fred returned home to his aunt's belittling abuse. "It was all I knew," he told me, "and at least it felt familiar." By now, Fred's belief in his stupidity and inadequacy had turned into THE TRUTH: "I am less than other people." Two failed marriages, several lost jobs, and a small try at a business venture finally confirmed THE TRUTH to Fred, and he attempted suicide. Placing the gun in his mouth and shooting himself twice in the roof of the mouth, Fred managed not only to survive, but also, basically, to suffer little ill effects. With a wry smile he told me, "I couldn't even do that right."

Listening to Fred talk I began to hear a thinker under all the self-doubt and hatred. It became apparent that he was not "stupid" or "dumb," but rather uninformed. This was a man who had not tried to read, since he didn't believe that he could. Avoiding groups of people where his inadequacy might show, he isolated himself, leaving his education to game shows and old situation comedies.

Once a belief becomes THE TRUTH, it is very difficult to wedge it out of place. Not only does it take a lifetime to put THE TRUTH in place, you are programmed (remember the previous chapter) to not mess around with it. Your programming (mind) tells you, "THE TRUTH is there for a reason: to take care of you—so leave it alone."

The tragedy in all of this is that while change is possible, it is never seen as such. THE TRUTH is not fixed in concrete. It just feels that way. Much of this dilemma is based on our perceptions of our childhood experiences, along with the conclusions we have reached. No one escapes this problem! The brightest and healthiest among us carry the family legacy into beliefs, and then, into THE TRUTH (Your Truth). But as we shall see, change can only occur with *awareness* of the way YOUR TRUTH impacts and directs your life.

WATCHING YOURSELF

When I was a teenager I decided to become a golfer. Probably because my father was taking up the sport (and partly because few of my friends played), I thought I had a chance to be a "big fish in a little pond." In my fantasy moments, I imagined myself walking down the 18th hole toward the victory cup and several thousand dollars. Unfortunately, my form, swing, and unwillingness to spend hundreds of hours in practice worked against the fantasy becoming a reality. Because I was tall and gangling with long arms, I could hit a golf ball a "fer distance," as my barber used to say. Unfortunately, that "gangliness" did nothing to help my tendencies to lunge at the ball. Well-meaning adults with whom I played kept telling me that I was lunging with every swing, particularly when I was driving. Because I hit the ball 250 to 300 yards each time, I ignored their advice. I also ignored the fact that the ball seldom landed in the fairway.

One afternoon, my best friend and I decided to make a "movie" of our golf game. Since the old Super 8 camera was a hobby of mine, I hauled it around the golf course taking pictures along the way. He filmed me putting, chipping, and driving. Weeks later, when I finally got around to developing the film, there I was in colored footage, lunging with each drive. It looked awful, and my form was worse than that. So, on that summer evening of my 16th year, I decided that God did not want me to be a professional golfer. Watching myself on film was a revealing seminar on how not to swing a golf club, and how to realistically choose a career.

Since those days, I have been amazed at how easily we can ignore ourselves in life. Have you ever noticed how seldom you "notice" yourself? It's possible to go from year to year, and decade to decade, without ever watching yourself in relationships, behavior, and decision-making. Many people find themselves at a dead end in marriage or employment wondering how they got there. Lives fall apart daily in our society and people stand around scratching their heads wondering how this ever could have happened.

Some people blame television, which tends to numb our minds and annihilate family communication; others blame affluence and technology. Regardless of the reason, we live in a time where few people even bother to "think". Sitting on the porch swing or lying under the stars allows people to think. Working ten hours a day and falling asleep to the predictable jokes of late night TV does not. There are even those who say to me, "I try not to think about things so that I don't get upset or fearful. Instead, I work hard at keeping busy."

If you are unhappy or distressed with your life, it will not get better by pretending otherwise. While it may be upsetting to think about things, it is the beginning of awareness, one of the major ingredients for change in your life. In Alice In Wonderland, when Alice was wandering aimlessly about, the White Rabbit asked her where she was going. Answered she, "I don't know." "Then," said the White Rabbit, "it doesn't much matter if you get there or not, does it?" Roaming about through life without thought or awareness leaves your life and future in the hands of an unfamiliar automatic pilot.

THE LEGACY AND PERCEPTIONS

Doesn't it seem to border on the insane to live your life without knowing what's going on? What advice would you give to a friend who got lost every day because he took the wrong turn at the corner? Wouldn't you suggest that he turn another direction? But what if he kept doing the same thing because he wasn't thinking, or because he forgot where he was? You might begin to suspect he didn't mind getting lost, or that perhaps he was going around with his eyes closed. If you cared about him, you would probably suggest that he open his eyes and watch where he's going.

Although I should be used to it by now, because I have done it in my own life and have listened to countless stories of others doing it in theirs, I still find that a lot of people stroll along in life with limited vision and no awareness. It is only in watching yourself that you will begin to take charge of your life and find ways to bring change into it. Patterns are impossible to see without looking, and life is filled with patterns. If three or four relationships break down and you are told the same thing over and over, it might pay you to stop for a minute, look where you are, and watch yourself. Perhaps some thinking is in order. There may be some destructive patterns just waiting to be seen by you before they rear their ugly heads again.

Many people enter therapy because they feel they are powerless in their lives. Problems are seen as insurmountable and relationships are so filled with pain that many clients see only hopelessness. In most situations, healing occurs not through learning any more *stuff*, but rather in *unlearning*. There is a myth in our society that if you can just learn enough *stuff* you can get "better," presuming there is something wrong with you. Unfortunately, most of us have more than enough stuff in our heads. The need is to dump some of it out, especially the junk that is unhelpful and destructive. However, how are you ever going to know what to get rid of if you don't take the time and energy to watch yourself in action so that you know what beliefs are running your life? Beliefs are uncovered by noticing yourself in every situation. If you constantly step into the background each time an opportunity comes your way and then wonder why you never get anywhere, you should be aware that there will never be a change until you notice what you are doing.

Whatever is true for your life—Your Truth—based on your beliefs and rooted in your family legacy, will remain constant until you explore the whole picture. Watching yourself is a major step in letting go of the beliefs in your life that keep you stuck. In a sense, to watch yourself, you don't have to read any more books, attend any more lectures, or write in a journal; all you have to do is stay in the present time and *notice* your actions, behavior, and feelings.

When you watch and discover yourself "lunging at the ball," or as you see destructive patterns in your life, you will begin *unlearning* automatically. To notice yourself is to begin the journey toward change.

THE LEGACY AND FAMILY TYPES

*"Infancy isn't what it is cracked up to be.
Children, not knowing that they are having
an easy time,
have a good many hard times.*

*Growing and learning and obeying
the rules of their elders,
or fighting against them,
are not easy things to do."*

Don Marquis

THE LEGACY AND FAMILY TYPES

Children seem to enter the world with a blank slate. Awaiting the wisdom and teachings of parents, their minds stand ready. Poised with a piece of chalk in hand, and no eraser within reach, children are in the "classroom" at their port of entry. Long before studies can tell us what they are learning, they quickly fill chalkboards with our ramblings and proclamations. Coinciding with a hind-end smack trailed by a gasp, school is opened.

Over the years I have discovered that family legacies seem to have a pattern. Since they all tend to blend together, it is not possible to clearly distinguish one type of legacy from another. However, for purposes of clarity I have divided them into four major types: The Guilt- or Critical-based Legacy, The Shame-based Legacy, The Legacy of Denial, and the Fear-based Legacy.

Section II defines each Legacy type with particular focus on the impact to children. It is critical to remember that children are eager learners in the early years. The modeling and conversations of parents are the strategies or expressions of the "curriculum," namely, the Family Legacy. "The kids are all ears," is only a partial truth. They are also all "feelings," taking in what is said and done through every cell in their body. Children learn by simply being with their parents.

Two major points cannot be overemphasized: First, parents teach what they know, and they know their family legacy. Being raised themselves in a powerful belief system, parents understand it is their duty to pass on this knowledge to the children. Unexamined legacies become part of the mandate of parenting, and falsehoods get taught with just as much power as truth. Whether right or wrong, healthy or unhealthy, parents teach the legacy with the absolute belief that it is their job. Expressed through love or fear, the legacy is taught by parents who are convinced of its value and importance.

Secondly, children do not have the ability to separate fact from fiction. They believe what they see, hear, and feel. To expect children to process the helpful pieces of the legacy while dismissing the unhelpful is asking the impossible. When pushed toward the illogical or ridiculous, children will automatically assume that they are the ones with the faulty thinking. Few children ever consider the possibility that their parents might be misinformed. Even adult children seldom examine this likelihood.

Legacy patterns shape families as well as family members. Some of you reading of these patterns may discover that your family exhibits all of them. Others will find one major pattern that feels very familiar. Less important than figuring out your family legacy is understanding the ways in which it was helpful or not helpful. Holding on to the helpful parts and letting go of the unhelpful is a major step in self-growth and healing. It is your legacy and your life. The question is, how do they work together for you in giving you a more joyful and celebrative life?

CHAPTER VI

THE CRITICAL LEGACY AND THE GUILT-BASED FAMILY

*"The conscience is the still small voice
that makes you feel even smaller."*

J. A. Sanaker

*"I could see by the way she sniffed
that she was about to become critical."*

Wodehouse

"Bob never does anything right; he never thinks," Sharon said to me in a marriage counseling session. Bob, her husband, sat in the chair looking at the floor, his eyes rising to meet mine and then quickly dropping to stare at the bottom of my desk. "If he didn't have a Ph.D., I'd wonder about his brain," Sharon continued. "I go out for an evening and he decides," she looked at me, "I mean, he finally makes a decision, to strip the dining room walls so I can paper them." She stared at Bob angrily.

"And?" I asked.

"Just this." She looked back at me. "The wallpaper is on order and won't be in until the end of next week. He knew that," she gestured in his direction. "Of course, he also knew that this weekend my boss and his wife are coming for dinner and the evening."

"I forgot," Bob said weakly, his voice almost a whisper.

"You forgot," Sharon mimicked his voice, "You forgot. Of course, you forgot. It's not your boss, so what the hell difference does it make to you if the dining room looks like shit."

Bob looked at her, "I told you I was sorry. I can give it two coats of paint before the weekend and it'll look OK."

"And that's supposed to make it all better?" Sharon's voice was rising, "God, what did I ever do to deserve this? I thought I was marrying a man, someone who could think and make decisions, but instead I ended up with Elmer Fudd." She was referring to a book she had recently read about husbands who play out the roles of cartoon characters.

In a surprise move, Bob suddenly stuck his middle finger in the air in a gesture toward Sharon and said, "Up yours, Bbbb-ugs Bbbb-bunny." While I worked hard at holding back my laughter, his imitation of Elmer Fudd only served to further infuriate Sharon.

Standing up, her purse falling off her lap onto the floor, she shouted, "That's it! I've had it! I want out of this damn marriage and I want out now." She grabbed her sweater off the back of the chair and stormed toward the door. "Find your own way home, Mr. Fudd; you're out of the house this weekend." She pushed the door open and left, slamming it shut behind her. Just as suddenly she pulled it back open, "And don't worry about my boss for dinner this weekend, I'll take them out." She slammed the door again, this time for good.

Bob sat still, the silence almost overwhelming and his wife's anger still swirling its energy throughout the room. Finally he said to me, "Well, I guess I really did it this time. But she really pissed me off. I suppose I should have just sat there and kept my mouth shut; every time I open it I get into trouble. That's the way it was when I was a kid and that's the way it is now."

Later on that evening, I sat down with my notes and reflected on Bob's family history. The oldest of three children, Bob was the first child born into his mother's family system. His grandparents took an inordinate interest in his life, filling him with praise at every accomplishment from Little League to his junior high school band concerts. Each holiday they pushed him to the head of the table where he played his trumpet, and, what is more important, without any mistakes. Equally, his grandparents filled his head with high expectations. "You're going to be somebody!" his grandfather would tell him, "…the first person in this family to really amount to anything."

Unfortunately for Bob, his father was a pleaser, a man who spent himself and his money trying to keep everyone happy. When Bob's mother was upset, his father immediately began the task, no matter how difficult, to make everything better. "Sometimes when dad came home from work he was so tired he could barely stand. But he never took time to sit down and rest because there was too much to do—too many chores my mom had waiting for him. Sometimes I felt my mom was really unfair to him, but he would just look at me, shrug his shoulders and wink. I always felt he was saying, 'This is what it means to be a man: keep the old lady happy.'"

Bob's mother was a very capable and sensitive woman, just like Sharon. Both women were also angry at the males in their lives, men whom they called "wimpy" and disappointing. Sharon often said that she truly loved Bob, she just couldn't understand why such a capable man at work was so terrible as a husband and father. It appeared, she once said to me, "that he invites criticism—like he wants me to point out just what a failure he is. And you know me," she grinned, "I gladly tell him exactly where he's screwed up. He ends up walking away like a whipped dog with his tail between his legs, and I end up feeling guilty and worthless."

THE CRITICAL LEGACY AND THE GUILT-BASED FAMILY

While I don't have the statistical data to support this thought, I have noticed that on numerous occasions both people end up feeling guilt-ridden and worthless in relationships that reach a point of confrontation. It appears to be more by design than accident. Certainly husbands and wives would not consciously go around trying to get one another to feel bad; yet that's what happens so often that it bears examination.

"Relationships are the seminars of life," I read somewhere. I wish I had said it, but I didn't. However, truer words have not been spoken. Our relationships all serve to bring issues of our past into the present to be worked through and healed. In this instance, Bob has a tremendous lack of self-worth; he does not believe in himself, but rather believes in his inadequacy.

Later on in the book we will be looking at ways Bob can use these confrontations as a path toward freeing himself from the guilt and poor self-esteem that seem to steer his life and relationships. He and Sharon, in a true sense, are gifts to one another as they both bring out, into the open, the unresolved issues from the past. It is almost as if much of our past is hiding in the shadows waiting for situations in the marriage to shine sun into the dark corners. Even terrible scenes, such as the one in my office, can be a marvelous way of moving the clouds aside and ushering in the sunlight.

WELL-MEANING BUT SCARED PARENTS

There are family legacies that end up teaching children the very opposite of what was intended to be taught. By using guilt and criticism, parents are not trying to injure their children; instead, they are trying to point out to them the errors of their ways so that their lives will work better and be more fulfilled. Unfortunately, the strategy backfires and the children end up with lives less fulfilled and feeling more guilt-ridden. Bob's family was filled with loving parents and grandparents who truly wanted the very best for him. There was, however, no space to make mistakes, to fail, or NOT to do it right. In a sense, there was great permission to excel but no permission to be HUMAN.

My step-son recently attended a week-long retreat experience that entailed living and swimming with dolphins. Upon his return, filled with enormous "insights" as to the order of importance of God's creature, he told me that dolphins were "persons." "All mammals are persons," he said, "Some persons are dolphins, some are whales, and some are HUMANS!" While I tended to give him a hard time over his zealousness for that which I considered a fish, it did allow me to think about how important it is for us to see our HUMANITY as a freeing condition. We are not God, nor will we ever be. If we define God as perfection, pure and holy, that certainly is not who we are. While the thought that you are not God may seem obvious to many of you reading this, there are a large number of people who cannot give themselves permission to live out their HUMANITY and all that it means. To be HUMAN means NOT to be God. Making mistakes and doing it wrong is part of how we express our HUMANITY.

Now, this is not to say that we simply run around messing up everything and then say "I'm HUMAN." It means, instead, that when we make a mistake, we allow ourselves the luxury of accepting that mistakes are a part of the HUMAN condition.

In guilt-based or critical family legacies, mistakes, however, are seen as far more serious. Instead, they are thought to be the very things that can not only damage you, but can also destroy all you have worked for. The reasoning in a guilt-based system goes like this: "You are my child and you MUST learn. If I don't teach you and point out to you the errors of your way, how will you learn? Furthermore, if you are not punished for doing things wrong, or for failing, how will you ever know that I am serious about this? And how will you ever learn?" "HOW WILL YOU EVER LEARN?" is a common motto in every guilt-based system.

Since guilt-based systems do not just occur but are inherited from one generation to the next, parents know exactly how it feels to experience guilt. While you might think that because parents know guilt feels so terrible and is so controlling, they would do everything in their power to avoid it—just the opposite occurs. Guilt is like the common glass in the bathroom, or the one towel in the kitchen; everyone uses it because it works.

In many ways, guilt comes into play because parents experience fear when children begin to grow, try new things, and rebel. It is also important to remember that parents are living out the legacy of their own families. Parents of parents expect that children, their grandchildren, will "turn out right."

THE CRITICAL LEGACY AND THE GUILT-BASED FAMILY

Your mother and father not only have a vested interest in your future because they love you and want what's best for you; they also need to carry out their own charge from a family legacy that came from your grandparents. This is why it is almost impossible to understand your parents if you don't have some kind of knowledge of your grandparents and the relationships they had with your mother and father.

Criticism, then, is used by parents to point out exactly what it is that children have done wrong. Guilt, on the other hand, is the feeling that occurs as a result of that "helpful" discovery. The hope of parents and well-meaning adults is that because children now know how uncomfortable it is to feel guilty, they will "stay in line," and not do wrong things. The fear that parents have as they see their children make mistakes pushes them to critical parenting, which in turn leaves the children feeling filled with guilt. This guilt, unfortunately, leads children into feelings of badness and inadequacy. "I never do it right," is the cry of most guilt-ridden children of the critical-based legacy.

BUT WHAT ABOUT THE KIDS?

Growing up in guilt, the kids get a very clear message: If you do it right, you're real lovable, but when you are bad, you're a real bad penny, and nobody wants a bad penny around. The message is said in a lot of different ways, depending on the family's communication style, the legacy of discipline, and the degree of fear carried by the parents. Nevertheless, whether given in Morse code or shouted loudly in the bedroom, the kids learn that their behavior is being watched and judged. Is it any wonder children of critical-based legacies so clearly understand that Santa keeps a list and checks it twice? They could write a book about it.

Anytime you hear a lot of *shoulds* and *oughts* coming out of someone's mouth, you know that you are talking with a child (adult or otherwise) of a legacy that used criticism and guilt. Once kids learn they can be good or horrid, and that some type of conditional love is sprinkled in with that lesson, it's just a short step to self-judgment and "shoulding" on themselves. I grew up in a small town without even so much as a traffic light. The year I started college, the first traffic light swayed over main street. Fifteen years later, McDonald's found a home there and now three traffic signals are needed. In that small town, a traffic jam consists of four or more cars; the folks can't understand the "tie-up."

One day, when home visiting my parents, my dad and I rode "downtown" to pick up a few things. Part way up Main Street, the water company had placed a barricade in order to fix a broken pipe. While cars were getting by, maneuvering room was narrow and so a traffic jam started. We were the fifth car back. Immediately my father said, "Boy that was really stupid. I should have gone up Walnut Street. Or, if I'd been thinking, I'd have turned up Grant Street." I didn't say anything and we sat a minute or two. "I can't believe this," my father went on, "I should have gone down by McDonald's and cut over to the Super Duper the back way. That was real dumb."

I couldn't take it anymore so I said to him, "Did you know the water company was doing this work today?"

"Well, no," he admitted.

"Then, how were you supposed to know to turn up Grant or go down the back way to the Super Duper?" It seemed like a good question to me.

"That's not the point," my father insisted, "I should have gone the back way and we wouldn't be stuck like this." By now we were through the traffic "tie up" and pulling into the parking lot of the Super Duper.

Not wanting to leave it there, I said, "Well, the next time you're going downtown, why don't you call the police station and ask them if there are any barricades up around town. That way, you would know about the traffic jams and you could cut around the back way to wherever you're going." He glared at me and we walked into the grocery store.

Thinking about this later on, and knowing my father's mother very, very well, I realized the depth and strength of the critical legacy in which he had been raised. It was so powerful that he believed he should be able to know what was going to happen before it happened. In talking with many clients over the years, I have been amazed at the number who feel they should or ought to be able to see around corners. Again, as far as I know, it is impossible for HUMAN BEINGS to see around corners or to know what is going to happen before it occurs. Compounding this insane, but understandable, thinking, is the fact that when they cannot see around corners, they feel guilty as they bump into a surprise on the next block.

Children raised in critical- or guilt-based legacies are rooted in fear. One of the primary reasons for this is that it is virtually impossible for a person to experience guilt without feeling that he or she will be punished. Punishment is a familiar experience in legacies of this type, and children grow to expect it if they do something wrong, something they should not have done.

"You just wait until I talk with your father, young man, and then we'll see just how smart you are." That is not an unfamiliar line in many critical-based families. For some children, it is more than an eternity before father comes home. The anticipation of punishment is cruel in itself, along with an almost irreparable damage to the father-child relationship. Of course, the opposite can be true when Mother is the heavy hand for whom a "bad child" waits.

Guilt is both insidious and vicious. In my view, it borders on the demonic, and yet, it is used in virtually every significant relationship, certainly in my own, as well as in the lives of my clients and friends. To understand it better, I tried drawing a picture of guilt as an interesting exercise. My picture had something that looked like a dragon with two faces; one with glaring fangs, fire breathing from its nostrils, and the other with a sweet smile, glassy eyes, and sucking on a breath mint. Sometimes guilt tricks you into thinking you will not get punished, only to nail you through the backdoor. Other times, there is no doubt about it and you face your punisher head on.

By the time children are adults, they have learned how to expertly use and misuse guilt in their lives. Using exactly a measuring cup amount of punishment, guilt is appeased. If you do something horrid, two cups of punishment may not even suffice; on the other hand, a minor infraction calls for only a teaspoon or two.

Alan was a politician who struggled his whole life with a weight problem. He was constantly fighting with his wife when she caught him sneaking food out of the refrigerator—a violation of his most recent diet. No matter how good his intentions were, Alan invariably ended up sneaking a Snickers Bar out of the cupboard, or a doughnut from the small box hidden under the front seat of his car.

During election time, Alan faced his weight problems constantly. Evening dinners and morning breakfasts were daily events. While he tried to keep his intake under control, the food was always delicious and plentiful. One evening, driving to a fund raiser in which he was the guest speaker, he made himself a promise. "Only one dessert tonight," he smiled at himself in the rear view mirror. Unfortunately, this was a smorgasbord affair featuring several homemade pies and cakes. Alan ate three pieces and picked up a brownie on his way to the car. Driving home, he could hear the voice of his deceased mother and father mingled in with his wife's disapproval. Together they pronounced him guilty as charged. As a matter of fact, like Alan, in much of our daily living, most of us carry around a small interior court. Easily, and quite willingly, it can be called into session—almost invariably the verdict is *guilty*. In fact, if you didn't feel guilty, why would you call court into session at all?

Alan now knows that he is guilty and therefore some type of punishment is necessary. If you knew him, you might think that a perfect punishment would be to contract to a 800 calorie-a-day diet, or perhaps to wake up early and exercise with the trim young athletes on ESPN. Guilt, however, is much more tricky than so simple a solution. Alan's punishment occurs the next evening, when, at the Councilmen's Annual Banquet, he eats five desserts. Within two months Alan had moved into a size 52 suit, and now hates himself even more. The important consideration here is that guilt has done its dirty work, namely, to get Alan to hate himself. Guilt is never interested in whether you learn anything or not. Quite impartially, it wants to destroy you.

Some of you reading this might wonder why Alan doesn't simply take better care of himself. This is a good question, but one that ignores another side effect of the critical-based family legacy: poor self-esteem and great self-hatred.

GUILT AND THE SELF-HATRED CYCLE

Several years ago, while in college, I sang in a small choir that enjoyed performing Broadway musicals and some of the smaller Off-Broadway shows. One time the director asked me to sing a part in a short operetta called "Speak Up!" It was a delightful musical rendition of a mother, father, and sister surrounding a subdued teenaged son, forced to sit in a chair while the rest of his family circled him, singing criticisms of his behavior. The big, basso father is growling: "When I was a boy...," while the boy's mother keeps wailing, "You will be the death of me, oh, what will I do with you?" After twenty minutes of this type of barrage, repeated over and over, the young boy stands up and sings, "What you say may be true, I have one word to say to you." There is a lengthy pause and then he screams "Help!", running off the stage as quickly as he can.

The audience laughed and applauded every place we performed this "family circus." Not only was it cute, but most of the people watching found a place to relate with the dilemma of this young boy, who was unable to do anything right. Indeed, there is a certain desperation experienced by children of the critical-based legacy. The same parent who asked "How will you ever learn?" while doling out punishment, also asked other questions such as "Why did you do that?" or "Why can't you be like so and so?" Regardless of the questions raised by parents in the critical- or guilt-based legacy, the children all get the same message: "You don't do things right!" Even very young children, when hearing this criticism, begin to arrive at conclusions about themselves. Most popular among the childhood conclusions is: I'm a bad person and I'm a failure. Children arrive at the same judgment of behavior as their parents have expressed. Kids, for the most part, are fast learners and they take seriously the admonitions of their parents. After all, "these are the people who 'made me.' They certainly know more about me than I do."

Children of the critical-based legacy quickly install their software of guilt and criticism. Room for errors or mistakes is limited since they "should know better." The "shoulds" and "oughts" of their parents become permanently installed as a living guide for the future. The cycle of self-hatred is now prepared to begin.

Since we live in a world of uncertainties and surprises, it is impossible for any person—even the brightest and most gifted among us—to know everything. Things happen to you every day that you didn't expect to happen. Predictability is a longing, not a reality. Companies and corporations come and go; so do family members. The wealthy can lose everything in a moment, as can the healthy. We live in a world of permanent change.

Logically speaking, how can you possibly do everything

right all the time when you live in a world of continual shifts? How can you do everything right all the time when you are a human being, filled with emotions, fears, and longing? The answer, of course, is that you can't. Nevertheless, this is the internal expectation of the child of the critical- or guilt-based system. "There are no excuses" rests at one end of the critical-based spectrum, while "one mistake is OK, but remember—only one," at the other end. Both ends, needless to say, are dead. It is incredible to realize that people who are intelligent and reasonable in every other area of their lives are so stuck and rigid in their insane judgments of themselves when they make a mistake, or "don't do it right." Bosses who would forgive their employees for an enormous mistake would not forgive themselves for a relatively simple one.

Critical to understanding the cycle from self-criticism to self-hatred is the leap that occurs in people's thinking when they make a mistake. Grace was married for twenty-three years when her husband came home one night and told her he was in love with his secretary, one of Grace's casual friends. Obviously, and quite appropriately, Grace fell apart that evening. She cried, screamed, and threw things. Feeling betrayed by both husband and friend, she raged through the night, until, exhausted and worn, she fell asleep near morning. The next day, her husband packed a few things and moved out. By then, Grace was too paralyzed to protest.

The next several months for Grace were filled with fear and anger. Within a week of leaving the house, her husband moved in with his secretary. Grace was livid and filled with thoughts of revenge. For years she had stayed home with the children while her husband built up his own financial and economic position within the work force. She, now, had to start over, beginning at a very low salary and forced into the work world out of desperation instead of choice.

Three years later I saw Grace in my office. She told me the story of her past situation, expressing her frustration at being so "stuck" in her pain, anger, and grief. "I feel exactly like I did three years ago," she told me. "While I am now fairly happy with my job, I just can't believe this has happened." She started to cry and through her sobs said, "I don't do this every night, but would you believe almost every one?" Grace talked on for an hour about the "rawness" of her feelings. She was particularly upset because she was not "handling" this problem better. "I talked with my mother last week and she said I just had to get my life under control, that I've moped around long enough."

Grace told me that in her childhood, one of the things she got the greatest praise for was her ability to solve problems. A great planner, Grace constantly avoided difficulties in her life, and, if by chance life threw her a curve ball, she always managed to hit it. "I don't strike out," said Grace. She talked about her father's strong teachings to "be prepared." Her brother, Tom, came to one session with her and told me about a conversation he had with his father on his seventeenth birthday: "Dad said to me, 'This is the best advice I can give to a young man about to explore the world: If you ever get caught with your pants down, be sure the lights go out at the same time.'" Grace nodded her head in agreement with her brother's story. Later on she said to me, "I guess I got caught with my pants down but no contingency plan. What a dope I am. God, I hate myself!"

Exploring this thought with Grace, it was fascinating to hear her reasoning, the logic of the critical-based legacy. "You should be prepared and handle whatever happens. If you caused it, and you probably did, then cure it." As Grace examined the breakdown of her marriage, even though her husband had left her, she concluded that it must be her fault. In the critical-based system, fault is important. If it's not your fault, then you're OK; however, if it IS your fault, definitely, you're NOT OK. Grace arrived at an entire cycle of thought, ultimately leading her to feelings of self-hatred and inadequacy. "My marriage broke up because of things I didn't do right. Beyond that, I'm not handling anything right, not 'curing' things. I'm screwing up at every turn so I must be a failure, or even a bad person. God, I hate myself!"

There is a huge, but nevertheless understandable, leap from Grace's judgment of behavior to her self-hatred. "If I do bad things or fail, then I must be a bad person or a failure. No one likes or loves a bad person like me. I hate myself for being so bad, for not being prepared, for not handling things right, and for failing." Feelings of self-hatred emerge from judgments of bad behavior or failure. While the internal court, the judges of the critical-based legacy, may make pronouncements regarding behavior, the little child within leaps to the next ledge called self-hatred. "I do bad things therefore I hate myself," is a creed for many children from families of guilt and criticism. These children are easily named "Self-condemners."

Sometime ago when my wife and I were driving to visit a certain shop I wanted to see, I got lost. Before we left home, I was positive I knew exactly where we were going. Obviously, I didn't; instead we found ourselves driving around in a strange section of the city with nary a clue as to the location of the shop. Pulling over to the side, I rummaged through the glove compartment for the necessary map to lead me to my destination. There was no map! I couldn't believe it; I had driven into "foreign" country without a map. I would NEVER do that. Yet, I had. I ranted and raved at myself for my stupidity for about an hour while we drove around searching for my shop. I hated myself for my stupidity; I should have called the shop before we left home. I should have checked the glove compartment to make sure the map was there. I should have asked the kids which one had "stolen" the map. What a stupid fool I was. What an idiot!

It is possible, at this point, to see the vulnerability opening up in children from critical-based systems. Once you have made mistakes (preventable, of course) and messed up your life by doing bad things (what other kinds of things are there you do?), then you must see yourself as bad and, therefore, hate yourself. This thinking now leaves the child (adult) wide-open for the insertion of guilt, punishment, and self-condemnation. When you hate yourself, you are more than agreeable to a visit from guilt. In fact, you may even invite him to stop in for coffee. Guilt finds easy access in self-hating people. Of course, if you hate yourself enough, you may even be willing to provide the necessary punishment to yourself. Grace punished herself nightly by NOT letting go of her perceived mistakes. Sitting up at night in her pain and grief, holding on to her list of "faults" for a broken marriage, she has invited guilt to remain and the punishment to continue. Grace is a victim of owning the judgments of her critical-based system; she is also poorly named since she so opposes the very concept her name reflects. To suggest to Grace that she show herself a little "grace" is immediately met with protestations and self-flagellation. "I don't deserve kindness," she told me when I suggested that she try to be as kind to herself as she was to others, "I've screwed my life up so bad. I just hate me."

Critical- or guilt-based legacies then, lead children to

judgments of themselves that invariably are negative. Out of these self-evaluations and conclusions, guilt is born, with its continual cry for punishment. Self-hatred, self-abuse, and stuckness, then become the products of the Self-condemning child. Unfortunately, the cycle will continue until the pain gets so hurtful that one either turns another direction or stagnates into oblivion.

Sometimes children from a critical- or guilt-based legacy will try to avoid the downhill slide into self-hatred and guilt by becoming overly productive and successful. Just as the Self-condemning child punishes himself by using inner guilt and criticism as fuel, the "Efforting" child pumps the same fuel into a similar engine but steers down another street. Trying with great energy to be the opposite of the Self-condemning child, the Efforting child strives with double strength not to make mistakes. Straight "A's" on the report card, a 4.0 grade point average at college, the collector of awards, and the youngest executive at AT&T are hallmarks of many Efforting children. Attempting to prove they are NOT inadequate, they resort to behavioral success as a way to convince themselves the critical-based legacy was false.

Authors and therapists John Bradshaw, John and Linda Friel, and Melodie Beatty have so wonderfully shown us the role of the Family Hero as the one who redeems the family system. It seems that every family needs a *hero*, someone who leads and takes charge of things. But, not only are Efforting children promoted to hero for the system, they become top salespeople because it is a hallmark of their "okayness." They do it for themselves, as well.

The over-productive child and the under-achiever can both come from the same critical-based legacy. Both, however, choose to express their feelings of self-hatred and inadequacy in different ways. The Efforting child becomes a success in the world, thus receiving praise and promotion; the Self-condemning child keeps falling down as a result of his/her negative self-judgment and guilt.

Brad and Mark were brothers born into a middle-class family in the suburbs. While their father was a child of a critical-based legacy, their mother grew up with much more grace. Both seemed to do well in elementary school, although Brad was often described as "immature" by his teachers. Mark was very much into sports and his peers; Brad, more introspective and private. When their parents divorced, both Mark and Brad moved away with their mother. For several years, connections with their father were limited and few. Brad later wondered if this was due to "conditional love."

Their mother remarried a recovering alcoholic, who slipped back into his addiction shortly after her marriage. Mark, feeling betrayed by his father, moved into his own addictive behavior. Brad embraced his mother and a higher path. The criticisms of their stepfather, even when given in drunken stupors, were taken seriously by both boys. Brad said, "One day I just made a decision not to believe him anymore. I was going to prove to him and everybody that I was somebody special." From that time on Brad excelled in everything he attempted. Graduating from high school with awards, he entered college with scholarships and high visions. His experience in college was marked by complete success, academically and socially. Brad was on his way to fulfilling his decision of years ago, to become somebody special. Forgotten was the criticism of his childhood, replaced by the markings of success.

After graduating from high school, Mark, on the other hand, joined the Navy, but was disillusioned there, also, leaving after his two year tour of duty was complete. Bouncing from job to job, he entered young adulthood filled with self-hatred and feelings of inadequacy. His self-condemning childhood led him to a life of punishment and self-hatred. Mark was as much a self-proclaimed failure as Brad was a social success. Both, however, were fueled by criticism and guilt. Brad simply steered down that "higher" street; he traveled Fifth Avenue while Mark visited the Bowery.

In understanding the impact and effects of the critical- or guilt-based legacy, it is important to recall the following: (1) Parents want their children to grow up and to do things right; (2) Criticism, guilt, and punishment are used as a way to be sure kids get the message; (3) Children install software into themselves to keep alive the messages and concerns of their parents; (4) Self- criticism leads to guilt and negative judgments; (5) The consequences of these negative judgments will be either Self-condemnation (punishment) or Efforting (success).

CHAPTER VII

THE SHAME-BASED LEGACY

"You ought to be ashamed of yourself."

Miss Snyder

"And when they saw they were naked, they hid."

Genesis

THE SHAME-BASED LEGACY

Several years ago I was invited to give the keynote address at a conference on family life. Because of travel difficulties, it was necessary for me to arrive the night before the formal start of the conference. Traveling light, since I was planning on flying out immediately after my presentation, I had only an outfit for the evening prior to my speech, and my new suit, especially purchased for this occasion.

I rose early and enjoyed coffee in my room before leaving for the auditorium. My new shoes fit a bit snugly, but I reasoned that they would soon stretch into a more comfortable shape. I picked up my travel bag and briefcase and walked out the door. Since the elevator was stuck a floor below, I decided to walk down the stairs to the main lobby. While I'm not exactly sure how it happened, I was about halfway down the stairs when my new shoes decided to turn on me, making me more clumsy than usual. I fell the rest of the way down the stairs.

As I jumped to my feet, my knees smarting and the knuckles of my hand throbbing, the first thing I did was look around to see if anyone happened to see my flight. Thank God, no one was in sight, allowing me the opportunity to give myself a body check. There was good news and bad news. No bones were broken but both knees were scraped and bleeding; that was the good news. The bad news was to be found in two large tears right in the front part of my pants. Wool that had covered the left knee now dangled down almost to my shin. The right pant leg had a hole in it about the size of a golf ball. My new suit pants were ruined, my knees were bleeding, and I had only a pair of casual tan slacks in my overnight bag. My suit was light gray.

I rushed back into my room and tended to my wounds first. The priority, however, was what to do about my clothing. I found a sewing kit in the bathroom basket of goodies—thank God for the Hilton—and, as best I could, tried to mend my slacks. The hole, however, could not be closed; I never could figure out what happened to the material that had been there before the hole. I did manage a halfway decent repair of the rip. Standing in front of the full length mirror, I examined myself. My shoes were banged up with scuff marks on the tops of both, my right pant leg had a small hole in it with my white, untanned skin shining through, and my left leg was covered with light gray material sewn in an uneven semicircle in bright, white thread. I was a mess.

I managed to check out (without anyone seeing my limited seamstress abilities), and walked over to the convention auditorium. I quickly found that if I carried my briefcase in front of me instead of at my side, it covered up my holes. Protected by leather, no one could see my flaws, the torn trousers, or evidence of my clumsy nature. Since I sat in the front row until introduced, and stood behind the full length podium while speaking, I actually completed my assignment and left without anyone seeing my hairy legs.

Driving to the airport in my rental car, I thought through the entire matter. Why was it such a big deal that no one find out what had happened to me? Why did I care if these people, most of whom I would never see again in my life, saw me in ripped trousers? I could have explained my fall to them. Certainly everyone has fallen down sometime in his or her life. Maybe they all would have had a good laugh out of my story. Two words kept running through my mind as the airplane taxied down the runway: shame and embarrassment. But, why should I be ashamed of falling down and tearing my pants? Why should it embarrass me to explain my ripped trousers to others? And yet I clearly felt both feelings.

Over the years I have recalled the "ripped trousers" episode many times. It is a vivid example to me of the power of shame. I used the word "power" because shame seems to have a life and strength of its own. It can propel people into all sorts of actions from running away to depression. Shame is the feeling people experience as a result of being "found out." It is the emotional outcome for people when they believe that others have seen through the curtain that hides "all which needs to be hidden." Shame is exposure.

In the previous chapter, I discussed the power and impact of the critical- or guilt-based legacy. Guilt and shame often get confused since it is very difficult to have one without the other. Guilt, on one hand, says that I did a bad thing; shame, on the other says that I am bad. Guilt claims, "I made a mistake," whereas shame shouts, "I AM A MISTAKE." Guilt points to behavior, shame to "being"; guilt looks at actions, shame stares at worth. Guilt tells you that you did something wrong; shame shakes its heads and says, "There's something wrong with you."

Oftentimes, critical-based legacies and shame-based legacies go hand-in-hand. It seems almost automatic in most families for shame to follow guilt. You may recall that in critical-based legacies, which use guilt as a way of teaching children, a primary question often asked is "Why did you do that?" In legacies rooted in shame the questions change slightly to become: "What's wrong with you?" or, "What's the matter with you?" Both questions imply that not only have you apparently done something bad, but obviously there is something bad about you. Your very being is brought into question.

Certainly there are many behaviors that you can control, such as biting your fingernails or sitting still during church. You can learn to be polite at the dinner table and to greet your aunt with a kiss. If the threats are strong enough, you can learn to come home on time and to do your homework. Maybe you can even get good grades. Most behavior is in your hands; it is in your power. On the other side, however, your *being* is your *being;* you can't do much about it. You are who you are. When parents criticize a child's actions, new ways of behaving can be introduced and the negative conduct changed. How can a child change his *being?*

As you can imagine, when you do something wrong you may hate yourself for not thinking, or for doing something stupid. In Chapter Six, it was easy to see how this reasoning can lead to self-hatred as a way of punishment for bad behavior. However, what happens to a child who believes that something is wrong with him or her goes even deeper. Such children end up believing that they should not be.

THE SHAM AND THE SHAME

Carl Rogers and his disciples very helpfully pointed out that children were looking for two basic things early on in their lives: one, to be self-actualized (fulfilled); and, two, to be unconditionally loved. I sense this is very true: All of us want to do whatever it is that makes us happy, and we want to be cared about. Kids learn very early, however, that life is not always a bed of roses. Sometimes you want to do something, but your parents are not in favor of your choice. It could be something as simple as crossing the street to visit a friend. The trouble is, however, that crossing the street is not permitted and, if you do, Mom and Dad will become angry. They may even punish you. The question is, "Can I cross the street and do whatever I want to do (fulfillment), and still be cared about by Mom and Dad (unconditional love)?"

While this may seem like a simple example, it is only one of many different situations that children find themselves in as they begin the task of growing up. Sometimes it is a very unimportant thing, such as wanting to watch a television show when Mom and Dad say it's time to eat. At other times, it may feel like something very critical, as in dating a young man whom your parents feel is "bad" for you. How can you please them, and please yourself? This is the dilemma Rogers talked about in his understanding of personalities.

Early on, then, we learn that sometimes, if we are authentic (truly ourselves), we may not feel loved by the important people in our lives. Can I do what I want to do and still be loved? It is important, however, to understand that parents are not quite so quick to withdraw love as children might believe. In fact, many parents love their children quite unconditionally; the difficulty is that the children equate parental disapproval with withdrawal of love.

Because parents are unhappy with a certain behavior does not mean they no longer love their children. Many children never figure this out; thus the confusion between *behavior* and *being* occurs. And, to support the way children think from time to time, in response to a child's unacceptable behavior, and in frustration, parents DO ask such questions as above: What's wrong with you, anyhow? The kids, of course, cannot separate what they have done from who they are. "Because I have done something wrong," they reason, "there must be something wrong with me. After all, didn't Mom and Dad just ask me that?"

Early on, then, SHAM is born into the lives of children. Apparently a necessity, sham is the counterfeit masquerade created to cover up the flaw in our character that our parents have so cleverly spotted. Children get the message from the start that if they continue behaving in an unacceptable manner, there will be serious consequences to follow. The unspoken message the kids carry is one of conditional love and the possibility of abandonment. "If you're not lovable, then you're certainly 'leavable,'" is what they hear. To protect themselves from the loss of love, and all that loss might mean, most kids develop a sham to hide their reality.

THE SHAME-BASED LEGACY

The anthropologist, Jules Henry, back in the 1960's, in a speech given to the Hahnemann Medical College, spoke eloquently about sham in the Western World. He quoted Albee as saying, in the play "Tiny Alice," that whoever refuses to believe in the sham should be shot. In particular, he argues that children need to learn early the importance of pretending. A child who refuses to develop and support "The Sham" will probably not survive, he claims.

Countless books and articles have been written on the "False Self" and the "Authentic Self" but the bottom line is always the same: A child creates an *artificial self* to cover up any unacceptable things that may lead his or her parents to withdraw their love. Just as Henry writes, it seems to be a survival issue. Without this sham the child is always at risk—at least in his or her own mind—and, therefore, goes into hiding.

Walter's father was a musician of sorts. He had played in a dance band while in high school, and for a few years, he joined a semi-pro band to play at wedding receptions and local clubs. His father had played the saxophone, but his first love was the drums. So, when Walter came home one day with the school band news sheet inviting sixth graders to join, it was an exciting time for his dad. While Walter had some interest in the band, he was more fascinated with the shiny trumpet, which he loved to hear when the band marched by or played in school assemblies. Instead, Walter signed up to learn to play the drums.

Almost immediately, Walter discovered that he hated the drums. First of all, he was not given a drum to play, but rather a rubber-coated board, a practice drum. It didn't make any noise and seemed just plain boring. His father, however, was excited about Walter's drumming career. Pulling the drum sticks out of his book bag, his dad would play on the car dash board or on the kitchen table. Wherever his dad could find a place to beat the sticks, he did. Meanwhile, Walter was falling behind in his drumming class. Without any interest, he did not learn how to keep time or even how to hold the sticks properly. Soon he started skipping lessons altogether.

One day the band teacher happened to spot Walter in the school lunch room. Coming over to him he asked, "Where have you been hiding, Walter? You've missed the last three weeks of lessons?" Red-faced, Walter said, "Well, my folks wanted me to give up the drums since I need to work harder on my studies. I was going to come and tell you and I just forgot." Looking somewhat puzzled, the band teacher went back to the faculty table and Walter continued eating. He also continued carrying his drum sticks back and forth to school, pretending to his parents that he was still busily learning how to be a drummer. Walter was living his sham. Not wanting to disappoint his father, he kept the facade going, until the Parent Teacher's Organization sponsored a Parent's Night.

As luck would have it, both Walter's father and mother decided to go to Parent's Night. Usually his father wasn't particularly interested, but for some reason or other, he chose to attend. Walter went to bed early, hoping against hope that his parents would not talk with the band teacher. Although he was still awake when his parents came home, he never moved a muscle in his bed, trying hard to breathe evenly as though asleep. However, it wouldn't have mattered because his father pushed into his room, clicked on the light and started to shake his shoulders. Sitting up in bed, Walter felt himself go numb. His head seemed to be spinning, and it felt as though the blood was rushing through his brain in a speedy current. Walter felt he could not catch his breath; and, amazingly enough, this was before his mother and father said one word to him.

A confrontation followed in which his parents tried to understand why Walter lied and pretended to both them and the band teacher. Feeling cornered, Walter tried to tell his parents that he didn't like the drums, while at the same time trying desperately hard NOT to upset or disappoint his father. Walter's SHAM was uncovered.

When a SHAM is exposed, the result is SHAME. It is no mistake that both words come from the same root word meaning, "to cover." Shame is the feeling that something is wrong with you; sham is the attempted cover-up. With the exposure emerges another shame, not the type that comes from within as a judgment of your being, but rather the feeling that you are now "known," "seen," and "uncovered." This felt shame leads to a feeling of being ASHAMED, the "A" before the word "shame" coming from the Old English preposition "in," or "into." Shame, exposed, means that you are "in" shame.

Shame is first of all a condition resulting from your own beliefs that you are NOT acceptable as you are. The attempt to hide your authentic self becomes your SHAM. When your sham is uncovered (the curtain lifted), and you are seen by others in all your *realness,* you feel ASHAMED; you blush, and for some it feels as if you die.

Walter felt that he would not be acceptable to his father if he did not learn to play or enjoy the drums. Liking the trumpet was evidence that something, indeed, was wrong with him. "Every kid should be as lucky as I was," Walter told me. "The drums are a wonderful opportunity." As strange as it may seem, Walter felt shame since he didn't want the opportunity his father was presenting to him. Because he was afraid that his father would see his flaw (not liking the drums), Walter developed his sham. He pretended and created a deception. Unfortunately, one sham leads to another just as one falsehood calls for a supporting lie. When his parents attended the Parent's Night program, Walter was "found out." His resulting feeling of numbness and inability to breathe were his physical reactions to the uncovered sham—he was ashamed.

AND WHAT ABOUT THOSE NEIGHBORS?

If you spend any time in book stores or watching television talk shows, the word "co-dependent" is a familiar one. Entire books are written in an attempt to define this very slippery condition. At its simplest level, however, if you are a co-dependent you are dependent on others to determine how YOU should act. Critics of the "recovery" movement, designed to bring healing to people in whom co-dependency has been diagnosed, claim that everyone is co-dependent. I suspect they're right. We live in a culture that teaches co-dependency. "Be sensitive to the needs and wishes of other people" is quoted by both the adult family world and the school. It is almost impossible to grow up in the Western World and NOT have some degree of co-dependency tucked away under your belt.

However, there is a big difference between being sensitive to the needs and wishes of others, and allowing that discovery to control your life. For some people, what others think is more important than what they, themselves, think. Obviously, this is a very deadly condition since it leads to the possibility of a total loss of the self. There are a large number of people in our culture who have abandoned themselves in favor of the needs and wants of others.

Brad and Helen, a couple in their 50's and married thirty years, came to see me for marital therapy. Brad's complaint centered on the fact that no matter how nice he tried to be, Helen was always treating him poorly. She was friendly and pleasant to the neighbors or a stranger on the telephone, but seemed to be "angry" at him all of the time. "I'll come home from work and she'll be on the phone," Brad said. "And she sounds so kind and agreeable, but the minute she hangs up the phone, she speaks to me like I was some snake that slithered in the front door. I don't understand it."

"I'm sick of him never making decisions," Helen glared at Brad. "He can't choose a restaurant or decide what tie to wear without looking to me to do it for him. Whenever I ask him what he would like to do or where he wants to go, he always says the same thing, 'I don't care.'"

"Well, I don't," Brad looked at me and then back at Helen, "It's more important to me that you're happy. When you're happy, then I'm happy." He looked at me again, "I don't see what's so wrong with wanting to make your wife happy. Why does that make her mad?"

Helen turned toward Brad and pushed her finger into his chest, "Because I would like to know, at least once, if anybody lives in there." She poked his chest, "Hello! Is anybody home? Does anybody live inside there?" Dropping her hand in her lap, she said, "For thirty years I've been married to this man and I haven't the slightest idea who he is. I don't know what he likes, I mean really likes, to do. I don't even pretend anymore to know how he feels about anything. And I'm just sick of being married to a stranger."

In the many sessions that followed this one, it became clear that Brad had a strong belief in his own feelings of inadequacy. Raised in a family that demanded he be a "nice boy," Brad's fear of doing something wrong became so overpowering that he made a decision to avoid potential difficulties by abandoning himself. The critical parenting he received in those early years led Brad to a belief that something was wrong with him. He experienced a sense of shame; something was wrong with his being. "What's the matter with you?" became internalized and placed into his software.

As soon as Brad realized that he was "damaged goods," he assumed that meant that if he followed his wants and desires, he would only further expose his "flawed" being. For Brad, the safest and smartest way to travel was in disguise: he would want only what others wanted. Tucking away his self in some deep, hidden corner of his childhood, Brad became a "nice guy." He did whatever anyone wanted him to do. Since he no longer had a self, it didn't matter to him where he went, what he ate, or how he was treated. His disguise was complete and all the more effective, since he himself began to believe in it. He forgot all about the authentic part of himself that he shut away in childhood. Brad's shame, his belief in himself as flawed, had developed a wonderful sham; his acting career was launched.

In order for Brad, and others like him, to keep their facade in place, they must take their cues from others. Brad could not afford to "go inside himself" to make decisions. Since he thought of himself as damaged goods, it absolutely necessitated that he look to others for decision-making and guidance. He lived a life of external focus.

There are thousands of people like Brad, people who have shelved themselves because of feelings of inadequacy. For the most part, they are the highly productive and pleasant people of society. They work hard, since they don't want anyone telling them they're lazy (they already know that), they are good citizens since they can't stand to have anyone think otherwise, and they try to make everybody happy. Obviously there are degrees of self-abandonment due to shame. For some, it is only a partial abandoning of the self; for others, it is total. It also is true that not all self-abandoning issues emerge from shame. There are other reasons for going into hiding. Shame, however, is apparently the number one cause for a flight into external focus.

When Helen met Brad, he was such a wonderful man it was impossible for her to imagine that she would ever grow to detest his niceness. His pleasing personality and obsession with meeting her needs were only evidence of how deeply he loved her. In reality, it was, instead, a powerful expression of his fear of not pleasing her and her uncovering of his sham. Brad completely fooled Helen, a condition she eventually uncovered. As Helen became more and more aware of Brad's hiding, she also became more and more angry. Unfortunately, Brad's response to Helen's anger was to double his efforts to please her, abandoning his own needs even further, but to no avail. Helen's anger only intensified—a predicament Brad could not understand; he was trying so hard to make her happy.

If you had an opportunity to meet Brad's parents, you would probably like them. They are loving and caring people who only ever wanted the best for their son. Unfortunately, they came from legacies that judged their worth by the successes and failures in their lives. A successful son or daughter meant, obviously, that they had been good parents. On the other hand, a troubled child meant only one thing: they were not doing it right. The family picture, presented for all to see, must be bright, happy, and in focus. No dark shadows or blurred images would be allowed. The kids, Brad in particular, got the message: "look and be sharp." Brad's father used to laugh and tell him that the Gillette road signs were the best mottoes for life.

In a very real sense, the "neighbors," the external world, became the judge and jury for Brad's parents. When Miss Kennedy, the neighbor next door, would tell Brad's mother what a polite little boy he was, it was the equivalent of a verdict of acquittal. However, when Mr. Scott mentioned that Brad had been running through his backyard making foot tracks in the soft earth, Brad was found guilty as charged and his "flawed" thinking pointed out once more. The only solution, of course, was for Brad not to run. It didn't matter that young boys like to run; what was important was not upsetting anyone.

"What will the neighbors think?" is a hallmark question of the shame-based legacy. Since shame is never acknowledged unless the sham is uncovered, those ever-watching, judging neighbors become critical. Neighbors can uncover you; they can see your flaws. In a powerful way, they can even be elevated to the position of a judging and uncovering god. As a child, I recall attending a church service with my grandparents. This little fundamentalist church, nestled on the corner in our small town, was featuring a series of services on the book of Revelation. While I had never read the book, I did have a fascination with the beast and the dragon stories my grandfather had shared with me. That evening, the speaker was thumping the pulpit and pointing out to us sinners the meaning of the word "stand," as in standing before God. He said, and I believed he was saying it to me and only me, "...the word 'stand' comes from the Greek word meaning to be 'fixed,' as in cement. When you die, you will stand before God and it will be as if your feet are 'fixed' in cement; you will not be able to move. All around you will be others you know and love. Your mother and father will be there, as will your aunts, uncles and cousins. Your Sunday School teachers and neighbors will all be there. At that time (and by now I wanted to disappear from the church pew but I couldn't run away since I was sitting in cement), your life will be presented for ALL to see—as on a large drive-in movie screen. Every thing you ever did will be flashed on the screen for your parents and teachers to see. Nothing will be left out; every lie you ever told, every sexual thought or indiscretion will be RIGHT THERE for everyone to see!"

I almost died in that service as I thought about the time Barbara Henry and I were fooling around in the field behind my house. Would my parents see my hand gently graze her breast? The fear was absolutely overwhelming as I imagined God and my grandmother watching my life on a movie screen.

As silly as that memory may be, it represents, without question, the power of shame and sham in our lives. Those neighbors represent God to parents and children. The all-watching, ever-mindful eyes of the neighborhood can spot your sham if you're not careful. Once that happens, they will, of course, KNOW about your damaged goods and flawed character. You will be "A-shamed," living in shame.

KISSING THE SHAM

In mythology, Narcissus was a handsome young man who refused to respond to the love of the nymph, Echo. This so angered Venus, the goddess of love, that she caused him to fall in love with himself. Narcissus spent virtually all of his time trying to embrace or kiss his reflection in the water of a stream. Since, no matter how hard he tried, he could not kiss his image, he pined away and died.

Like Narcissus, some children from legacies of shame attempt to "kiss their image." They are embracing the other side of Shame: self-exposure. Most children who emerge from a legacy of shame attempt to go into hiding. It seems to be the sensible way to deal with shame. In the Old Testament, Adam and Eve, after eating the forbidden fruit, discover they are naked. The writer(s) of Genesis claims that when they saw their nakedness, they were "A-shamed" (in shame). Shortly after this discovery, God went for a stroll and stopped by the Garden to visit. In their shame, Adam and Eve hid from God (love). Most children of shame hide from love for fear of being "found out," and, as a result of the uncovering, abandoned.

Narcissus was under a spell—an illusion—about reality. His life, then, was spent in trying to capture that illusion. There are children from shame-based legacies who try to embrace an illusion that says they are NOT damaged or flawed. I deliberately use the word "illusion" since, deep-down inside, all children of shame-based legacies believe there is something wrong with them. Pretending otherwise, either through hiding or self-exposure, is embracing an illusion. If you decide to hide, it is because you feel that if others truly saw you, they would determine you unlovable and no longer want to be around you. Those who decide, instead, to be "out front" with their shame, use another strategy. "This is who I am," they say. "Take me or leave me." This, of course, is a gamble of enormous consequences; nevertheless, the thinking is that if I expose myself, others will give me credit for my courage and will like me.

In our culture, hiding is quite acceptable because it embraces the sham, which we all know is necessary for civilization to continue. Henry says in his book, On Sham, Vulnerability, and Other Forms of Self-Destruction, that children who do not learn to embrace the sham should be shot. This, he writes, was the thesis of Albee's play I referred to earlier in this chapter. While hiding is somewhat acceptable, self-exposure creates a certain amount of difficulties for people. Sharing too much stuff about oneself can be viewed as a personality defect by those who are forced to listen. The dilemma for the child from the shame-based legacy who chooses to self-expose, is to decide where the infamous line is which ought not to be crossed. How much can I share without making others too uncomfortable?

George was a father of four children; he was also a very moody man. Growing up in a shame-based system, he decided that he would NOT hide himself; rather, people would have to accept him just as he was. In a family session, his wife said, "About 5:30 P.M., George comes home from work, and usually we're all in the family room." She motioned to the children sitting around my office, ages 17–26. "We all listen carefully to how long George sits in the garage before he gets out of the car. If we hear the car door slam immediately after he pulls in the garage, we all relax and know that he's OK. But, if he sits in the car for awhile, we know that he's in a bad mood. When we hear the car door slam, everybody heads for his or her bedroom, and I head for the kitchen."

"How does that make you feel, George," I asked him, "knowing that you family jumps up and hides if you're in a bad mood?"

George moved toward the front part of the chair and sat up straight. "Now listen up, everybody," he said, "and get this straight. There's nothing wrong with me; I like me just fine. In fact, I think I'm a really OK guy. I'm more than an OK guy. And if any of you have problems with the way I close the car door, and with the way I am, that's just too bad. That's tough. I like me peachy-keen, so there." He sat back in his chair, held his hands up toward the ceiling and smiled at me.

In a private session, George confided to me that he did not have to apologize for his "way." "I am who I am," he told me, "warts and all." Sharing some of the ways his father had belittled him in front of his uncles at a family reunion, George said that he had to learn to cope with these idiosyncrasies of his dad. "He really loved me, though," he told me, "he just didn't know how to teach us to do things right. I was always screwing things up but never seemed to be able to learn from him. I bet I really frustrated him."

"How did you cope?" I asked him.

"I told him, 'I'm sorry dad, that's just the way I am. I guess when God handed out the old hands to cut and nail wood, he forgot to give me a good pair.' He'd listen, shake his head, and walk away. God, I still hate that today, when somebody walks away from me, like the kids going to their bedrooms, as though I've got the plague or something. So," he looked at me, "you want to see my flaws, my skin rash, go ahead and look. I'm not ashamed of anything. My grandmother used to say, 'It doesn't matter if they laugh at you; you're from Prather stock, so hold your head up high and walk right through them.'"

George is a perfect example of a man trying to embrace his own image. Unfortunately, no matter how hard he tries to kiss his reflection, he does not believe in himself. It is true that he is not in hiding, at least not the way that others choose to hide, through performance and niceness. George hides his flaws by pretending they don't bother him; therefore, and obviously, they are not worth looking at. They are so meaningless that he points them out to others. His thinking is that if he points them out, surely they must be minor, and we all have minor problems. The problem is that, in his flaunting, he alienates. He is a living illustration of "Me thinks thou dost protest too much."

In reflection, then, of the shame-based legacy, it is important to recall that: (1) Children of shame-based legacies believe they are damaged or flawed; not only their behavior is bad, but their being is also; (2) In an attempt to cover up the shame of being bad, children develop a sham; (3) When the sham is uncovered, children are in shame, "A-shamed"; (4) Children who choose not to hide develop a sham of self-exposure as an attempt to let the world know they are lovable; (5) All children of shame-based legacies fear being abandoned.

CHAPTER VIII

THE FAMILY LEGACY OF DENIAL

"Gee, I feel really bad about what happened today."
"Now you know you don't feel that way."
"Gee, I thought I felt really bad about what
happened today."

The Kitchen Table

"This world is not my home, I'm just a-passin' through."
"Where is my home, pastor?"
"Just sing the song, son."

The Church Pew

THE FAMILY LEGACY OF DENIAL

I was eight years old when my father's father died. Walking up the street toward our house on my way home from school, I saw the parked hearse. My grandparents only lived two houses above ours, and there was no question in my mind as to what had happened. For several weeks he had been ill, and as my Sunday School teacher had told me, "One of these days, he'll just decide to go home." While I knew of heaven, his home was the brown house some 100 feet from our front door. Walking in the door of their house, I was met by the funeral director, who smelled like my grandmother's lilac bush. He, my mother, and my grandmother told me that, indeed, Grandpa had gone home. A little later, I went home (a different "home"), grabbed my ball and bat, and headed for the ballfield.

The next three days were interesting ones in my childhood memory. For some reason, which I never knew for sure, my grandfather's body was placed in a casket in their living room. Friends, neighbors, and relatives "called" on Grandma as she sat on the living room sofa. During that time we stayed in the house with her, eating together and receiving visitors. Time after time, when no one was in the living room, I went in to touch and feel the body of my grandfather, who by now, sort of smelled like the flowery funeral director. His body was hard, not the soft hands and arms I remembered feeling when he read to me, and his skin was ice cold. To this day, I can recall the sensation of touching his forehead.

One time I walked into the living room to see my father standing in front of the casket, looking down at his father. Walking over to where he stood, I looked up at my dad. That image is one of those imprinted on my memory circuits; I stood, looking up at my dad, who stood looking down at his. I suppose it would have made an incredible photograph. What I remember most about that scene, however, was my father's Adam's apple, bobbing furiously up and down in his attempt to hold back his tears. I went to school that day on my father's denial of his right to express his pain. Like my dad, I didn't cry at the funeral either. I denied my feelings.

To deny is to say no to your feelings, your thoughts, your wants, or your needs. It is to look at the truth of a situation and yet see something different. Living in denial is pretending that what "is," is something else. Rather than being an objective reality, truth becomes whatever the situation and circumstances call for.

THE FAMILY LEGACY OF DENIAL

Although my father was not raised in a legacy of denial, he was rooted in both a cultural and family legacy regarding the expression of feelings. From talking with hundreds of men, my suspicion is that my father was behaving as a "man should behave." By denying his feelings, he was being strong not only for himself, but also for those around him. He was also being loyal to his family and community in terms of the lack of permission for males to express their feelings. In that we never saw my father express his feelings, how much fear would have been generated if we had watched him break down in his grief? What message would we have received from seeing his humanity? Would he have felt it would have been too much for us to handle? Equally, his legacy had taught him about being strong, another way of saying that a real man does not give in to his feelings. Instead, he denies, categorizes, and overcomes his feelings as a way of expressing his manhood. This, of course, is the way of the adult world.

My father, however, like all of us, did not come into the world a grown up. We all enter, through our mother's wombs, as infants. Unfortunately for many parents pleading for a full night's sleep, babies are not at all interested in behaving like grown-ups. Instead, they are incredibly sensory beings, without any concept of denying their feelings. When they are hungry, they *feel* hungry and they let you know. When their bottoms are wet, they *feel* wet, and scream to be changed. Babies *feel* happy just as they *feel* safe; they do not interpret data, search their memory banks, and arrive at conclusions about appropriate behavior.

Even as you enter the world a sensory being, in touch with your feelings, you also come in as authentic. Little children haven't the slightest idea how to pretend or lie; it is not in them. They haven't learned anything about the sham discussed in the previous chapter. Infants and children are authentic in feelings and expressions; they are too young to be socialized or civilized. They see no harm in walking around naked or touching their body parts. When they itch they scratch—it really doesn't matter where. Children do not understand there are some things you just don't say or do. How can they, when they are primarily sensory beings, and not as mental or verbal as their parents? Yet, the lessons start early.

"Don't do that! You know better." Well, truthfully, the child does not know to stay out of the dog's water dish. It looks pretty, the light reflects off the water, and the child feels the need to touch it. The cool water feels wonderful so why not put your finger in your mouth? And the water tastes delightful!

But, mother has different ideas, "Oh, icky! Don't ever do that. That tastes awful!" But it doesn't taste awful, and you haven't the slightest idea what mother is saying, but you sense or feel something is wrong. A tiny, little police officer is being born in that second, along with a critical question. Unable to be expressed, it is only felt. "Something's the matter here; is it me?" While the lesson takes a while to learn, after several trips to the dog's water dish, followed by several reprimands about how "you don't want to do that," you begin to "learn." The dog's dish becomes off limits; so, of course, does the joy of the wet finger in the mouth. The child has learned to deny his or her desire not out of any mental process, but rather out of a felt experience of disapproval from the parents. Denial is sometimes as simple as saying "no" to your desires; other times it may encompass feelings, behavior, and thoughts.

Almost everyone grows up with a legacy of denial. The only question is one of degree: how much, and what did you learn to deny as a child? In some families, children are taught to deny their feelings and emotions since such expressions may be seen as weak. In other systems, children are taught to deny themselves as a witness to their faith or an example of good manners. "If there are three children and only two cookies, you be a good little girl and go without." Whether you want the cookie or not is immaterial. The issue is that good manners take precedence over desire. The clear message is: deny your feelings and pretend you do not want the cookie.

There are also many families where children learn to deny what they see because to believe it would be too overpowering and threatening. Examples of this might be the family where alcohol is misused, or where physical or emotional abuse is present. For a child to admit the family is out of control is so frightening that the only alternative for survival is denial, to pretend what is being seen is not really happening. To accept the chaos of the family as reality would place the child at such risk that the mind must find a way to deny the truth. For these children, and there are many, life is hell but the fires and pain are replaced with pretense and denial.

"I just want to get something straight, right away," June

said to me in our first therapy session. "If you're going to spend a lot of time bashing my father, there's no point in our even getting started."

"I don't even know your father, or anything about him," I said to her.

"He was a good man," she looked at me.

"I'm sure he was."

"Well, that's good," she wiped at her eyes, "I just wanted to get that straight. He may have had some problems with drinking but that doesn't make him a bad person."

"I agree with that."

A woman in her late forties, June had called for an appointment to discuss some difficulties she was experiencing in her marriage as well as in relationships with her adult children. "My husband is a cruel man," she told me later on in the first session. "I guess I'm one of those women you read about who get called 'abused wives.'"

"Does your husband abuse you?" I asked her.

"Well, I'm not sure if you would exactly call it that because most of the time I have it coming; you know, I sort of ask for it." She lowered her head.

"I don't understand."

Her voice lowered a little, "Just the other day he had to push me through the door because I didn't fix his eggs right." She smiled a sort of weak grin, "He likes his eggs a little runny and I got busy folding the wash and they overcooked. He got really mad because he feels I don't think about him enough."

"What happened?"

"He was pushing me around the kitchen and I lost my balance; it happened just as he gave me a shove and I fell into the door, and it broke. I guess I really am too fat." She looked at me with some embarrassment. "I told him how sorry I was about the door and that I would pay to have it fixed."

"And did you?"

"Well, it's not fixed yet, but the man is coming over tomorrow afternoon to put on a new door. And I can paint it. I'm pretty handy with painting." Her face brightened a little,

"So, yesterday Bill and I had a talk, and I told him that I was sorry I got him so mad he had to hit me. He was real nice about it and said he was sorry, too."

During the next several sessions, June told her story to me. The youngest in a family of four, June had the worst of her father's addiction. Finances were bad and so were the kids. "He told me lots of times that he wouldn't have to drink if we kids weren't such hellions. After that, I really tried not to fight with my brothers; I always gave in so they wouldn't start anything." She lowered her face into her hands and started to cry, "I really tried to be a good girl."

Describing her father as a "good man," as long as he wasn't drunk, June told of a life of constant fear that he would get out of control and hurt her mother. "At night I would lie in bed and listen to him when he came home. I used to pray and pray to God that he would be sober and come home safe; then I would pray that he wouldn't hurt my mother. Sometimes I would squeeze my eyes real tight and hope that everything would just go away."

"How did you survive all of that?" I asked her one day.

"It was easy," she smiled at me. "I just pretended we were the Grace Kelly family. I used to make up stories at school about my dad traveling all the time in this real important job; that's why he wasn't able to be at the plays and stuff. I told the kids about all the neat things he brought back to me from his travels, expensive stuff that I wouldn't bring to school. I don't know if they believed me or not, but along the way I almost convinced myself. And from time to time, Dad was real decent. He could go for weeks at a time without a drink; then I could really pretend we were a normal family. Of course, I never could bring any of my friends home because they would see right away that we weren't exactly a normal family."

"Not the Grace Kelly family?" I smiled at her.

"Only in my mind," June said, "but you'd be amazed how far you can get with that fantasy. It really helped me. I always promised myself that if I couldn't grow up in a Grace Kelly family, someday I would make one for myself."

"What happened?"

"I'm not sure. Bill seemed so nice when we first started

dating, and I tried so hard to please him. Whatever he wanted, I gave to him. He had a hard childhood, too, you know," she told me.

"Did you ever tell Bill about the things you wanted in your marriage?" I asked her, "The things that would make you happy?"

"Not exactly," June said, "I didn't want to put any pressure on him, you know. Besides that, I'm not sure I know exactly what I want in a marriage. All I know is that I'm tired of not having it."

In June's case, as in many, the fear and unpredictability of her childhood was so overwhelming that she had to pretend it was normal in order to survive. To allow herself to feel and experience that terror on a daily basis would have been too overpowering for her body and emotions to endure. June learned, early on, to deny the reality that surrounded her, and thus she blocked the connection between her mind and emotions. In John Lee's words, she became a "Flying Girl," one who cuts off her feelings and "flies" to her head to survive. In her mind she can pretend, fantasize, and become Grace Kelly. As long as she doesn't feel the fear and terror, June can get through each day.

It, of course, almost goes without saying that June is unable to allow herself to touch reality. Her ability to be authentic in her relationships with Bill, or her children, is severely impaired. She has learned to dream of her wants instead of expressing them. Pretending her needs have been met, when in reality she is far removed from feeling her needs, June gives everyone the impression she is happy. Her children believe her when she says she doesn't want anything for herself; sadly, June also believes it.

June's mother, combined with her life experiences, became her greatest teacher. Watching her mother pretend in order to make her father happy, June learned to deny for the sake of safety. The lesson of the legacy of denial is clear and implicit: "Hold your feelings in, do not state the truth, and give other people what they want; then you will be happy (safe)." For the person who lives in denial of feelings, reality, or truth, safety and sanctuary become the overriding goal. "If I give you what you want, you will be happy, life will become somewhat predictable, and I will not get hurt." This is the thinking of the child, raised in a fearful setting, and desperately trying to create a safe and sane world for himself/herself.

COLORED GLASSES

To live in a family legacy of denial is to make an agreement that everyone looks through colored glasses. It is almost as if a deal is struck in which the entire family decides to pretend that something quite different from reality is happening. Another example of "co-illusion" is presented in denial-based families as all members agree to look at the illusion together. Children quickly learn of subjects or family matters that are never to be mentioned. As far as the family is concerned, Aunt Margie's marriage and quick divorce when she was nineteen never occurred. Uncle Fred's "condition" is treated with silence, if ever referred to in conversation by outsiders. The denial is understood.

An incredible result of the denial-based legacy is that, after a period of time, as truth is denied, the denial actually becomes the *truth*. The lies becomes believable. "Daddy is seen as a heavy drinker, but it was not a problem. He certainly was not an alcoholic. Mom's sickness was 'not that bad' and really didn't affect us."

It is very important, in understanding legacies of denial, to know that denial is a strategy to deal with pain. It is not something bad or wrong that parents do. Often, parents want to protect their children from pain, and so they offer such advice as, "It's not that bad," or "Don't think about it." Because children see parents as wise and all-knowing, many times they take their advice seriously. Unfortunately, at times, IT IS THAT BAD; and at other times, IT IS critical to think about it. In fact, not thinking about it could get you into a lot of difficulty. Even though parents know that avoiding problems can often cause struggles of a more serious nature, they may still advise their children to "think about something else."

While denial is a very human condition and is probably built into the emotional body's system of self-care, if encouraged in a family as a strategy to avoid pain, it becomes destructive and damaging. Sometimes, such as when the doctor says you have cancer, denial kicks in as a way of keeping your whole being from short-circuiting. If taught, however, as a way of life, the results invariably are relationships that bust apart at the seams. Pretense in relationships weakens every fiber and ultimately leads to a bleed-out, and many times to the death of the relationship itself.

Gerald grew up in a rural community in the Mid-west. His father was a successful business man, working long hours and earning a wonderful income for the family. From his earliest years, Gerald had questioned his sexuality, finding himself attracted more to males than females. Raised in the Bible-belt region, Gerald feared that any movement toward the homosexual lifestyle would destroy his family. He more than knew the community's attitude toward homosexuals, since his father held forth long and passionately on the subject at the dinner table. Gerald recalled listening to his father belittling one of his employees, whom he called "queer" at the company picnic. Shortly after that episode, the man was fired, mostly because of Gerald's father's intervention and demands.

Margaret, Gerald's mother, was a very frightened woman, insecure in her self, and feeling extremely inadequate in the shadow of his father. Secretly, she told Gerald that she hated his father, and no matter what, did not want him to grow up like his dad. Gerald didn't need any encouragement to be different from his father, since his sexual feelings already gave him the message of "not fitting in." The marriage between Gerald's mother and father was obviously a facade, more for convenience than intimacy. Yet, the community and church saw them as a happy and wonderful family. Gerald, his sister, and mother and father always sat together each Sunday in church. They certainly looked the part of the successful and happy nuclear family.

Playing basketball and baseball to please his father, Gerald was surprised at his athletic ability. His skills allowed him to fit in with the other boys, putting further distance between any suspicions his father might have about his sexuality and the truth. Gerald appeared like a "real man;" he also continually lived a lie. Watching his parents handle his unmarried sister's pregnancy, and her shame at the forced silent abortion, Gerald knew that he could never share his real self within his family structure or the community. He left home at 18 to begin college. Other than a few visits at holiday times, Gerald never went back home again.

THE FAMILY LEGACY OF DENIAL

In his early twenties, Gerald found a lover and the two of them moved in together. Everything was wonderful for several months until Gerald's father called to say he was coming East on a business trip; he assumed he could stay a night or two with Gerald. This, of course, created tremendous anxiety and conflict between Gerald and Robert, his lover. Insisting that Robert move out for a few days, Gerald gave a clear signal of his inability to be authentic in his relationship with his father. He could not afford to tell his father the truth. It also presented a subtle issue of shame, something Robert was unable to understand since he and Gerald were public in their relationship.

When the invitation arrived for Gerald to attend his sister's wedding, he chose to attend by himself. Seeing the RSVP note with only one name listed on it, Robert grew furious. The ensuing battle was so great, and Gerald's fear so powerful, that he could only handle it by immediately calling his sister and declining the invitation. His lie to his sister about a critical business trip only further angered Robert. As his sister's wedding day came and went, Gerald was filled with guilt and shame at his inability to act in his life. He could not leave Robert for fear of that relationship breaking apart, leaving him only the alternative of disappointing his parents and sister. Because his relationship with Robert was a daily affair, he chose to be disloyal to his family, an act for which his sister never forgave him.

Neither could Gerald tell the truth to his family for fear of their judgment and potential abandonment. Even though he seldom saw them, the cost of exposing himself was simply too great. In a tragic sense, he denied his nature not only to protect himself, but also his family system. There was no room in his family for any violation of the sexual legacy. Eventually, Gerald and Robert parted, both expressing resentment and guilt for the pain each had caused the other.

Gerald's story illustrates that legacies of denial are not only limited to families of alcohol or drugs. Rather, denial-based legacies are found in virtually all families in our country, particularly those in rural and small town settings. The closed legacies mentioned in Chapter 3 often use denial as a way of maintaining the values and traditions of the family system.

WHAT THE CHILDREN SAY

Growing up in a family legacy that encourages avoidance, rather than facing issues, creates a progressing problem for children. Sometimes the admission of truth is so frightening to families that another way of living is adopted, namely, the denial of what is. Out of a fear that the system could not withstand the truth, that it would collapse if family members authentically spoke aloud, denial becomes a daily strategy in relationships. In the middle of this confusion, the children must find a way to survive and make sense out of things. Unfortunately, when the truth is denied, all else seems to be nonsense and things do not fit together.

A workaholic father, promising his daughter to come home early for her birthday party only to become so engrossed in his work that he forgets the time, nudges his child one step closer toward denial. Only the evening before, he sat with her on his lap, nuzzled her, and told her how much he loved her, but the very next night he forgets to celebrate her birthday. For his daughter, how can she make sense out of this? If her father loved her, how could he forget her birthday? And if he didn't love her, why did he tell her that he did? Since these questions are so overpowering and fearful, her only alternative is to reach another decision. She will not allow it to bother her that her father has forgotten her birthday party. In a sense, she will numb herself against the pain and confusion. By administering an internal shot of Novocain, she does not feel the hurt and disappointment. She has learned to deny her feelings, and with enough practice she will be able to move through life on a daily basis without pain. The next time her father forgets a date they had, or fails to keep his promise, she will not allow it to hurt so much.

The Chinese have a proverb about the conscience. Imagine, they say, that your conscience is like a metal triangle spinning around inside your heart. Each time you go against your conscience, it spins one turn, forcing the points to pierce your heart and cause you pain. However, if you keep going against your conscience, allowing the triangle to continually spin, eventually the three points will be worn smooth and the turning will not bring you any pain. In some ways, denial is exactly like that triangle. Each time a child denies his or her feelings, it gets easier. Soon, nothing is felt except numbness;

the child is on a permanent "fix" of internal Novocain.

When a child from a legacy of denial says, "I don't care," in response to a question, he or she is telling the truth. If asked how they feel about something, and the answer is "I don't know," the child is speaking as best as he or she can to the situation.

Dale was the youngest of six children. Raised in a chaotic home with a strict father and an overprotective mother, he learned never to say how he felt about anything for fear of retaliation from his father. The father's mood and anger created a fear level among all the children, forcing them to "walk on eggs" whenever he was around. The kids learned they could freely talk to their mother without fear or punishment. On the other hand, withholding or lying became the primary strategy to deal with their father. When Dale came along, adding stress to both the financial and space needs of the family, he felt no choice but to go into hiding. Keeping to himself and staying out of his father's way became the primary purpose of his life. Whatever Dale wanted he quickly shelved for fear it would cause more problems. He reasoned that his very existence had caused problems within the family, so he certainly wasn't going to add to that by expressing his desires.

It is impossible for anyone to exist in this world without desire. While some are overpowering, all desires are felt within our emotional being. For Dale, the only way to survive was to NOT FEEL his desires, to deny they were there. By the time he was ten, he had isolated himself so much that he seldom felt anything and rarely spoke. His world was within himself. For Dale, his survival depended on not wanting anything, on not allowing his desires to be felt for fear they would lead him to ask for something.

Dale's parents divorced when he was twelve, and his world suddenly became safe. Supported by a loving mother who wanted him, and who gave him permission to express his feelings, Dale found hope. It is, however, a long road back from hiding and denial, even for a twelve-year-old. By the time Dale started high school, he was beginning to let his feelings trickle through into expression. A smile appeared on his face when his brother asked about a girl who spoke to them in the shopping mall. At a football game, his mother watched him jump up and down in his excitement, another small step in his attempts to connect his feelings with his outer expressions. Denial was becoming less and less a strategy for Dale.

When his first marriage ended in divorce, however, Dale quickly fled back into hiding. As we talked together, he shared how easy it was for him to allow himself not to feel. "It's like all those years of hard work to get in touch with myself washed away down the drain." As he looked more closely at his behavior, Dale concluded: "I'm fine as long as I feel safe. As soon as I find myself threatened in the slightest, I go underground. When that happens, I really don't know how I feel, and even more frightening to me, I don't care."

Recalling one time when he told his father that he wanted to play soccer, his father said to him, "You don't want to play that stupid game. Why don't you go out for football? That's a real sport."

"When I told him that I liked soccer, he said, 'Don't be crazy. You know you don't like soccer; what's wrong with your head, anyway?'" Through that conversation, and many others of a similar nature, Dale arrived at the conclusion that something was probably wrong with his feelings. As in all legacies of denial, the children never even consider that their parents may be the one with the problems. Living with the criticism that they seldom do it right, children assume they are the ones, and certainly not their parents, who are mixed up and wrong.

"I only had one choice," Dale told me, "and that was to go into hiding. So I hid from my dad, my teachers, my friends, and eventually my wife. All she had to do was disagree with me and I would retreat. She always complained that we never fought; she was right. I was too afraid to tell her how I felt or what I wanted."

Dale represents the child who feels so afraid of his feelings or desires being judged, that he has made a decision NOT to allow himself to feel or want. He says, "I don't care," and means it. He lives the legacy of denial on a daily basis, as the only way for him to feel safe.

A man once told me that when attending a class he was asked to draw a tombstone, print his name on it, and write a brief epitaph. "I drew the tombstone, printed my name in large block letters, and underneath it I wrote: Here lies So and So, HE

DIED SAFE." Recalling that event, he said, "This was a tremendous discovery for me. I never realized that my whole life was dedicated to safety and denial. What's the point in surviving so that you die safe? I don't think that's living at all."

Children of legacies of denial are seldom living; instead they are hiding from life, which to them has become so frightening and confusing, retreat appears to be the only option. Sadly, they survive without joy or pleasure because they cannot afford the risk of feeling.

Family legacies of denial, then, are often created through the generations by the need to look good to the community and to avoid the shame of exposure. The strategy of the system is to: (1) Keep the system intact by denial of any issue that appears threatening; (2) Present a united and wholesome front to the community, and, (3) Remain loyal to the denial. In the legacy of denial, children survive by: 1) Denying feelings; 2) Hiding; 3) Looking the other way. Eventually, the consequences of the legacy of denial to the children are: 1) Inability to be authentic in relationship; 2) Inability to feel, or to be in touch with feelings; 3) Unwillingness to express desires; 4) Constantly seeking safety through hiding, lying, or an inner retreat.

CHAPTER IX

THE FEAR-BASED FAMILY LEGACY

"Present fears are less than horrible imaginings."

Shakespeare

"When you don't have any money, the problem is food.
When you have money, it's sex.
When you have both, it's health.
If everything is simply jake,
then you're frightened of death."

J. P. Donleavy

"There's nothing to be afraid of."

Parents Anon.

"For God's sake, be careful."

Parents Anon.

THE FEAR-BASED FAMILY LEGACY

One of the dreadful parts of growing up is suffering through all those childhood diseases. Lying in bed with chicken pox, I still remember clutching my hands in order to keep from scratching myself. "You'll scar yourself if you dig at those things," the doctor had warned me. "And you don't want to grow up with your face all pitted and marked, now, do you?" Of course, I didn't; so I twitched and itched, but I didn't scratch. Later on in the month, there was some joy as my sister suffered the same fate; she had caught my chicken pox. Not that I wanted her to suffer, mind you, I just wanted her to know what I had been through. In looking back, I suspect she got the message.

Unfortunately, childhood diseases are not the only things children catch. There are many contagious family lessons tossed around the household, such as prejudice, gossip, and suspicion. One of the worst and most paralyzing lessons children catch is fear. Many times, born out of ignorance and rooted in the history of parents and grandparents, children are handed the fears of the generations. With little explanation, and oftentimes, no wisdom, children are taught what to fear as an extension of the terror of their parents. Fear is contagious, and especially vulnerable are the children, whose minds and thinking processes are too immature to sift through the "disease."

If you see your parents afraid of something, how can you approach it with curiosity or boldness? Most children can't. Instead, they accept the judgments and conclusions of Mom and Dad as "gospel." "If my parents are afraid, I should be afraid, too," is the thinking process of the child. Fear breeds fear within the family system.

Consider, for example, Mary Ellen, who comes home from school with her homework assignment. "I have to memorize this poem and say it in front of the class next Friday," she tells her mother. "Oh my God," her mother says as her face turns white. Immediately, Mary Ellen's heart starts to pound as she realizes something is wrong. She is picking up her mother's fear.

"Why do they do that to children?" her mother asks, to no one in particular. Mary Ellen is the only one within earshot.

"Do what?" she asks her mother.

"Oh, I don't know," she says. "Why do they put children through such torture? Standing up in front of all those kids like that. I mean, all you have to do is forget a line, or make one little mistake and you're the laughing stock."

By now, Mary Ellen is becoming very unnerved. "What's a 'laughing stock'?" she asks her mother.

"Oh, you know, a fool. Someone the kids pick on because they forget their words." She looks at Mary Ellen, "Kids are cruel. You certainly know that by now, don't you, dear?"

Looking at Mary Ellen's worried face, her mother realizes that she is talking about her own bad experiences. She too vividly recalls the day she forgot the words to "The Village Blacksmith," and the reprimand from her teacher, followed by the hilarious laughter of her classmates. Her memory had gone blank when she pronounced "sinewy" incorrectly. One of the kids had snickered and, at that moment, her memory had kicked into overdrive and stalled.

"Oh well, dear," she attempts to smooth things over, "I'm sure you'll do just fine. You have a marvelous memory."

Mary Ellen, however, is now very uncertain. Fear has started its contagious work on her mind and confidence. Perhaps she does NOT have such a good memory after all. What if she does forget the words? What if the kids DO laugh at her? It's never happened to her before, but she saw what happened to Sylvia Davis when she tripped while walking to the pencil sharpener. The entire class laughed at her sprawled body, Mary Ellen included. Since that day, Sylvia seemed to keep her eyes down all the time. The scene began to burn in Mary Ellen's mind.

By the time Friday arrives, Mary Ellen is sick. Her stomach is in knots and she begs to stay home from school. The fear of making a mistake, or making a fool out of herself, is so powerful, it virtually bends her at the waist. She has caught her mother's fear of inadequacy, shame, and failure.

Children are not born afraid. Fear is always learned, either by experience or education or both. Infants have nothing to fear; they know nothing of the world and its dangers. In all probability, they know little, if anything, about pain.

In the early years, before children are able to verbalize their feelings and thoughts, fear is more absorbed than programmed. Pulling a cat's tail, a toddler gets scratched. Crying and running to his father for comfort, he is warned to stay away from kitty. He may or may not remember the warning. Fear, certainly, will not keep him away from kitty; he has not yet learned. Two or three scratches into the future, however, he becomes apprehensive and begins to keep his distance. This kind of fear is a part of the natural order of development. An internal "wisdom" is born in the toddler and he becomes careful. Any fear he feels, however, is not a paralyzing kind; instead it is more of a cautious lesson about cats. He learns to approach kitty from the front, and to reach carefully toward her fur. The child and kitty work together in a self-taught lesson. Fear, in this instance, had led the child to a new approach; it has been his teacher.

Fear as *teacher* is almost always helpful, leading children to movement and growth in their lives. Fear as *paralyzer,* however, keeps them stuck and unable to take charge of their lives. It freezes children in place. In the family legacy of fear, this is the fear that needs examination and change. When fear is a teacher, children are programming themselves to creatively use it for self-improvement. When it is presented through the legacy, the fears of the parents and grandparents are passed on. No longer does the child do the programming; instead it is being done to him/her. This type of programmed fear is invariably paralyzing; the child feels frozen and unable to learn from it. The fear is simply too frightening.

GIVE ME SAFETY OR GIVE ME DEATH

When my youngest son was four years old, he had a burning desire to be a farmer. Perhaps this was fueled by the small green tractor he carted with him wherever he went. Joking with my father, he said that he was going to be a rich country farmer, and with all his money, he would take care of my father when he grew old. This was a standing joke in our family for years in reference to "my son, the farmer."

One day, he and I were swinging together on the front porch glider when he said, "Can I ask you a question?"

"Sure."

"I've been thinking a lot about being a farmer, you know, and driving my tractor, stuff like that." He turned the green tractor over in his hands. I waited for him to go on.

"And?"

"Well, I was wondering what would happen if I was driving my tractor out on the highway, you know, the road in front of the farm, and some cars wanted to pass me. Tractors go pretty slow, you know." He looked up at me.

"What do you think would happen?" I asked him, thinking we were really communicating here.

"Well, I guess I would have to pull off to the side of the road and let the other cars go by." He looked at me again.

"That sounds like a pretty good idea," I told him.

We glided back and forth in silence for awhile. Finally he said, "But I was thinking something else." I waited again.

"Go ahead."

"Well, what would happen if there was no place to pull off?"

At that instant, I realized that I was having a conversation with myself. My son was me in his thinking. How could that have happened? This was a six year old child, much too young to be frightened by the possibilities of nowhere to pull off, no place to be safe. He was expressing one of my greatest fears: being caught with no way out, being trapped.

Later that evening, I thought back over the conversations we had shared together. Knowing that I had never told him to be wary of being trapped, I knew that he had *caught* this one. Somehow, from observing me in my behavior and relationships, my fear had become contagious. He had watched me try to escape from conflict with my wife, as I maneuvered the conversation in another direction. I was suddenly aware of how many times I used the expression, "I just want out of here," whenever I felt upset at work or home. He had been going to school on my driving, when I refused to park even for 30 seconds in a no-parking zone while I picked up the family. My fear of doing something wrong and getting caught (and therefore punished) had become his. Tractors don't belong on the main road; he had heard that from me, along with other non-repeatable lines about Sunday drivers and people who should either park their cars or blow them up.

The message to my son was clear: don't be anywhere

you're not supposed to be; you might get caught. Going unspoken was the imagined and terrible things that would happen to anyone who gets trapped in a "no-permission" zone. His fear was a reflection of my own. A dread of punishment for being in the wrong place had been transferred to my son through my behavior, words, and feelings. Until that moment, I had never seen it.

Most parents are not aware of passing on fear to their children. Far from it, they are deeply concerned that their kids NOT be as ridiculously frightened as they have been. In fear-based legacies, the children, sensing the fear in the system, pick it up and carry it as their own. They sense the emotions and warnings they feel surfacing from their parents, and it becomes a part of their programming.

In legacies of this type, fear is transmitted in two ways. First, it is often the anxiety and worry of individuals based on their own personal experiences. A mother, for example, growing up with three brothers, gets frightened again and again as they chase her holding a live snake. As an adult, then, it is with a pounding heart and sweaty palms that she approaches the glass display in the reptile house in the zoo. She relives her fears while holding the hand of her child as together they stare at the Cottonmouth. Even if she is silent, and does not verbalize her fear, the child senses it. Almost in a cellular fashion, the fear is caught. In this illustration, the legacy of fear is only two-generational, from mother to daughter. Nevertheless, it is highly contagious and easily caught by the kids.

The second type of fear-based legacy is far more powerful. It reaches back into the generations, pulling the beliefs and values of the great-great grandparents into the present. In this powerful expression of fear, the entire system is programmed. Attitudes about the city, or "people not like us," are found here. Issues surrounding the wealthy, the poor, the old, or the retarded are housed in this type of fear. An entire system of trust and mistrust is created out of the programmed beliefs of this system. You learn exactly who you can *stand with* or *stand against* in this umbrella of fear. Hate is born to aid in defining your enemies. Without fear, how would you know from whom you need to be protected? It becomes a very powerful god, pretending to protect you, to keep you advised, but in reality shoving you further into the walls and hiding places of life. As Shakespeare said, "In time, we hate that which we fear." In legacies of this type, fear becomes a demon-god.

THE NEGATIVE MOTIVATOR

As children are growing up, much of their fear is experienced through punishment and criticism. The "big people" in their life, who know so much more than they do, seem to hold the power of life and death in their hands. In a manner of speaking, a father or mother literally can destroy the life of a child either physically or emotionally. Children, although they cannot articulate any awareness of this fact, *still feel it.* They clearly know of their own vulnerability. If you can imagine living 24 hours a day with some giant who has the ability to break you in half, and you also know of your tendency to mess up, you, too, would live in terror of an impending doom. In the following chapters, we will be discussing the many ways in which this type of thinking impacts our concepts of God.

The fear of punishment can be a powerful motivator. It can turn a normal, spontaneous child into a frightened and self-restricting robot. Consider, for example, two seven-year-old boys who live next door to each other. Fred is a bright, delightful boy who loves to draw. Even at this early age, his art teacher has praised his ability to his parents, trying to encourage Fred to continue his animal sketches. A pleaser, Fred works hard at keeping everyone happy, and is thrilled when he wins first prize in the "Hire The Handicapped" poster contest.

Gordon is a bundle of energy. He gets in a lot of trouble with his teachers, but most of it is an expression of his boredom. His two older brothers are active in scouting and Little League. Gordon can't wait until next year when he will be able to join the Cub Scouts. Unlike Fred, Gordon does not worry about pleasing others; he is far more interested in enjoying life himself.

One day, both Fred's and Gordon's fathers come home with a surprise: the first bicycles for the boys. They are very excited and, almost immediately, both begin to learn to ride their bikes. At the end of the day, Gordon and Fred wheel their bicycles out to the rear of their respective houses, each leaning them against their back porches. A little later in the evening, it begins to rain; obviously, the bikes get wet.

Gordon's father asks him to go outside and put his bike in the garage, promising to meet him there. Inside, his father takes an old towel and begins to wipe down the bicycle. "Gordon," his father says, "a bike is not just an opportunity to have fun, it's also a responsibility. If you don't take good care of it, it won't last. You certainly know how hard your mother and I work for our money, so I'm asking you to take good care of your bike." He then shows him how to dry off the spokes and chain. "Rust is no friend to a bike, believe me," he says to Gordon. Standing in the garage, the two talk for awhile about several things. As they dash from the garage to the house, Gordon's dad has his arm around his shoulder.

Fred's father also tells him to get his bike and meet him in the garage. As he wheels it into the garage, he sees his father standing there with a towel. His heart begins to pound because he has seen this look on his father's face before. "Now look, kid," he father says, twisting the towel in his hands, "I work damn hard for my money, and if you think I'm gonna toss it away on you, you're screwy. I told your mother you weren't old enough for a bike, but she said you'd be responsible." Snapping the towel against Fred's cheek, he said, "Well, I guess we know the old man's not wrong all the time." He threw the towel at Fred, "Now you wipe every damn drop off the bike; I mean every drop! I'll be out in ten minutes to check it. Mister, it better be dry." As he walked out of the garage, Fred's father said, "And I better not find this bike EVER left out again, or you won't have a bike."

Fred quickly began wiping the water off his bike. The minutes passed as he rubbed as carefully as he could, jumping each time he heard a sound that might have been the back door. Finally, the bike was dry; there was not one drop of water anywhere. Still, when his father returned to examine this bike, his heart pounded and his throat was dry.

Two sons and two fathers were presented with an opportunity to teach and to learn. One boy learned the importance of taking care of his bike as an extension of his responsibility. Gordon felt treated with respect by his dad. Fred, on the other hand, learned not to do something wrong because he was in incredible terror of his father's anger. Keeping a bike dry was only important to avoid punishment. It certainly is true that Fred will have a dry bike, but his motivation is fear, not stewardship or responsibility.

Fear as a motivator is bad enough in the life of any child,

but, unfortunately, it does not stop at that level. Because he is so afraid of punishment, Fred will be "frozen" in much of his life and behavior. Many of his decisions will not be made out of wisdom, trust, or desires, rather they will be decided out of the fear of making a mistake, followed by the punishment that always occurs. His ability to be spontaneous or have fun will always be tempered by the possibility of things going awry—things for which he will have to pay, and pay dearly.

Imagine Fred and Gordon riding their bikes on a warm summer morning. Just as they turn to pedal towards the ballfield, it begins to sprinkle. Immediately Fred says, "Oh God, it's starting to rain. We better head home."

"What are you talking about?" Gordon looks puzzled at him. "It's just a warm shower. It'll be over in ten minutes. Come on, we can park under those trees."

"Unh-Unh!" Fred shakes his head, violently, "Our bikes will get wet! We've got to get home."

"So they get wet," Gordon says, "We'll wipe them off. Come on, let's go."

"What do you mean, 'wipe them off'?" Fred asks, he's almost shouting now, "We can't do that! We've got to get home." And with that, Fred begins pedaling furiously in the direction of home. Sighing, Gordon turns toward the ballfield.

This summer shower scene illustrates the paralysis that Fred lives in. He is so frightened of punishment, and so vividly remembers the reprimand (and towel snapping) of his father, he "polices" himself out of fun. A normal, spontaneous bike ride in a summer shower is impossible for Fred. Add ten years to his life and he will find himself avoiding all unpredictable events and experiences. With another ten years, he will be raising his own children in the same legacy, creating another generation of frightened people.

So often, in therapy, clients will ask me, "Why is it so important for me to have control in my life?" As I have looked at this issue, it seems to me that the fear that gets generated without control or predictability is so overwhelming that control, or the attempt at it, is the only solution. Even though we all know that life is filled with curve balls and the unexpected, many of us still pretend we are in control, because any other position would strike terror in the core of our hearts.

THE FEAR-BASED FAMILY LEGACY

Fred needed to be in control because he was afraid of the consequences of making a decision to ride his bike in the rain. If pushed too far and frightened enough, Fred will not ride his bike AT ALL. It is possible to imagine him sitting inside all day, in safety, drawing pictures of horses and dogs.

Whenever fear motivates people (except in physical safety issues), the result is always negative, no matter how successful they become or how dry they keep their bikes.

Although it is not easy to see, Fred's father is also fueled by fear. In all probability, it may be economic fear, which always is rooted in a basic fear of survival. While it may seem ridiculous to consider that one little bicycle could be the cause of economic ruination, the important concept here is NOT the bike, but what it represents in Fred's father's legacy and belief system. As discussed below, the bicycle just might be the "ruination" of Fred's father, as defined by his legacy's thinking pattern.

SPINNING THOUGHTS OF FEAR

Fear-based family legacies tend to leave a lot of open-ended and unanswered questions. In this way, the children are left to arrive at whatever horrid conclusions might be the most controlling and protective. You know that you're in conversation with a person raised in a legacy of fear when you hear a lot of "what ifs." "What if we can't find another gas station and we run out of fuel? I mean, we only have three quarters of a tank. What if that happens?"

A young woman told me that each time she walked into a public rest room, whether in a fine restaurant or a department story, she was filled with anxiety over the possibility of finding a body inside, the victim of a mugging. "What if they thought I did it?" she asked me, "What if they arrested me and I couldn't prove it wasn't me? What if they took me to the police station and my name appeared in the paper as the 'alleged' killer?" While you may find this a type of nonsense thinking, for children of fear-based family legacies, it makes perfect sense. It is an expression of their fear of the unknown and terrible.

There are few of us who have not tossed and turned at 3:30 A.M., the victim of our own thoughts. We can re-examine conversations, plan retaliative strikes, re-think a bad experience, or begin to sweat in anxiety. At 8:00 A.M. the next morning, we may laugh or be furious at ourselves for losing so much sleep over something so ridiculous. For children of the fear-based family legacy, there is no next morning. The fear of the unknown and terrible travels with them 24-hours a day; they live IN fear.

Seldom do children of fear-based legacies follow their thoughts to the end. They simply spin them for awhile, in their minds, until the fear is felt enough to be paralyzing, or to cause stomach flip-flops and diarrhea. If not careful, they can become addicted to the fear; it is so familiar that they are uncertain how to live without its presence and control. As in all addictive persons, left unexamined, the pattern seems normal and natural. One primary reason the thinking of fear-based children rarely moves to a conclusion is the thinking pattern of the legacy itself. Most parents say the same things that Fred's father said, "Take good care of what you have. Money doesn't grow on trees, you know. You never know what can happen, and you may not have another chance to buy a bicycle. We've been lucky so far, but you never know. What if something unforeseen happens? What then?" Certainly the child can't answer those questions. First, the questions are too fear-inducing because of what they imply—the unknown and terrible—and because they are children, their thinking processes are too immature.

If you could get inside the head of a child and try to follow the spinning thoughts, if might sound like this: "What if something bad happens, like my bike getting damaged so that it costs money to fix it? And what if my dad spends money to repair it, but runs out of money for food? What if we have to go hungry because he spent all that money on my bike, and the same week he loses his job, so no more money comes in at all? And what if he can't get another job so we have to lose our house? Will that mean we have to move in with my grandma, and if we do, where will I sleep because there's not enough rooms? What if Dad and Mom decide to send me over to sleep with Uncle Henry because there's not enough room at Grandma's; and besides that, they're already mad at me for breaking my bike? What if Uncle Henry gets mad at me like he did Larry Ross? Would he get so mad that he might hurt me, or maybe even kill me? But, if all of this doesn't happen, would we just stay at home and starve to death because there's no more money?"

The spinning and fearful thoughts inside a child's head are

very present and real. Unfortunately, because no adult in the legacy helps the child examine his fears, only silence is experienced. But how can the adults help the children when they carry the same pattern of fearful thinking? Adults are only more sophisticated in their thoughts of fear. In the fear-based family legacy, adults and children, however, do arrive at the same conclusion: death and loss by the unknown and terrible. No one dares to think beyond that.

Arguments and disagreements in the fear-based family legacy are seldom focused on the true issues. For that matter, few people, regardless of type of legacy, have learned how to look under the surface of a conflict to discover what is actually being discussed. The bicycle and keeping it dry is not the issue for Fred's father; rather, he is deeply afraid of the loss of things and what that might symbolize in his belief system. If his children do not learn the value of things, the price of a bicycle, they will become careless in their treatment of all objects. Not only does this increase the possibility of damage and loss, it raises the potential problem of replacement. If Fred's bike rusts, will another one have to be purchased? His father fears this dilemma since it strikes at the heart of one of his major terrors: We may run out (of money). Especially at the economic level, fear-based family systems have a core belief of scarcity and loss. Stated simply, it says, "There is not enough to go around."

The belief in scarcity and the fear of loss forces children of fear-based family legacies to develop strategies for survival. To avoid running out, a strong "police force" is needed to assure the pantry will stay full. In children, this police force is found in the adult community. Parents police the children to be sure they understand the philosophy of scarcity. Monitoring the children's behavior and desires, the parents create an ongoing system of "responsible" thinking. "You need to learn responsibility," says Fred's father. "Money doesn't grow on trees, you know." Parents, then, model for their children various ways to avoid "losing" things. Proper storage of equipment, from automobiles to something as inexpensive as a bottle of car wax, is preached with vigor and enthusiasm. "A penny saved is a penny earned" is not just a quote from a wise saver; it can also represent a belief in scarcity in the fear-based family system.

As children develop and grow, they no longer need an outside police force to point out the pitfalls and possible catastrophes of life. Having gone to school on scarcity and the fear of loss for much of their life, they now have, living within, their very own police officer. Rooted in fear but justified by economic wisdom, this police officer never goes off duty. On vacation, a hard working woman who has saved all year for this one-week fling cannot allow herself to order the $4.95 piece of chocolate cheesecake. No matter how much her mouth waters, her belief in the scarcity and the possibility of loss are too great.

Self-denial is not only born out of a sense of poor self-esteem, it also is created in children of fear-based family legacies, as they learn to deny themselves in order to protect their limited holdings. In a very true sense, to be that firm in self-denial calls for a tremendous sense of self-control. One hallmark of children in fear is their ability to be in control of themselves, and if possible, their environment. In trying to teach his son to take good care of his bicycle, Fred's father was showing him how to avoid loss. The garage roof collapsing on the bike would be an unavoidable loss, but a rusted bicycle chain can be avoided.

Fear-based family legacies teach children to take every step possible to control their environment, and everything in it, in order to keep scarcity and loss at a distance. If, indeed, the garage roof falls in on the bicycle, Fred's father is well-insured. "No responsible person would not have insurance" is not only the motto of Fred's father, it is echoed in every fear-based family legacy. "Control what you can control and leave the rest up to insurance," is an accurate reflection of this legacy.

Over-controlling people are not stiff or unfeeling; they are simply afraid. If you need desperately to control your surroundings, the only question that needs to be asked is, "What are you afraid of?" There would be no reason to police yourself so fiercely if you were not afraid of what would happen if you did NOT do so. A watchful and disciplined eye is seen as critical to your safety and well-being.

If this reasoning of the fear-based family legacy seems strange and unfamiliar to you, then so will the "logic" of the system. A forty-nine cent item can send a well-educated, successful man into a rage. Driving twenty miles to save thirty cents while spending two dollars for fuel, is an example of the logic of scarcity. Nevertheless, it is never the *truth* of a legacy that motivates the children; it is the *belief* in the teachings. Unfortunately, these lessons burn their way into the hearts and emotions of the children, pushing truth far to the rear, too threatening and frightening to be examined.

Although I have chosen to use economic fear as an example of this legacy, all fear-based legacy teachings ultimately boil down to the fear of loss. It may be the loss of money or things. In some legacies, it is the loss of the children if they move away to a distant state, or even to the next town. Although seldom articulated, there are many who struggle with the loss of purpose as children age and marry. A similar difficulty for a man or woman facing retirement can occur as the several issues leap forward: the loss of identity, purpose, or income.

For children of divorce, the fear-based legacy adds another powerful dimension: the loss of a parent. Even though visitation rights are lovingly set-up and custody is not an issue, the children will experience abandonment by one or both parents. The ensuing fear is staggering for these children. "Will I be okay? What will happen to me if Mom and Dad get so angry with each other that they do something terrible?" While never followed to its end point, as is consistent with the fear-based legacy, the potential for horror is ever-present.

Eventually, if strained and filtered down to a fine point, the ultimate fear of loss would be uncovered: the LOSS OF SELF. To some children, this may mean something as simple (and destructive) as a life of total people-pleasing: "I don't want anything; the important thing is, 'what do you want?' You can be certain I will give it to you. In exchange, please never, never leave me, for I will not be okay if left alone." For these children, the self fades away in the light of the needs and desires of others. More important than anything is NOT losing other people, the lifeline of existence. Like oxygen, others become critical for breath and life; their presence is a necessity in order to continue living.

When examined closely, the fear of the LOSS OF SELF may very well be the fear of death. Certainly, if not the actual fear of death, it may represent such fear symbolically. Children have a very difficult time contemplating death. They, however, have little trouble in experiencing or feeling dread, as in an impending doom. Running out of money or food, mother or father moving out, failing to keep others happy—all are lead-ins to the drama of doom. At age eight, to articulate about death may be an impossibility; however, "something terrible will happen" takes little imagination at all.

Warnings from parents are never taken lightly by children; neither do they come from parents who are without a belief in the wisdom of the warning. Even those parents who frighten their children into submission or discipline do so out of their own fear. "If they don't learn, something terrible will happen to them, or to me," is the thought behind the punishment. The child who is fearful of forgetting her lines in front of the class, in reality is most afraid of not being okay, and WHAT THAT WILL MEAN. Will she die from her blunder? Probably not, but a piece of her may "die" in the dread, sending her further underground in her ability to express and enjoy life.

In fear-based family legacies, then: (1) The system is deeply afraid of something(s)—unknown and terrible; (2) To avoid the unknown and terrible, children need to learn quickly how to survive properly; (3) Punishment and warnings are vital to prevent catastrophe; (4) A system of right and wrong, good and evil, and an ability to recognize the villains in life are critical. Children in this system learn:(1) Something dreadful can happen at any time, so be prepared; (2) Think ahead to avoid anything bad that could happen; (3) Police yourself wisely; (4) Self-denial, people-pleasing, and anticipation can help keep the unknown and terrible from your doorstep; (5) The most important thing in life is to be okay (safe).

THE LEGACY AND SPIRITUALITY

*"Try and be a sheet of paper
with nothing on it.
Be a spot of ground
where nothing is growing,
where something might be planted,
a seed, possibly,
from the Absolute."*

Rumi

THE LEGACY AND SPIRITUALITY

This section will illustrate the old fundamentalist adage of moving from "preachin' to meddlin.'" Exploring religion and spirituality in any form is risky business; linking it to the sacredness of family is quite another. Yet, so much confusion has been generated through the intersection of the family legacy with religious teachings, that it cannot be ignored. Grandparents, parents, priests, and God can easily become blended together in some type of family theology, which generally ends up serving neither community nor institution very well.

The truth of the matter is that family legacy is sacred ground. In like manner, religious traditions proclaim the same thing about their teachings. The fact that both merge together in a sort of arranged marriage is certainly understandable. There are, however, difficulties which quickly surface as the pronouncements of religion clash with the beliefs of the family legacy. In particular, this is evident when the legacy's definition of the *self* becomes unable to open to the offerings of the grace, forgiveness, or mercy of religion.

Section III will examine the ways in which God is viewed in the light of the teachings of the family legacy. As parents are seen as *gods,* children become baffled, and the teachings of religion become insufficient. Seeing God as a police officer, judge, or executioner does not stretch the imagination, particularly for young people who have experienced similar roles at home. The leap from the "grounded" family to the concepts of the "Heavenly" Father is not unusual.

This section may raise more questions than answers; if so, it has served a purpose. Most of us struggle with our religion and spirituality. In my view, this dilemma carries a great deal more power than we realize or care to admit. In a world filled with everything from addiction to denial, there is an ever-present drive toward that which will satisfy. In our Western culture, we seldom name our desires, nor peel them back to see the force behind them; however, the universal thrust toward feelings of satisfaction, happiness, and peace continues. To see the connection between our family roots and any perceived conclusions about our self, as they intertwine with our religious concepts of God, is critical.

For many people, a type of spiritual pain surfaces when the promises of religion and the proclamations of the family legacy clash. Feeling unlovable and unworthy due to legacy implications while listening to the promises of grace and forgiveness serves to leave many people in a quandary. How can God love me when I know better than anyone else exactly how unlovable I am? In effect, I am smarter than God. To deny the power of the family legacy in terms of its impact on spirituality is to deny what is. Too many people struggle with this issue to pretend it doesn't exist. It many situations, the legacy IS God, or, if not, is at least SACRED.

CHAPTER X

THE ORDINATION OF THE LEGACY

*"Some believe all that parents, tutors,
and kindred believe—They take their principles by
inheritance,
and defend them as they would their estates,
because they are born heirs to them."*

Watts

THE ORDINATION OF THE LEGACY

It is impossible to overstate the power of the family legacy. Rooted in an intergenerational march into time, the legacy carries an unrecognized weight into every decision and action of its most current family recipient. The man or woman of the 90's, although separated by generations from the past, mysteriously extends a connecting thread to the tribes who walked before. That legacy belief, which seems so easily dismissed in the mind, suddenly takes on astonishing power when faced with a major passage of life. Birth, initiation, marriage, and death, instead of stepping aside from the power of the legacy, most often embrace it. The tribe, indeed, is not so far behind us.

Obviously, as time passes, children are educated and learn to dismiss tribal superstitions. Science classes contribute to the unlearning process as the weather is understood in terms of clouds, jet streams, highs and lows. No longer is it necessary to dance to the rain god or offer corn to the wind. We all know better than that. Instead, the legacy offers us another approach: "If you're a nice person and don't do anything wrong, life will be good to you." Good behavior and kind thoughts replace the rain dance. In some cases the teaching is a bit more clear: "If you study and work hard, you'll be rewarded with a high paying job and promotions, after which you will be happy." In either case, the family legacy seems to offer an *if/then* clause of promise, sounding strangely close to the prophetic.

THE DEIFICATION OF THE LEGACY

A few years ago I attended a seminar offered by Pir Vilayat Kahn, the great Sufi master. During the question and answer time at the end of his presentation, someone asked him a question about God. He sat quietly for a few moments and then said, "I don't think we can talk of God this evening because we would only end up speaking of our *concepts ABOUT God.* You realize," he went on, "that all we can ever do is talk ABOUT God, for all any of us have are *concepts.* Who among us can *know* God, except in our own personal way, which, in turn, when spoken, gets translated through our concepts?"

For some people, God is an all-powerful Spirit who rules both heaven and earth. For others, He/She is a detached Force who set up the world like a row of dominoes, and now watches them tumble into one another toward a pre-planned pile-up. Some people embrace a very personal God who loves them and calls them by name; and then there are those who point to a punishing judge, who keeps a list and checks it twice.

God, however, regardless of your concepts and understandings, seems to be a power, force, or spirit, BEYOND you. Almost all persons, regardless of creed or faith, seem to learn of the presence of something beyond themselves which has power and impact on their lives. This "something" may be as simple as a creed of love, or as complicated as a theological text book on the "ground of all being." The attitudes of both superstitious and sophisticated people alike point to God as some type of mystery BEYOND themselves. Even those who choose to accept God as a power WITHIN, still view something which transcends their own limited humanity.

Much of the first two sections of this book focused on the ways in which the family legacy provides a *belief system* for the children as they enter adulthood. Designed to guide the children with the wisdom and teachings of the generations, the family legacy can be seen as an intergenerational "Bible." Filled with prophecies, teachings, and proverbs, the "Legacy Bible" gets carried by the children into every avenue of life. Unlike the bedside Bible, or motel room Gideon gift, the Legacy Bible cannot be lost or forgotten. Dropping it is unheard of without considerable noise from the invisible parenting forces which not only helped write it, but are charged with seeing that it remains holy.

The Legacy Bible contains the beliefs of your family. Given to you by your parents and grandparents, arranged in order of priority and importance by any and all significant adults in your life and filtered through your own vision and thinking patterns, the Legacy Bible is your "friend" for life. "Don't leave home without it," is a motto you never have to hear since it will never happen.

When I was eight years of age and attended Sunday School every week, I always carried my Bible with me to class. Each week, for those of us with "good memories," since we had brought our Bibles as good "swordsmen," we received gold stars beside our name on the class roster. Above the list of names was a sticker of a Bible with some fancy printing on it about the "Sword of the Lord and of Gideon." One Sunday, as I was walking home from class, I decided to play catch with my Bible. Tossing it up in the air, I would make magnificent catches, not unlike my hero, Willie Mays. As I passed under a tree I spotted a branch probably twenty feet above the ground. It seemed like a challenge to see if I could throw my Bible over that branch and catch it on the way down. Two or three tries later, it barely cleared the branch, flipping and flopping as it fell towards the ground. Like Willie Mays, I caught the Bible. Unlike a baseball, however, the first ten pages ripped out in my hands.

I recall standing in shock at the unforgivable thing I had just done. Never thinking for a moment that the Bible was a book, I could only imagine that if God didn't strike me dead, my grandmother, who gave me the Bible, would. Racing home, I grabbed the scotch tape and crawled under the bed. As best I could, I repaired the "word of God" with yellow scotch tape. It was a messy job with the first ten pages easily sticking out from the rest of the Bible. My fear was overwhelming for the next several weeks as I conveniently "forgot" my Bible, bringing to a screeching halt my string of gold stars. Even my teacher's murmuring about her disappointment in me didn't come near the fear I had of being found out. At night, however, lying in my bed, I knew that God knew that I had damaged "His word."

It was years later before I started to realize that I was deifying the Bible, making the book into God. Never viewing the Bible as an attempt by people to express their concepts of God, I did not see a book with glue, paper, and binding; instead I saw God with ten pages ripped out.

While we may never consider it, the family legacy easily turns into a Legacy Bible, with all the superstitions and fears of my childhood Bible-tossing experience. Filled with the critical and important beliefs of our family, the Legacy Bible can become God. In a very real sense, our beliefs, then, can become our God, a force beyond ourselves which impacts our lives and destiny.

For children, it is almost impossible not to view the legacy as the rules of God. The Ten Commandments cannot hold a candle to a critical-based legacy, proclaimed by a strict or frightened parent. Beliefs become sacred within the Legacy

Bible and, therefore, easily turn into guidelines for life and decision-making.

George was raised in a critical- and guilt-based legacy. His mother was a highly successful attorney who repeatedly reminded him that "time was money, so handle a piece of paper only once." Taught the importance of good management, George had his own stock portfolio by age twelve. George's father, the head of surgery at the city's largest teaching hospital, often pointed out that "mistakes cost lives, even beyond the operating room." This type of teaching, along with a fear of letting his parents down, led George into high school as a frightened young man. Always feeling inadequate and seldom believing he could even live up to his parents' expectation of perfection, George found it easier simply NOT to try. In school, he received B's without studying, and ignored his parents admonitions to rise above his mediocrity. Choosing to settle for "second place" rather than risk open failure, George moved into adulthood feeling like a living disappointment to his mother and father.

In place, however, was a legacy of perfection with a built-in system of criticism and guilt. As long as George could pretend or lie to himself, he did not have to try. In adulthood, though, it became more and more difficult to look the other way, or to relax in the completion of his tasks. Soon, although he fought against it, George became very much like his parents. His children's grades became overly important to him, and he found himself sounding suspiciously like his own father when he was reprimanding his daughter for a "B" in math.

Things came to a head for George when his wife insisted the two of them enter marriage counseling. During the first session together, his wife, Dot, told a story about the way she saw George controlled and driven by his need to do things right. "We had made plans to take the kids to the zoo," she said. "And George was busy painting the bathroom. He'd been at it all morning, so around noon I went in and told him that we were going to leave in about an hour. I suggested that he stop and get his shower so we could leave on time." Dot wiped at her eyes with a tissue. "Fifteen minutes later I went in and he was still painting. At 12:30 he hadn't stopped so I said, 'You'd better hurry up or you'll be late.' Finally, at one o'clock, when we were planning on leaving, I went back upstairs and he was still at it. I was so disgusted, I took the kids and we left without him." She was quiet for awhile, and then said, "I feel so bad that the kids can't enjoy their father on a beautiful day like we had; and just as bad that he is missing out on their growing up."

For some time, George sat quietly, then he said, "Painting is not easy to do, you know; it HAS to be done right. You don't just go to Sears, buy a gallon of paint, and start in. The walls have to be washed and prepared, and I don't mean a quick swipe, I mean WASHED. Then you have to be sure you have the drop cloths everywhere, and things masked that need masking. Also, the brushes are real important. You need the right brush for the right job and you have to take care of them." He looked at me, "You know, if you take good care of a paint brush, you can use it over and over again." I nodded that I understood.

"The problem was...," George continued and then he faltered as his voice broke, "The problem was that I just couldn't stop painting because I wasn't finished. You can't quit something in the middle, just like that! The brushes would have needed cleaning and the paint can wiped off. Everything had to be put away, and... well, don't you see, the bathroom wasn't finished." George started to sob, "I really wanted to go the zoo with Dot and the kids." He looked at her, "I really wanted to go, but the bathroom wouldn't let me, don't you see."

George is expressing a deep and profound belief in how things are supposed to be. There seems to be no maneuvering room for him—no space to compromise his beliefs. Trapping him against his will so that he cannot do even that which he desires, his beliefs have become his God, the legacy has been deified. One of the commandments of his Legacy Bible is: Everything you start MUST be finished; there are no exceptions.

It is important to understand that most parents never INTEND that children turn guidelines into sacred beliefs. Because children are who they are, with all of their openness and receptivity, the family legacy, when presented with either power, guilt, or fear, easily falls into the realm of the sacred. Gradually, the legacy becomes deified. After all, how could this be avoided when children are raised by gods?

THE PARENTS AS GOD

THE ORDINATION OF THE LEGACY

Every major religion of the world has certain teachings to guide behavior, values, and decision-making. Whether the Ten Commandments, the Sermon on the Mount, or the Five Hindrances of Buddha, rules and guidelines were presented to followers in order that they might walk the "right" path. Sometimes the teachings were written down for future generations; other times, stories were passed from father to son with one purpose in mind: the continuation of the important dogmas and creeds of the early founders.

Scriptures, oral tradition, and written words were all designed to point beyond the message to the hidden Source. The Ten Commandments, for example, offer a series of rather explicit rules to live by. Stealing, lying, and adultery is forbidden; honoring of parents is revered, while coveting your neighbor's dairy farm is not allowed. The critical issue, however, is the POWER, believed to stand behind the teachings. The reasoning seems to run somewhat like this: If the Ten Commandments are not from God, then what point is there in adhering to them? God stands behind the teachings of Jesus, says the believer, or why bother to struggle with loving your neighbor or turning the other cheek?

All religious teachings point beyond themselves to a Force or Power, Ruler or Judge, who is seen as sustaining and guiding the totality of life. Viewed as an all-knowing and all-seeing power, God holds you in the palm of His hand with the apparent option of crushing you, if He so chooses. On the other hand, He might wish to shower you with blessings, gold, or wisdom. And while this might seem to present God as functioning on His whims, viewing God as whimsical is absolutely unacceptable to most religious people.

As sophisticated as we supposedly are these days, many people still adhere to the belief that says, "God blesses the good and wallops the bad." The so-called "good" person who struggles with endless problems has probably done something to deserve it, the story of Job notwithstanding. Breaking one or more of the Ten Commandments clearly puts you at risk for a divine spanking. On the other hand, while honoring the Sermon on the Mount may not guarantee that you will hit the lottery, the odds of blessing are apparently much more in your favor.

The significant factor in all of this rests on the

understanding that religious rules are sacred teachings of a very powerful and enforcing God. Given to creation to guide everyone onto the right path, religious teachings assume the inability of the peoples of the world to know enough to function correctly without them. In a religious sense, God viewed the foolish and unwise thinking and behavior of His children, and designed instead a divine plan to guide the little ones back onto the narrow way.

In a very profound manner, the family legacy is exceedingly like the Ten Commandments. Expressing the rules and guidelines of the generations, the legacy is passed to the children, not unlike the tablets of stone to a frightened and bewildered Moses. Etched in stone are the teachings of God, while carved in the minds of little children are the programmed legacy beliefs of the parents.

Just as God, with all of His power and authority, stands behind those Commandments, your parents, with the absolute ability to destroy or preserve your life, stand behind the legacy. To make matters even more difficult, God tends to hide rather invisibly in the rainbow and roses of your backyard. Your parents and grandparents, on the other hand, loom tall and broad beside your bed at night, their voices booming with power and threat each time you turn away from the correct path. As one man told me, "Ask me about my fears in childhood, and I'll not tell you of a God of the mist, but instead give you a narration of my father, who squeezed my shoulder in disapproval. My catechism teacher's proclamation about an ever-present God does not carry the weight that my grandmother's ever-watchful eye did. While waiting for the punishment of a God that I may have disappointed, my pinched ear reminded me of a very flesh and blood grandmother whose wrath most certainly matched that of a raging God."

Somewhere along the way, however, things get very confusing for children. The power of parents gets confused with the strength of God, while the teachings of religion ends up blurring with the family legacy. Soon, God, parents, legacy, beliefs, and religious teachings all melt together in some kind of stew pot. Children find themselves unable to separate parents from God. Virtually every attribute assigned to God is found in parents. The ability to reward or punish and the overpowering strength to control the destiny of the child, along with the sheer physical size of parents, lead most children to a conclusion that "parents are indeed gods."

Imagine yourself at age four, standing a little less than three feet tall with a father twice that size. For the child, living with a giant is a reality. Can you consider the fear or terror a child must feel when that giant gets angry? Violate a legacy belief and watch the giant react. Standing behind the legacy, ready to dole out the necessary punishment or earned reward, the giant has become God to the child, and the belief a commandment. No wonder children, educated or not, grow up to believe in an *if/then* system of life in which God hands out blessing to the good (those who follow His teachings) and metes out pain to the bad (those who are disloyal). "If I am a good boy and do what Daddy says to do, then he will be proud of me. But if I am a bad boy and don't follow Daddy's rules, then he will punish me."

Because much of what a child understands of God is learned from his or her parents, is it any wonder that our concepts of God are so confused with those of the human condition? Many of the religious writings describe God as having nostrils, arms, and teeth, just like our parents. Certainly Mom and Dad can smell our messy pants from a distance, or our newly-shampooed hair when they tuck us in bed. The arms of God which sweep away the enemies of His people can be seen in the arms of an angry father who traps and holds us firmly in an act of discipline.

"Turn the other cheek" carries a certain amount of power to children, especially when taught by "big people" at church. On the other hand, "Don't trust uneducated people," is a legacy belief which has *Family Commandment* proportions. As a part of your Legacy Bible, it flies right past any minor religious teaching. And, since the enforcers eat supper with you every night, you'll be more likely to take it seriously—very seriously.

For children, the family legacy is accepted as a mandate from God, namely the parents. Its holiness and truth quickly become a part of the Legacy Bible, as children inherit the intergenerational scriptures. To change or delete the Legacy Bible is to place yourself at enormous risk in the eyes of the Parent-Gods. Disloyalty to it is not only dangerous, it is heresy.

To understand the ways in which children create a Legacy Bible out of the beliefs of their parents is only to begin to comprehend the power of the family legacy. As we shall see in later chapters, when children enter adulthood and seriously begin to explore their spirituality, the Legacy Bible is very present and equally frightening. God and Mom and Dad are so very intertwined that it takes much more than educational awareness to unravel the threads.

Raymond, a forty-five year old husband and father, was arrested for punching a lawn-mower repairman who parked his truck in a "No Parking" zone at a neighborhood Seven-Eleven store. Entering therapy, Raymond told me of his confrontation with the repairman. "I pulled into the Seven-Eleven lot first," he said, "and immediately saw the narrow alleyway running beside the store. There's a big sign there which says 'NO PARKING: DO NOT BLOCK ALLEY.' As a matter of fact, I pulled into that spot first before I saw that if I parked there, no one could get out of that alley; it's a dead end. So, I backed out and moved to another place. Then, this other guy pulled into the same spot where I was, and he saw the sign, too, so he backed out and parked on the other side of me. There were two or three spaces next to mine so there really was no reason for that repairman to park in the 'No Parking' spot."

In somewhat bitter tones, Raymond went on, "Well, anyway, I was just getting out of my car when this lawn-mower repairman pulls up in his truck. Just as big as life he swung into the space, right in front of the sign, and he jumped out of his truck and started to go into the store. It wasn't that he couldn't see the sign. He almost walked into it when he came around in front of his truck." Raymond grinned at me slightly, "Course, just because he could see the sign doesn't mean he could read it!" He laughed at his own joke.

"So I said to him, 'Hey, buddy, can't you read that sign?' He just looked at me and walked into the store like it didn't even matter that he had broken the law. Course, I realize it's not a real law just because a sign says 'No Parking,' but still, what would happen if everybody in the world decided to go around ignoring all the signs? My dad used to say that somebody printed up that sign for a reason; it wasn't just stuck there for something to do."

Shaking his head, Raymond said, "I really don't know what happened next; I just know that I was furious at that guy's casual attitude about something as important as considering all those cars parked down the alley. It was like it didn't matter to him at all that he could be blocking someone's exit. I mean, what if there was an emergency, or something? So, anyway, when this guy comes out of the store with a couple of hot dogs and a coke, I went right up to him and said, 'Don't you have any respect for all those people who are parked down there?' He just shrugged his shoulders and grinned at me. Then he said, 'What's the big problem? I wasn't in there five minutes. They could have waited.'"

By now, Raymond's voice was rising in a fresh anger, as he relived the scene in his mind, "I don't really know what happened but I was absolutely sure that I was right, and this guy needed to be taught a lesson. How else are people like that ever going to learn anything? So, I poked my finger in his chest and said, 'Well, asshole, I hope someday you get blocked in somewhere so you can know how it feels.' I guess that must have got him mad because he sort of bumped me with his elbow, probably because his hands were full with the hot dogs and coke. That was all it took, I guess, because I just hauled off and hit him with all the anger I was feeling. It really wasn't all that hard, at least I don't think it was, but he fell backwards and tripped over one of those cement parking blocks and fell down. He was quite a sight with hot dogs, mustard, and coke all over his repairman uniform. To tell you the truth, I don't know what it's going to end up costing me, but that one moment may have been worth it. The guy needed to be taught a lesson."

Over the next several sessions, Raymond told me about his legacy upbringing. Using the term "rigid" to describe both of his parents, Raymond talked about the rules of his household. "There was NEVER permission to even bend the rules, much less break them. When I was a teenager, I was allowed out one night a week until 11:00 P.M. It didn't matter which night I wanted, but once I picked the night, it HAD to be that night no matter what. One time, when I was about sixteen, I had decided to go to the movies on a Friday night with my friend, Tom. So, I told my parents on Monday that I was picking Friday for my night out. Then, on Wednesday, Tom's grandfather died and he had to go out of town. It just happened that the next day at school, a friend of mine invited me over to his house on Saturday night because the foreign exchange student was going to be there, a girl I really liked. She was going to show us slides of her village in Sweden."

"Well, anyway," Raymond went on, "I told my folks the next night that I wanted to change my night to Saturday because I had been invited to this special party with our school's exchange student. My dad said that I had made my bed and now I would have to lie in it. He said that maybe I would learn not to commit myself to anything that I couldn't keep. No matter how much I argued with him, it was no use. For me, the problem was that I couldn't understand my parent's reasoning, but they were the boss."

"I always promised myself that I would never be as rigid as my parents," Raymond told me, "but my wife has been telling me for twenty years that I am 'unbendable.' I never saw what she meant before, but maybe she's right. It's just really hard for me to see any other way to deal with the Seven-Eleven sign issue. You either follow the rules or you don't. Is that rigid? I sort of see it like your morals; there's a right way to live and a wrong way to live. How can there be an in-between with morality?"

For Raymond, the teachings recorded in his Legacy Bible were called forth at the Seven-Eleven parking lot. "Following the rules" is one of his commandments; it is a sacred teaching. To violate such a rule, for Raymond, is equivalent with committing adultery. The sacred overtones of his legacy emerge everywhere in his life from home to the office, and even to the golf course where he never takes a mulligan.

Without ever realizing it, Raymond has taken the power of the legacy and made it his sacred commandments. A leap has occurred from the teachings of the family to the wishes of the Almighty. In spite of their protests, children from strict or rigid legacies will most often carry that rigidity into their own lives and relationships. Viewing their parents as rigid is many times followed by a similar view of God. With the passing of time, the parents and their teachings merge with God and scripture. If the opportunity arises, Raymond could easily embrace a fundamentalist religion which offers the continuity of his family legacy.

As we shall see, children from legacies of forgiveness will be much more likely to embrace the grace of God. As in the rigid family system, the teachings of a legacy of forgiveness will create a Legacy Bible, but with more grace-filled beliefs.

THE ORDINATION OF THE LEGACY

All family legacies present beliefs that the children accept as sacred. The key issue for growth is the uncovering of the teachings of each individual's Legacy Bible. Your Legacy Bible will be different from every other person you know; it is highly personalized.

Seldom are parents aware of the power of their teachings, or the children's creation of a Legacy Bible. In fact, all parents have to struggle with their own Legacy Bibles, recognizable as such or not. Raising my children to be Protestants is a sacred line in my Legacy Bible. When my grandmother asked me about my intentions for the children's religious training, I realized this was a sacred trust handed to me by my parents, who were handed the same commandment by my grandparents.

What cannot be documented, then, by statistics, nor proven by the courts, nevertheless occurs. Because of the incredible power of the family belief system, children make their own leap toward an ordination service of the legacy. No one ever suggests that children connect the teachings of the family with the sacred; they make that leap by themselves. Seeing parents as God, what else can they do?

CHAPTER XI

RELIGIOUS CONFUSION AND THE SELF

*"The most difficult thing in life
is to know yourself."*

Thales

*"The height of all philosophy is to know yourself,
and the end of this knowledge
is to know God."*

Quarles

RELIGIOUS CONFUSION AND THE SELF

"I'm not afraid to die, I just don't want to be there when it happens." Among his many wonderful lines, I find this to be one of Woody Allen's best. He so wonderfully echoes the predicament of humanity; we are mostly living in a dream of unawareness; we're not "really there." Seldom do any of us take the time or energy to pinch ourselves or to jerk our minds out of the constant stage of numbness that we wander around in. Paul Reps, in his thoughts on meditation, says that "we are most asleep when awake."

Up to this point in my writing, I have carefully tried to place a groundwork of understanding regarding the family legacy and its power in our lives. The different "types" of families have been discussed in an attempt to help you recognize parts and pieces of your own system. In the previous chapter, I began to nudge toward a recognition of the power of the legacy as it impacts the religious beliefs of children and adults. I want to consider, now, the intersection of the legacy and spirituality.

Writing about family is always risky business. Everyone is already an expert, not unlike our expertise on food. We all eat every day, and we know what we like, food critics notwithstanding. Equally, few have escaped the joys and tribulations of living in a family, regardless of how healthy or destructive the relationships might have been. You're an expert in your family, and while you may or may not have agreed with the concepts presented in the preceding chapters, it is my hope that you are considering the impact your legacy had on your own growth and development.

If writing about the family is risky, how much more dangerous is it to look at religion, spirituality, and God? I don't know of any better way to stir up the pot than to raise issues and questions surrounding God—thoughts and religious beliefs. In a way, along with the legacy information we received as children, many of us were "inoculated" with a sort of antibody against "messing around with our faith." Several years ago I was involved in a heated debate surrounding the ordination of a woman to the ministry. Unfortunately, for this woman, she had two strikes against her as she entered the process of examination. First, she was a woman entering a primarily male profession; and secondly, she was on the far "left" edge, theologically speaking. As a member of the Examination Committee, I felt it important to request one of the members to disqualify himself since he had already made a statement that regardless of the candidate's theological position, he would vote against her based on her gender. He refused my request, and a rather severe debate followed in which we "Christian brothers" showed exactly how easy it was to put the love of Christ aside for the sake of winning our position.

Reflecting back on the meeting, I found myself puzzled as to how a very intelligent, well-read man could be so hard-nosed when it came to issues that seemed to me to be neither black nor white, but gray. Walking one evening with a well-known theologian and author, I asked him this question: "How can bright and articulate people put aside their brains and hold on to half-truths like a dog holding on to the last bone of summer?" This conversation took place on a summer evening walking through a park. Although it was over twenty years ago, I have never forgotten his answer: "Some schools or churches give inoculations against openness," he said, "It's like a vaccine against new thoughts." We walked together until the sun went down, and it still didn't make sense to me.

Years later, when I was truly getting a hold on the power and loyalty of the family legacy, I understood what he was saying. The legacy, no matter how open it may attempt to be, does not want to be replaced or done away with. As though it has a life of its own, the family legacy finds its own way of vaccinating the children against change. Using a vaccine of fear, guilt, shame, and punishment, the children learn how to avoid any and all diseases which might undermine the basic beliefs of the legacy.

Is it any wonder, then, that we wander around in life as though we are asleep? Waking up is paramount to shaking the very foundation of the legacy belief system. It is pinching yourself out of the well of numbness to look at life with vision instead of ordinary sight. Waking up is opening your eyes and looking around.

The remaining chapters in this book are dedicated to a waking-up process, a looking with vision at your spirituality and your concepts of God. For some, this will not be an enjoyable section since it may too greatly threaten your Legacy Bible. Nevertheless, if you wish to *know yourself* and how your lack of vision has affected your spirituality and religion, then, as Martin Luther wrote, "Sin on, boldly!"

RELIGIOUS CONFUSION AND THE SELF

DEFINING YOURSELF

By now, you have clearly seen the power of the family legacy. In all probability, you have wondered about your own family and the ways in which your legacy has shaped you. I encourage you to continually look at and explore your legacy. By doing so, you will be opening new possibilities for yourself as you discover parts of the legacy which have not been helpful to you, as well as those pieces which have been exceedingly beneficial. Take great care in your legacy exploration that you do so in kindness, recognizing that parents were doing the best they could as they taught you, given their own history and legacies. Be gentle in your discoveries. Attacks and confrontations are rarely helpful in working through your own issues; instead they are more likely to produce added guilt and shame, two dynamics none of us need to add to our already large pile.

Although some of the people in my past might question it, I am big on love. This is what I mean when talking about the need to see *with vision*; it is a way of examining your family legacy and roots *through the eyes of love* instead of judgment or criticism. The whole world looks through the ordinary sight of blame or punishment; by now we all know that never works. Instead, looking through love transforms plain, ordinary sight into vision, a way of seeing things that not only *grows* you, but lifts the burden of guilt off the shoulders of the generations before.

The chances are great that you have followed the same path that countless generations before you have marched. Accepting the teaching of your parents as gospel, you have probably owned the legacy's concept of your self. Until you choose to "wake up," the only way you will possibly look at yourself is through the ordinary sight of your belief system. By the time you have heard two to three hundred "shame-on-you's" in your life, coupled with one or two thousand "why did you do that's?", you might possibly have arrived at the conclusion that "just a little something could be wrong with you." What other conclusion could you reach? When your parents (God) ask you questions, or point out the "obvious," surely they must see your flaws. After all, didn't they make you?

Chrissy was six years old the first time she discovered something was really wrong with her. On that day, she was playing in the kitchen with her cat, Nelly, attempting to dress the unwilling victim in her doll clothes. Nelly, squirming and kicking, scratched Chrissy and leaped from her arms to "cat freedom." Just as Nelly dashed out from under the table, Chrissy's father entered the room, accidentally stepping with his full weight on Nelly's front leg. Meowing in pain, the cat fled to safety back under the kitchen table, and began shaking her paw.

"Daddy," Chrissy protested, "You hurt Nelly."

It's unfortunate for Chrissy, at this point, that she did not understand her father's legacy. Continually criticized and shamed every time he got into an argument or fight with his younger brother and sister, Chrissy's father was super-sensitive to causing pain to anyone, including a cat. He had spent more than one evening sitting in the corner because he had "hurt" his sister. Not only did he cause his sister pain, his father had explained, but the pain was shared by his mother as well, who wanted him to be a good boy. Chrissy's father was a walking "shame factory," as well as being overburdened with guilt from the previous three decades.

Unable to carry any more shame or guilt, nor even to acknowledge that it was an accident, Chrissy's father said, "Don't be silly, the cat's not hurt."

Looking at Nelly huddled under the table and shaking her paw, Chrissy says, "But daddy, you hurt her."

Feeling the pain and shame again, her father says, louder this time, "Now listen, Chrissy, the cat's not hurt. Forget about it."

Moving closer to the table, Chrissy sees Nelly lick her paw. As Chrissy draws nearer, Nelly begins to move away, battered enough for this occasion. As she backs up, Nelly is obviously limping. "Daddy, she is hurt. I can see it."

"Now look here, young lady," Chrissy's father is no longer friendly or kind. "If you want to see some hurt, I'll show you some real hurt! Now get this, and get it clearly; the cat is not hurt!" He pronounced the last four words slowly and distinctly. "Do you understand?"

Chrissy is now growing afraid of her father. After all, he is so much bigger than she is, and when his voice gets loud she can feel a vibration in her chest. To Chrissy, her father is representative of God; he is the creator and sustainer of her life. There is a part of her that realizes that if he wanted to, her father could crush her.

What happens next gives a very powerful clue to how children think and reach conclusions. Chrissy looks at Nelly and sees the cat is still shaking her paw. She then says to herself, "It looks to me like the cat is hurt, but Daddy (God) says she is not hurt. Even though she is shaking her paw, Daddy (God) tells me she is okay. *THERE MUST BE SOMETHING WRONG WITH ME AND THE WAY I SEE THINGS.*"

Never for a second do little children believe that something might be wrong with the way Daddy *sees things*. Rather, they understand that the big people are always right. Chrissy obviously must have something wrong with her, or she would be able to see and understand the way her father does. Unable to comprehend her father's legacy of shame, Chrissy cannot see past the moment nor arrive at any other conclusion. Perhaps if she was older, she could find another way of looking at the event. Nevertheless, Chrissy is beginning to define herself, based on her father's need to avoid any more shame in his life. She concludes that she is damaged and flawed.

If you could follow Chrissy through other experiences in her life, you would soon see that there are more and more times she arrives at a similar conclusion. By the time she is fifteen or sixteen, she cannot trust that what she sees or feels is accurate or on target. To avoid shame, she seldom comments on anything. On her dates with boys, she lets them talk, hoping to avoid being "found out." Leaving the movie theater, she has no opinions on the film, opting instead for her boyfriend's analysis, and then agreeing with him. When asked how she feels about something, she deflects it back and convinces someone else to share. Chrissy has been defined by the fear and inadequate feelings of her father. Worse, she now believes the conclusions at which she has arrived are the *truth.*

Unfortunately, Chrissy's dilemma is shared by most children. Through the criticisms and judgments of parents or teachers, it becomes virtually impossible for anyone to arrive at the magical eighteenth birthday without struggling with enormous feelings of inadequacy. Is it any wonder that the self-help sections of bookstores are loaded with books on self-worth and self-esteem? It is the tussle of the 90's. Listening to the voices of the past keeps the belief of inadequacy alive in most adults. As you know, it is very difficult, at times, to remember that you are a grown-up.

Like Chrissy, a large number of clients who enter my therapy room carry a powerful disbelief in themselves. Converting the judging eyes of the past into their own personal critic, many clients will not even allow themselves to consider that their conclusions about being damaged goods might be false. It is my personal conviction that because children see parents as God, they cannot accept any alternative suggestions regarding their goodness. To do so would be to usurp the Almighty, in this case, their parents, teachers, or other adult authority figures.

As you might imagine, one of the "battles" of the therapy room is the contention between the judgments of the *internal critic* and the *authority* of the therapist, who dares to suggest that the harsh voices of the past may be false. For most people, to consider a new evaluation of the self will not occur unless there is permission to see the critics of the past in a new light, *through the eyes of vision.* This means there needs to be an awareness that parents will not be torn apart or destroyed in this new vision. To the degree you believe that your history or legacy is under attack, the walls of your defense system will be built. The greater the perception that the system is under siege, the thicker the walls.

Regardless of how much you may want to change, until you look at yourself through the vision of love, and at your parents through the vision of understanding, nothing much will happen. To discover the humanity of your parents, and to see their fear, which we all share, is the beginning of healing. Even parents, or other authority figures who may have appeared to be cruel or abusive, need to be understood in the light of their own fear and history. When a child discovers that his mother's criticism of his choices grew out of her own fear of making mistakes, a giant shift can occur in his sense of self. Such discoveries do not grow out of anger and violence, but rather out of a small desire *to see things differently.*

While it may seem to be a small thing to decide to look at the past through another window, such is not the case. Your entire sense of self, as well as the foundation of your belief system, is dependent upon the view outside the window through which you have always looked. Raising the possibility that there is a vision which can open your eyes to another scene may sound inviting; however, in reality, it is a very fearful task. If touched with fear, the small desire to see your past differently can grow even more tiny. I cannot overemphasize how much power and authority we all have given to the gods of our history. To question their commandments or authority takes enormous courage.

Ken had been living with a woman for three years before his problems began. "We had a wonderful relationship until recently," he said, "and then we decided to get married. That's when all of our problems began."

"How can that be," he asked me, "that we could be so good together and now it's so terrible? We used to have fun and good times; now all we do is fight. Our love-making was terrific, but now we hardly even touch each other anymore. I don't know what to do."

Ken had arrived for "crisis" work, as he called it. He didn't want "therapy;" he just "wanted Sheila back." Recently, Sheila had suggested to Ken that he leave and move in with a friend of his. When he refused, she said that she would go stay with a girlfriend. Ken stood by while she packed her bags, but when she started for the door, he refused to let her leave. As she persisted in her attempt to open the door, Ken wrestled Sheila to the floor. "I didn't hurt her," he said, "All I did was hold her." He started to cry, "I just couldn't stand to have her leave me."

Eventually, of course, Sheila did leave Ken, moving in with her girlfriend. Desperate to get her back, Ken agreed to get "help," as Sheila had screamed at him as she was leaving.

"I'm nothing without her," Ken admitted to me in our first conversation, "She's the best thing that ever happened to me in my life. I don't know what I'm going to do."

Ken's history was filled with abandonment, Sheila being his third significant female relationship in the past ten years. At twenty, while in the Navy, Ken had married a girl he met in one of the ports where he had been stationed. Although a son was born almost immediately, the relationship was stormy and she "ran away." Two years later, Ken married again but the relationship only lasted three years. His second wife left him because she said he was too "suffocating" to be with. He seldom saw his son and daughter from that relationship, since his ex-wife lived a distance. When he met Sheila, he "knew" this was "it." "She was the woman I had been waiting for all my life," he told me.

"What about your parents?" I asked him.

"My parents have nothing to do with this," he said, "I'm not a child. Maybe if I was fifteen years old, or something like that, it might make a difference, but I'm a grown man. What's that the Bible says, something about leaving your parents to take a wife?"

As time passed, so did Ken's reluctance to talk about his past as he shared a remarkable story of his mother and father. The youngest of four children, Ken recalled a night when he was five years old. "During the night my father woke us up and said we were all going on a trip. I was hardly awake, but I noticed right away that my mother wasn't with us. 'She's coming later,' my dad told us, but she never did." Ken told of a long ride through the night, and most of the next day until they arrived at an orphanage, Ken's home for the next twelve years. "My father left us there and I never saw him again." Ken relayed this story without emotion, talking in matter of fact tones.

"What about your mother?" I asked him.

"It was almost a year later when she came to visit us," Ken answered. "It was just about Christmastime and she brought us some gifts."

"Well, what happened?" I felt like a child waiting for the ending of a story.

"Nothing happened. She left us some presents and came back to see us about once every three or four months."

"You mean your parents just dropped you off in an orphanage and left you there?" This was one of the more unusual stories I had heard.

"That's right. And with the stipulation that we couldn't be adopted unless somebody took all four of us. So we stayed there until we were eighteen. Except when I was seventeen, I ran away and joined the Navy. I lied about my age and they didn't really bother to check up on me too much."

"Are your parents living now?" I asked Ken.

"My dad's dead—not that it matters," he answered, "And my mom lives in the city, about a half hour away from me."

"Do you ever see her or talk to her?"

Ken's face lit up a little, "Oh sure, I'm down there once a month or so for dinner or a visit. We get along fine."

"Did you ever ask her why all of this happened?" I looked at Ken.

"No." He shook his head. "Why would I do that? It's over and done with. The past is the past and you can't change it. So, I say the best thing to do is leave it alone."

"But, Ken," I said, "wouldn't you want to know what happened? This has had such an impact on your life. Perhaps it would help you to see things differently, including yourself."

Ken refused to discuss the possibility of talking with his mother about the unknown issues of his childhood. Adamantly stating that he refused to stir up the past, Ken wanted only to find a way to hold on to Sheila and to win her back. Agreeing that he had major issues with abandonment, Ken felt that if he could just behave "better," Sheila would be willing to stay with him. "Help me find out what's wrong with me, and fix it, and I know she'll move back," he kept saying time after time.

One day Ken seemed to be more open about the impact his legacy was having on his life. "You asked me once about talking with my mother about the orphanage. What happens if I don't like the answer?"

"What do you mean, Ken?"

"I mean, suppose that she gives me an answer I don't want to hear." He looked directly at me, "Don't you understand? Suppose she tells me that she let my father put us in the orphanage, and she left us there because..." he began to weep softly, "because she didn't love me. Maybe she never wanted me or loved me."

"You know something," he pointed his finger at me, "this is why you should leave the past alone; you never know what you're going to find out. If the person who made you doesn't love you, what does that say about you?" Before I could open my mouth to respond, Ken raced on, "I'll tell you what it says: it says that you're garbage! And who the hell wants to be around garbage?"

In a single sentence, Ken stated the power of his legacy and the ways in which it had defined him. The person who "made him," in this instance, his mother, was truly a god with the power to punish or reward. How else could a child see this horrible experience? What other conclusions could he arrive at other than his sense of being "garbage?" Ken, like all children, never considered that his mother or father had a problem; he only saw his own unworthiness, as proved by his placement in an orphanage. "People do not want to be around garbage," said Ken's truth. He had concluded that his placement was the direct result of his being damaged or flawed. "Why else would parents do this to you?" was the only question he could have asked; but then, he already knew that answer.

Is it any wonder that Ken had a difficult time with the desire to see through another "window?" In this instance, he was so sure of his conclusions that another window would be pointless. He already knew "who he was": an inadequate man who, when found out, would be constantly abandoned by those he loved. Life had proven this to him, as had his relationships. To arrive at any other conclusion would be virtually impossible.

"FIGURING IT OUT!"

You might think that once you "figure out" your legacy and the ways in which you have made it sacred, all that remains is to de-mystify it. Paul writes that "when you were a child, you thought and reasoned like a child, and now that you are an adult, you put away childish things." Why not, then, allow the wisdom and logic of adulthood to erase the legacy beliefs? Certainly this makes sense, and, to a degree, there is some truth in it. Education and a new vision can help bring about change. Looking through another window allows a different view.

There are, however, at least two difficulties in bringing about legacy change. First, remember that early childhood learning is internalized through the emotions. Little children sense the teachings of their parents; they learn through their *feeling receptors*. Like radar, children absorb the legacy in various sensory experiences. Storing the teachings in their hearts, as they grow older, children add the verbal and intellectual legacy of their parents to this reservoir. Long before the written commandments are handed down, the children already have a fierce loyalty of the heart to the teachings of the system.

When a child begins to reason and think, legacy issues are bound to be raised. Not only is this normal, it is a part of the child's struggle for definition of the self. Along with each question, however, comes the emotional inoculation of the legacy. As my theological friend mentioned earlier in this chapter, there is a built-in sense of loyalty, a vaccine against disloyalty. There is a feeling of guilt which often surfaces regardless of how reasonable or sensible the questioning of the legacy may be. The adult part of a person may logically examine the legacy to discover various flaws and weaknesses. However, the child part of a person may adamantly refuse to allow any new discoveries to take root. The cost is too great, and the legacy too holy, to fiddle around with it, regardless of how crazy a parental teaching may seem.

Secondly, throughout the years of childhood, the legacy gets "owned." The beliefs taught or espoused by the parents and grandparents actually BECOME the beliefs of the child. Your grandmother's beliefs, for example, at a certain point, become YOUR BELIEFS. Questioning legacy issues, then, suddenly becomes dangerously close to an attack on yourself. It is not just the legacy you are defending, it is a very personal struggle with YOURSELF. This does not mean, however, that you accept every legacy issue from your family, but it does mean that every legacy issue has impact on your life, forcing you to deal with it. For most of us, though, accepting the legacy teachings of parents becomes an easier and more reasonable path through childhood.

Understanding your legacy, then, becomes crucial if you wish to change your life. But understanding alone will not do it. There is an old saying I first heard from an experienced therapist: "Understanding is the booby prize of therapy." Because you understand your legacy does not mean that you will automatically let go of the pieces that trouble you; it only means that you understand it.

Letting go of pieces of the legacy is akin to dropping a few of the Ten Commandments. Because parents are experienced as God by most of us, and since their teachings seem to fill our Legacy Bibles, questioning or change can be equated with being sacrilegious. Remember that it is not your mental conclusions that point out the heresy in examining the Legacy Bible, it is your *emotional storehouse* in which the legacy was first placed that screams out warnings. Years ago there was a science fiction show called "Lost in Space." It featured the adventures of a family hurling through space from planet to planet. Accompanied by a rather cowardly doctor and his somewhat cynical robot, this family flew from one adventure to another. Virtually every episode had one scene in which the robot would spin around in circles and cry, "Warning! Warning!" Immediately, the family would seek shelter or safety.

Just as the Robinson family had their security robot, we all have a built-in signal device. Screaming "Warning!" each time we poke around in the Legacy Bible, the robot suggests that we leave well enough alone and not mess with the *divine*. Figuring it out may be relatively simple—changing things is another matter; the warning lights may be just too bright.

THE SELF AND GOD

In the previous chapter, I discussed the ways in which you might possibly confuse your parents with God. Their strength, size, and authority carries enormous power into our lives. Imagining a father or mother as God is not a difficult concept to believe. What one of us, at one time or another, as a small child, did not fear for our very lives? These parents had power! Confusion is understandable in the minds of children when the teachings of the church/synagogue get mingled with their concepts of the original gods of life.

It is important at this time to raise a fascinating point: If your parents are your very first god, what happens when you begin to learn about the REAL God? How do you sort out the God of all creation from the god of YOUR creation? What about the conflict that may occur when the teachings of the "heavenly" Father are in dispute with the teachings of your earthly father? And if all that has been suggested in the preceding chapters has any validity, what if you now have internalized the commandments of your Legacy Bible, only to find them clashing with the commandments of your religious tradition? Which God is right: Mom and Dad who eat supper with you every night and warn you of dangers in the dark, or the other "god", whom you cannot see, but are assured is in your heart, bedroom, and backyard?

Consider Phil, for example, a man who grew up spending much of his childhood locked in a cellar because he was a "bad boy." After the death of his mother, Phil's father and stepmother couldn't be bothered with him. At the slightest problem between Phil and his two brothers, he was sent into the cellar. "Sometimes they would let my brothers bring me something to eat down there," Phil said, "And other times, I would just plain go hungry."

When brought up from the cellar, Phil's father and stepmother would patiently explain to him why he had to be punished. "If we don't teach you to behave, you'll end up in some reform school," his stepmother told him. "You're just bad blood."

While Phil couldn't understand the unfair treatment and abuse, he clearly knew that something was wrong. At times, he was sure it was his parents who were crazy, but there was another part of him that wondered if he really was "possessed" with something terrible. As Phil compiled his Legacy Bible, his list of commandments kept note of his inadequacy and worthlessness. It was not long before he truly believed that he was bad and perhaps should not have been born.

Phil's definition of his *self* was totally negative and unentitled. Trusting in his conclusions regarding himself, combined with his deification of his legacy, Phil made his belief into something holy and sacred. "I am an unworthy person" became his creed, as he recited it daily in his relationships and work. Obviously, in both areas of his life, Phil was constantly in trouble. Everywhere he went, he carried with him the locked cellar, the admonitions of his parents, and his own internal judgments.

One Sunday, on a whim, Phil turned the television to a religious broadcast. "Jesus died for you," the evangelist was crying, "because you are His brother, the beloved child of your Heavenly Father. You are precious in His sight."

At that moment, Phil broke down and wept bitterly. Unlike the many religious stories that tell you of a new life, this story is quite different. Regardless of how much scripture was quoted by this evangelist, or how powerful the preaching about the worthiness of God's creatures, Phil's Legacy Bible knows better. His own conclusions regarding himself tell him that these words are not meant for him. Phil *knows* that he is a worm since his legacy tells him so. He weeps for the "good news," which sounds so wonderful, but is not for him. The sacredness of his own BELIEF system carries ample strength to counter any attempt by the religious community to assure him of his preciousness in the sight of God. Phil is NOT precious, and he KNOWS it. It is important to remember that Phil's belief is internal and emotional. Regardless of his intellectual thoughts surrounding his worthiness, his internal and emotional conclusions carry the day.

For most of us, our first and primary SACRED experiences are with the family legacy and our parents (gods). If we learn our lessons well, and are loyal sons and daughters, our Legacy Bible will carry us properly through life. When any attempt is made to convince you that what you CLEARLY KNOW about yourself is false, the "Warning!" is sounded, the vaccine is re-injected, and you safely remain in the fold of the commandments of your legacy.

I have tried to convey in this chapter, as clearly as I can, the ways in which the family legacy shapes the definition of the self. When children arrive at conclusions about themselves, these quickly become the *truths* and *beliefs* of the Legacy Bible. When parents are viewed as gods, the sacredness of the legacy becomes even more powerful. It only remains now for the struggle to occur between the claims of the spiritual/religious community and the conflicting beliefs of the self, as taught by the legacy. In the following chapters, we will explore the ways in which these painful, and often paralyzing, clashes occur.

CHAPTER XII

SMARTER THAN GOD

*"It ain't what a man don't know
that makes him a fool,
but what he does know that ain't so."*

Josh Billings

*"Ignorance is a blank sheet,
on which we may write;
but error is a scribbled one,
from which we must first erase."*

Colton

When I was about six years old, I asked my father what would happen if I went downstairs at night, after everyone was asleep, to get a cookie. He told me that he would put the "kibosh" on me. At that age, I had no idea what a "kibosh" was; I only knew that I didn't want any part of one. Not understanding that he was telling me he would squelch my plans, I assumed the "kibosh" was some type of horrid instrument used to punish children. For the longest time, I imagined it to look like a small automatic sander that could be applied to various parts of the body. Rubbing vigorously back and forth, I saw the "kibosh" inflicting brush burns all over the top of my head.

For whatever reason, I also was led to believe the notorious "kibosh" was stored down in our cellar, on top of a series of shelves. Each time I walked past the shelves, I could feel the hairs on the back of my neck begin to prickle. What could be more terrifying to a young boy than the prospect of a dreaded "kibosh" sitting beyond my vision in a darkened cellar? I was petrified of this unknown and unseen instrument.

One day, when I was searching for my baseball glove, I saw the stepladder standing near the storage shelves. Normally kept in the garage, the ladder offered me my chance to finally catch a glimpse of the awful "kibosh." Pushing the ladder near the shelves, I climbed up to look on the top section. There was no "kibosh!" I was stunned; where could my father have put it? I knew there was no reason for him to have moved it, and yet, it was gone.

Perhaps, at that moment, I began to suspect the truth. The "kibosh" was one of my father's creations, an imaginary machine designed to keep young boys in line. While I never asked my father about it, from time to time he referred to the "kibosh," and regardless of my suspicions, it still filled me with concern and wonder. It was decades later when I finally discovered that the word "kibosh" was not my father's creation, but rather an uncommon noun, seldom used in everyday conversation.

The amazing thing, however, about the "kibosh", was that long after I knew it did not exist, I still was nervous around the storage shelves in the cellar. Even as a teenager, I did not like to walk past them; my neck still prickled with chills.

It seems to me this is an excellent example of the ways in

which our childhood beliefs, experienced at the emotional level, remain with us long into adulthood. Neither reason nor intellect seem to have much power over emotionally held beliefs and conclusions. By the time I was twelve, I knew there was no kibosh; my brain had stored that fact in its computer file. My emotions, on the other hand, were not so willing to let go of their initial conclusions. "There is nothing to fear here," my mind spoke to me as I walked through the cellar. "But there just might be something to all of this," my emotions screamed as I tried to be calm. The emotional conclusions of childhood hold enormous power; they are not so easily dismissed by mental awareness.

With each passing day in family life, the legacy is more and more deified; it is made sacred. Registered in the emotional body, or the "heart-mind," as it is sometimes called, the beliefs sit as if stored in a tabernacle. Lesson after lesson gets printed on the sacred scrolls of the heart, the "altar" of the child. Soon, the evangelized child enters the world with a core of beliefs which have prepared him/her for life.

It seldom matters if beliefs are true or untrue. There was no "kibosh;" nevertheless, my *truth* said otherwise. And since it was truth to me, I entered the cellar in fear and kept my distance from the storage shelves. Even after I realized a new *mental truth*, my altar-heart still held on to its early belief.

A neighbor of mine was in constant fear of spiders. Scouring his basement and walls, he searched high and low for the ugly looking bugs. The first warm day of spring, he would be flying around his house spraying chemicals in all directions. With heavy gloves, and a iron mallet in one hand, he would lift up large rocks around his lawn searching for any scurrying spider. In his house, he would enter rooms during the night and quickly click on the light, hoping to catch an unwary spider crossing the ceiling. Each time he found one, he immediately smashed it and then sprayed that particular room. Monthly, the entire house was bombed for insects.

One day he and I were talking about his bug problem when he said to me, "You know something, you probably think I'm crazy, all this nonsense I get involved in trying to kill spiders. I don't know what it is, but I can't stand to see even one of them. We don't eat out on the patio, you know, because if I see one, my whole meal is ruined." He talked on for awhile as we walked around the outside of my house, and he pointed out the areas I should attend to if I wanted to keep the bugs away.

"I hate this," he told me when we sat back down on the front porch, "because I know it's ridiculous. Just the other day I read an article in the garden news about how good spiders are for your garden. They keep the really destructive insects away, you know, sort of like security guards. And I've always known that they keep the house kind of bug-free. But, that doesn't even seem to matter. I guess it's not a matter of my brain but a crossed circuit in my feelings."

Emotions do carry a power of their very own. My neighbor was simply illustrating that regardless of how much he knew about spiders, his feelings seemed to be oblivious to those facts. The beliefs in his *altar-heart* carried the day. When he saw a spider, any data his brain carried about spiders got put away and the sprayer came out.

The altar-heart holds the beliefs of the Legacy Bible. Like the Ark of the Covenant storing the Ten Commandments, they get carried everywhere. Without them, the people are lost; they don't know what to do. Designed to guide children and keep them faithful, the legacy is an issue of the emotions; it does not respond well to logic or intellect.

WHO DO YOU BELIEVE YOU ARE?

At a Rotary Club meeting one day, I found myself sitting next to a visitor from Munich. His English and grammar sounded better than mine, and I remarked to him how well he was speaking. He smiled at me and said, "Well, my mother told me to always remember who I was and where I was."

"Are you able to do that," I asked him, "with all the traveling you do? I think I'd forget which country I was in."

He laughed, "I'm not sure she meant geography when she told me that. Perhaps she meant, instead, that I remember my place."

"Your place?"

"Yes, you know, my position in life. She was so proud that I was a surgeon. She would always say to me, 'Remember who you are.'" His eyes filled up with tears, "No matter where I go, I remember my place, and my mother's pride in me. I think she wanted to be sure that I would never do anything to embarrass myself or our family. Being proper is very important in our village. I only hope..." he swallowed with some difficulty, "that she is proud of me, always, and that I can be the man she meant for me to be. If I ever shamed her, I don't think I could go on living."

Driving back to the office after the meeting, I thought over this conversation. His legacy was clearly powerful; it had walked with him into every hospital operating room, as well as into each charity ball and speaking engagement. I was sure that his mother was, indeed, very proud of her successful and brilliant son. All of his education and wisdom would be useless to him, however, if he wanted to do something in his life that ran counter to his legacy. I tried to imagine this man falling in love with the "wrong" woman, or taking a position in an inner city hospital with little prestige. What space could there be for him to carve out a life that he wanted, or, to make decisions that were for his best interests instead of for the benefit of his legacy?

This surgeon cannot imagine being anyone other than who he is. His mother's suggestions have now become his own beliefs about himself. Stored in his altar-heart, they are deified. As a scroll in his own Ark, they are carried with him from country to country. If anyone would suggest a new goal or direction for his life, his emotional commitment to his legacy is so strong that, in all probability, he would not be able to entertain the suggestion, no matter how exciting or reasonable.

Your belief about yourself is sacred territory. But more than that, it is YOUR sacred territory. Created through your legacy and pumping through your emotional veins, your beliefs are now your own personal property. Regardless of what anyone may say or question, you know best who you are.

The most successful of business people or the most glamorous of movie stars will never be swayed by the public as to who they REALLY are. If raised in a shame-based family system, no amount of public adoration will convince you that you are acceptable just as you are. Who knows you best if it is not you? Others see the facade—they stare at the surface—but you know what is underneath it all. After all, didn't you learn who you were a long time ago? Votes, money, accolades, or awards will not touch your own conclusions about yourself. Your altar-heart carries the truth, and your Legacy Bible is printed by your parents' sacred hands. Holy tablets that define you are inside, and you know the words well—by heart, as a matter of fact.

Much has been written in recent years regarding the "Inner Child," that little one who lives inside and periodically sends you various messages. All of us have to contend with this character in our daily lives. Your Inner Child carries all of your earliest beliefs and fears. He or she knows of your weaknesses and strengths, your secrets and desires.

Depending on which book you read, the definitions of the Inner Child vary. Obviously, most of us know there is not a REAL child living within; instead you are simply aware, at a very deep level, of the feelings and memories of your childhood. They are housed inside your deepest part. If you were bitten by a dog when you were six years old, and one comes barking and rushing toward you when you're taking an afternoon stroll, all of the old fears will come rushing back. Your Inner Child will scream in panic. Depending on the level of your fear, you may run, or you might simply stand still. Either way, you will be hearing the sound of fear from within.

The family legacy is sitting deep down inside this child— residing at the deepest part of your emotional self. Defining you is literally "child's play" for this one who is in your heart and memory. Who knew you the best when you were growing up? And who, but this child, knows you best now? Is it any wonder that the legacy gets deified? Look at the age of the one who is in charge.

Your beliefs about yourself, then, were formed in the years you were most susceptible. Growing up with the wisdom and guidance of the gods who created you, your Inner Child has learned well. Most of the time you believe in the nudgings and whispers of this child. When he or she speaks to you from within, the words and suggestions are hard to ignore.

The important concept, however, regardless of how you choose to imagine it, is that your early history has carved out a belief system that daily impacts your life. Visioning it as an Inner Child, an altar-heart, or simply a deified Legacy Bible, is less important than grasping the concept and the strength that the legacy carries. It tells you who you are, and most of the time, you *believe* it.

WHO DOES GOD SAY YOU ARE?

To attempt to write God's view of creation is almost ridiculous. Thousands of books have been entirely devoted to this subject, and still no one knows much of anything about God's vision of His work. My theology teacher talked to me several hours a week for three years, but the most important line I ever remember him uttering was this: "When the creature can comprehend the Creator, you no longer have a Creator." Assuming this to be true, everything that follows is simply talk about God, as I understand Him. Unfortunately, my Legacy Bible and its impact will always be in the way, regardless of higher education and years of study.

Growing up, my minister reminded me that God saw me as a "worm," but if I confessed to my "worminess," He would be gracious enough to overlook it. This business about being a "worm" wasn't too hard to grasp, emerging from a critical- and shame-based legacy. The small town mentality, with its tribal customs, managed to keep an eye on me to be sure that my "worminess" didn't get out of hand. Sunday morning sermons gave me a weekly chance to stroll down the aisle, confessing to Jesus and the neighbor in the pew, that I recognized my lowly stature. Sometimes, I was given a chance to be a "confessed worm" on both Sunday morning and Sunday night.

Being Protestant, I always thought my Roman Catholic friends had it made. They didn't have to parade their "worminess" in front of others; all they had to do was go to confession. I really didn't know what that was, but I recognized it only involved one other person. What a relief it would be, I thought, to only have to admit your shame in one place before one individual. My Catholic friends used to talk otherwise, but I didn't believe them. They didn't know the power of the community eyes within the church.

One time I was taken to a youth revival where the speaker was billed as a man who understood the "private thoughts of youth." He gave a decent talk and then asked us to all close our eyes because our relationship with God was personal—it was our own business. I thought this was great stuff when he said, "I want every eye closed in this building. This is just a prayer between God and you." I closed my eyes and with several others held up my hand to confess my "worminess." I admitted to having evil thoughts—sexual ones, even—and waved my hand high. Reminding us that only God could see us, I acknowledged my brief wrestling match in the weeds with the neighborhood girls, as well as my pleasure in the body contacts. I was cooking with confession, just God and me.

Before his prayer was complete, he invited all of us to put our hands down, so that others wouldn't know who we were. As I opened my eyes, I was horrified to see several "adult clergy" walking up and down the aisle. One looked me in the eye, and I knew that he knew. "All right, now," shouted the evangelist, "are we going to be ashamed before God? Because if we are, the scripture says that 'in that day, He will be ashamed of us.' I'm going to invite all of you who raised your hands to stand up and come forward at this time. Come on now, are you ashamed to confess you need Jesus? He saw you raise your hand."

I wasn't sure if Jesus saw me raise my hand, but I surely knew that the parading clergyman did. He looked over at me and his eyes stopped. It took three verses of "Just as I Am" before my "worminess" wiggled out of the pew and down the aisle. My shame magnified that day, first of all since I had been duped in front of my friends, and secondly, because I compromised myself out of fear and guilt. Jesus and I grew no closer, and I never trusted evangelists again.

In many religious traditions, God is viewed as an all-knowing judge who sees through your outer skin and determines your degree of sinfulness. For children of critical-, shame-, or fear-based legacies, this is not hard to imagine. The gods of their childhood had already made note of their inadequacy. It takes little imagination at all to embrace the judging, black-cloaked figure proclaimed from the pulpit. If your mother caught you pulling your sister's hair, how much easier is it to understand that the Judging God caught your every evil thought?

If you lived in a fear-based legacy, the ever-watchful, punishing gods surrounded you. The Sunday school teacher's statement or your grandfather's word about the God who was omniscient could be terrorizing. "An all-knowing God certainly must be a punitive one," is the thinking of the child raised in fear. If He knew everything, He would be aware of your "wanderings" of thought and deed. As in all guilt, punishment would not be far behind; all you can do is wait in fear for the hammer of justice to fall.

I remember an occasion, when I was about eight years old, when I stole a flashlight from a cabin in back of one of my friend's homes. For a few days, I hid the flashlight behind our garage under one of the overhangs. After an appropriate time, I "found" the flashlight. Running into the house, I told my mother that I had discovered a flashlight behind our garage; did she want me to bring it in the house? Rooted in scarcity, and always needing one more flashlight, my mother agreed. I quickly ran out to the garage to retrieve it.

Stooping over to pick up the flashlight, I suddenly became aware that I was being watched. I sat down and leaned against the side of the garage, my heart pounding. Peering over the roof of the garage, and seeing me hiding under the overhang, was the awesome, imaginary, figure of God. Very tall, and balding, He saw my dastardly deed. His eyes told me that I was "found out." Nevertheless, I picked up the flashlight and ran into the house. My mother was delighted.

As happy as she was with the flashlight, however, my heart was sinking. I knew that God knew; and if He knew, it was only a matter of time before I would be caught and punished. "Crime never pays," said my father-god when discussing someone's plight if they were caught in a compromising situation. Three days later, under the most casual of questioning by my father, I confessed to my crime. The seven days of grounding, with the forced return of the flashlight to its rightful owner, felt far better than the dread of an impending doom I had experienced once I knew that God had "found me out."

How does God see you? Unfortunately, the answer to that depends upon how you see yourself. And, how you see yourself rests with the commandments and teachings of your Legacy Bible, which in turn is created by the gods of your childhood experiences. The child of the critical/guilt-based legacy views God as judgmental and authoritative. Those raised in a shame-based legacy feel God's disappointment, while children of fear-based legacies understand God as punisher or executioner. In the next three chapters, I will discuss these concepts in greater detail.

The notion of a God who simply loves is virtually unacceptable to everyone. Raised in conditional love, most children feel there are strings attached to everything, especially God. "There's no such thing as a free lunch" is applied to much more than supper. "Paying the piper" is not just reserved to the one who is followed by the children—it easily gets applied to the Almighty. The God who overlooks, or who is not interested in judgment and punishment, is foreign to most people.

The plain fact is that how God sees you is less important than how you see yourself. An absolutely fascinating phenomena to me is that *PEOPLE THINK THEY KNOW THEMSELVES BETTER THAN GOD KNOWS THEM!* This thought is perhaps the one major factor which led to the writing of this book. Your Legacy Bible has done such a superb job of defining you that it wouldn't even matter if God showed up for a chat with you in your bedroom, during which time He were to tell you how wonderful you were. "You'd know better! And that's that. After all, what does God know? Your legacy helped you to see your 'worminess,' and the church made sure you understood it. Let's not go off half-cocked at some notion about being wonderful in the eyes of God!"

Carl was seventy-one when he came in for therapy. At the strong urging of his daughter, he agreed to come in for one session to talk about his feelings of not "making it to heaven." "Why would God want an old fool like me?" he asked me early in our first conversation. "I'm just a sinner like everybody else, and probably worse than most," he said matter of factly.

When his daughter telephoned for him, she told me that her father had been an elder in the small Pentecostal church in his neighborhood. "He hasn't missed Sunday school in over ten years," she said, "and he is seen as a very holy man by all the people in the church. Even the minister told me that he goes to see my father when he gets a little down on his faith, or the work of the congregation gets too great. I can't imagine why Dad feels he's so unworthy."

"I feel like I'm betraying our pastor just by being here talking with you," Carl offered. "You know, if you have a problem, the Lord will solve it. It's just that I don't know how to tell the pastor how unworthy I am. He would be so disappointed in me. Besides that, our church doesn't believe in shrinks. They undermine the Word," he looked at me and grinned, "present company excepted."

"It sounds like you must be having quite a struggle," I told him.

He nodded, "I guess that's the word, all right. It's been a struggle for a lot of years now. I don't seem to be able to keep anybody happy these days, least of all myself. My wife is upset with me most of the time; course that's nothing new." He grinned again. "But it just seems a lot worse right now. Partly, I think, because she's not feeling good, and the other part because I'm not remembering things like I used to."

"Such as?" I asked him.

"Well, such as remembering to go the grocery store or to pay the electric bill. The other day after lunch I cleared the table off, carried the dishes to the sink, and then forgot to wash them. Nelly was really upset. I guess I was upset, too, since I wash the dishes every day, and always have. I couldn't figure out how I forgot they were there."

"Sounds like you've been a big help around the house for Nelly," I said.

He nodded his head slowly, "Yep, I've always done most of the housework. Nelly never did feel she could do a good job of things, so I sort of took over shortly after we got married. Course, I never told anybody I was doing 'women's work,' but it really never bothered me all that much."

"So what exactly are you struggling with, Carl?" I asked him.

"Well, I guess, sort of...like, should I be here?"

"You mean in here, talking with me?" I asked him.

"Oh no," he laughed, waving his arms around the room, "I mean, be HERE. You know, alive...in the world...HERE!"

"You're wondering if you should be alive?" I looked at him.

"Well," he said, "I've always wondered that ever since the accident."

I sat quietly, waiting for him to go on. Carl had a reputation for being a storyteller, and I thought one might be coming my way.

He settled back in his chair, "Most people don't know this, but I was a twin," he sort of sighed, "My twin brother, Cal, was born about ten minutes after me. We were the last two born in a family of seven. Our oldest brother was nine years older than me. Anyway, we lived on the old Benson farm out on Buckhill Road in those days, and pretty much kept to ourselves. Course, I don't much remember this story but it sure was repeated to me a lot as I was growing up. It was early in February and the house was real cold. I can remember being able to almost put your hand through the wall boards in my bedroom, they were so thin. My dad was a carpenter and he had made this special cradle for Cal and me; I still have it. It was wide enough to hold both of us, and he had put it on rockers, so you could rock it back and forth."

Carl paused for a minute, and pushed his white hair out of his eyes, "Well, on this particular morning, so I was told, one of my older sisters, Henny, was rocking the cradle back and forth. It was sitting on the kitchen table, since there was a draft on the floor. Anyway, Henny was working that thing pretty good, and she didn't notice that it was 'walkin' on her, you know, moving across the top of the table. All of a sudden the thing reached the side of the table, and fell off. As I understand it, I fell on the floor first, followed by Cal. After that, the cradle landed on him with one of the points of the rocker hitting him right smack in the middle of the back of his head." Carl was quiet again, "That's about it," he said, "I was fine; Cal died that afternoon. And ever since then, I've wondered why I lived and he died? How come it wasn't the other way around?"

Over the next few weeks, I learned a lot about Carl. Living with this horror story being repeated periodically by his siblings, as well as other family members, Carl seriously questioned his "right to be." This "rite of survivorship" issue was the same one raised by many Jewish survivors of the Holocaust. Questioning the right *to be* is the struggle of those who survive by fate or by accident. Being in the right place, or wrong place, at the right time is an issue of life's purpose and meaning. Is there intentionality in the universe? Does Someone up there know what's going on and pull the strings?

Carl's struggle with his right to be was his struggle with God. The question of why Cal had died, instead of Carl, was raised in the direction of God. No one could give Carl the answers he was seeking, or the permission to be alive. When his older sister, Henny, ran away from home in her late teens, the impact was even greater. By the time he was twelve years old, Carl was uncertain and doubtful of having any rights at all. His sense of entitlement was non-existent.

From the issue of legacy, Carl was questioning his right to have been born. While no one blamed him for Cal's death, he blamed himself for falling out of the cradle first. Equally, no one blamed him for Henny's running away from home; nevertheless, he felt responsible. Sometimes his mother would sigh and mention the loss of family happiness in the same breath as the "bad afternoon." This lack of entitlement came into play in a profound way the first time Carl visited the small Pentecostal church, where he still belonged. Listening to the minister speak about the "suffering servant," turning the other cheek and self-denial, Carl knew that he had come home. He already did all of these things; and he hadn't yet met Jesus!

If it would be possible to imagine there was no God or Jesus Christ, Carl would have been living the "Christian" life of self- denial and sacrifice, not because of embracing any religious doctrine, but rather due to his Legacy Bible, created in childhood by the death of his brother. There was no conversion experience for Carl, only an adapting of his lifestyle to the sacrificial tenants of Christianity.

For me, this was a tremendous example and discovery. One did not have to be a Christian to sacrifice, or to "walk the second mile." All that was needed was a legacy experience which produced questions of self-worth and entitlement. Carl did not need to hear the preacher proclaim him a "worm"; he already was one. The proclamation simply confirmed what he already knew to be true.

Most of us cannot begin to match Carl's story. It was profound and powerful in its way of shaping him, as well as leading him to embrace his faith with great zest and conviction. Carl preached self-denial and sacrifice, both in Sunday school class and in his family. For Carl, whatever sense of self he had was mostly negative and worthless.

In Carl's case, it is clear the way his family/life experiences impacted his sense of religion and God. The astounding thing about this is that each of us has arrived at similar conclusions. Rooted in our Legacy Bibles, regardless of the many various teachings we had, is the teaching that determines how we see God. How God sees us, then, becomes immaterial, since we will always believe that we know ourselves better.

SMARTER THAN GOD

The struggle for all of us in relationship with God is to get our Legacy Bibles and self-definitions out of the way. If you try to imagine how God views you by placing your belief system and family legacy in front of His eyes, what else will you see but the same view held by your system?

Fortunately, God does not bother with legacies nor childhood conclusions. His vision is a tad more sophisticated. I suspect that if God has a sense of humor, He finds our entire usage of the Legacy Bible and self-judgments in poor taste. As incredible as it may seem, we have decided that we are smarter than God in determining our worth and value. What a perfect illustration of the power and authority of the Legacy Bible. The legacy gets deified and God gets demoted to the office person who receives memos once cleared by the higher-ups. This is, indeed, the ultimate heavenly joke.

CHAPTER XIII

GOD AS POLICE OFFICER

Lennie: …human weakness takes many forms.
Desire, greed, lust —
We're all here for different reasons,
aren't we?

Fletcher: …With respect, Godber, we're all
here for the same reason.
We got caught.

**Dick Clement and Ian La Frenais
BBC**

"Whenever man commits a crime,
heaven finds a witness."

Bulwer

"Commit a crime and the earth is made of glass."

Emerson

GOD AS POLICE OFFICER

Children who emerge from a critical/guilt-based legacy know a great deal about getting caught. Living with the ever-watchful eyes of their parents peering at their activities, these children understand scrutiny. All you need to do in a critical-based family is wander off the appointed path or step out of bounds, and you'll be seen. *Caught* is perhaps the more appropriate word, or *captured, apprehended,* or *seized.* Regardless, the result is the same for children of these legacies; do something wrong and you'll be found out.

One day, when my oldest son was in second grade, he was given permission to ride his bicycle to school. This was a big decision on my part, and as I anxiously watched him pedal up the street, I wondered if I would live to regret it. At that time I was thinking strictly of his safety in traffic. Little did I know that there were other things to worry about as well.

I was just finishing some office work when my secretary spoke to me through the intercom; the elementary school principal was on the telephone. "Mr. Satterly, we're calling because Matt's not in school today. Several of the children said they saw him ride his bike up to the front entrance, but he's not in class. To tell you the truth, we're quite concerned."

My mouth went dry and I felt my heart start to pound. Just as I started to say something, my secretary pushed open the door to my office. "Matt's on line 2," she told me.

Putting the principal on hold, I switched to line 2. "Matt?" I said, hearing the anxiety in my own voice.

"Dad, it's me," he said. "I'm home and I'm sick."

"What do you mean you're sick?" I asked him, "And how did you get in?" I knew that he didn't have a key to the house.

"I pushed the picnic table bench around to the front of the house and climbed in your bedroom window," he told me. So much for neighborhood watch and the periodic security checks I gave the house.

Putting him on hold, I returned to his school principal and told her the "lost had been found." Expressing my thanks for her concern and call, I said good-by and went back to the poor, sick child. "Dad," he continued, "don't be mad but I threw up on the couch. I tried to clean it up but I don't know if I did a very good job or not."

"That's okay, Matt," I told him in my most nurturing voice. "I have a few things to attend to here, and then I'll be home in about a half hour."

Walking in the back door, I saw Matt sitting in his favorite chair dressed in his pajamas. He obviously had decided that he was sick enough to stay home for the day. After I checked him for a fever and assured myself that he was going to live, I switched my attention to the stains on the couch. It was wet, but certainly not clean. Finding the upholstery cleaner in the closet, I proceeded to spray and scrub the couch. The directions said to use dry paper towels to dab up the wetness. After finishing the job, I went into the kitchen to toss the wet towels into the trash can.

Perhaps it was my own suspicious nature, being raised by a clever father, or simply the sweet smell coming from the cushions, but I decided to poke down under the trash. Imagine my surprise to discover a whole pile of paper towels, soaking in what appeared to look suspiciously like chocolate milk.

Carrying one into the living room and holding it up, I said to Matt, "What's this?"

At that precise moment, he was nailed, captured, found out and collared. I had him cold, and he knew it. A rather lengthy story spilled out in which he shared his discovery that he had forgotten his lunch pail. Since he had time, he rode back home, pushed the picnic table bench around to the front of the house, (that part was true) and entered through the bedroom window. Enjoying the quietness of the house while at the same time remembering that Captain Kangaroo was on TV, he decided to have some lunch. Unfortunately, he spilled the chocolate milk on the sofa. The rest was obvious as he determined the necessity to create a story to match the evidence.

God, I was brilliant, though, to see through it all and apprehend him.

This is exactly how children of critical-based legacies learn a very clear lesson: there is no escape from the clever and watchful eyes of a resourceful parent. It wasn't that Matt had committed a horrible crime—he had simply been caught. And to tell the truth, it does not take a very wise parent to catch a child in his or her mistakes. It's a mismatch from nursery days, and children are losers every time.

How well do you remember your childhood? It is a time of great curiosity and exploration. The world is brand new; it looks exciting, and is filled with so many things that need touching, smelling, or throwing. Can you remember how it felt to pet a cat for the first time? Or to take your very first taste of a chocolate chip cookie? Everything seemed to be placed for you to discover and feel. An expensive vase meant no more to you than your plastic bottle. Why not toss it around in the air?

In those early childhood days, if you itched, you scratched. It didn't matter where and how. When something tasted bad, you spit it out. Why would you hold it in your mouth or swallow something that made you gag?

Unfortunately, manners and civility were not a part of your childhood. Rules and regulations seemed foolish and totally confusing. However, whether as a joke or not, God apparently placed these big police officers in your home to see to it that you learned what was "right" and "wrong." Not only were they real good at their jobs, they also meant business.

All children grow up in homes where they get caught. It is a fact of life when little ones are raised by big ones. Getting caught is not the real issue, but rather how the capture is made. Were you handcuffed, rough-housed, and hauled off to jail? Or were you handled with gentleness and care? This is the key to the emotional responses of children, who grow up in a world of "impossible" adults who always will outsmart and outwit them.

Parents hold enormous power in their hands when they first begin to catch their children in the normal activities of childhood. For those children who are supported and taught, even when caught doing something wrong, their emotions register a sense of okayness, a feeling of trust in the police officers in their lives.

However, for those children who are caught and critically reprimanded for exploring life, even if down an interesting trail, there is created an emotional registry of fear, shame, and guilt. Sometimes, the power of this scolding or admonishment is so great that these children not only spend much of their lives looking over their shoulder for the police to arrive, they gradually grow to expect it. Being caught becomes a familiar feeling, with all the resulting guilt and shame. Some actually become so used to being caught, they forget to think, leaving clues all over the place for the "police" in their lives to find.

So, when you're a kid, it's never an issue of getting away with anything, or pulling a fast one on your parents. You won't—at least not until you're old enough to be crafty. By then, the child living inside you has become so conditioned to being watched that all sorts of bells and buzzers will ring within each time you go against the rules of the legacy. In a very profound sense, this is the voice of your conscience. Talking to you like an inner mother and father, your conscience echoes the family legacy and the rights and wrongs of your system to remind you of good and proper behavior.

THE "VOICE" OF GOD

Oral Roberts and Jimmy Swaggart notwithstanding, it is never easy to hear the voice of God. Most of us struggle a great deal to separate our own wants and desires from the so-called "guidance" of God. I remember, when I was in my early teens, begging God to put in an appearance in my bedroom. "Even for five minutes," I pleaded, "so that You can clear up a few mysteries for me, Mr. Almighty, Sir." Perhaps I simply didn't stay up late enough or I looked in the wrong corner, but God and I never connected in any clear dialogue in those days.

This is not to say that God is not actively involved in the lives of people. I wouldn't want to get that "up close and personal" as to suggest what God does or doesn't do. The people I talk with, however, tell me that it is very difficult to determine the "voice" of God in their lives. For myself, discovering the wishes and will of God is a task requiring enormous energy and openness. Is it any wonder that Jacob had to wrestle all night with God in order to develop a sense of direction for his life, to hear and understand God's voice? In my opinion, he was lucky to get off with a bum leg.

To this point, I have focused my comments on the legacy which gets created and solidified in the family. There are, fortunately or unfortunately, legacies from other places in our lives. In particular, for those exploring this book, two other legacies carry extraordinary weight in life. The legacy of religious tradition seems to add to our concepts of God, heaven, hell, and so forth, while the legacy of culture through television, schools, and community, amplifies the teachings of family and church/synagogue. It is virtually impossible to talk about God without discussing the institution which claims to hold the *truth* about Him.

In our Judeo-Christian culture, God appears to be a blend of Santa Claus, Superman, Moses, Jesus, and the American Way. On the one hand, if you do things "right," God will be on your side. But, if you turn away from His rules, He will turn away from you. If you regret your bad behavior, though, He will cut you a break. However, He keeps an accurate list of your wanderings, and apparently, there is a limit. In the Old Testament, He apparently has a shorter fuse than in the New. Somewhere along the line, sacrifices and burnt offerings don't cut it; instead, mercy is required. In the earlier days, Jehovah seems angry a great deal of the time. Winning a battle isn't enough; slaughtering the unbelieving Philistines seems more acceptable.

He talks to Moses through a burning bush, to Gideon through the dry ground, and to Samuel in his bedroom. God speaks to Balaam through his donkey, to Joseph in a dream, and to Paul in a blinding light. The tenderness of a gentle Jesus gets a tad confused with the sword of battle recorded in Kings and Chronicles.

I realize that there are those who will speak to these difficulties in an attempt to have everything fit together. Perhaps, they will say, the earlier peoples weren't prepared for a more gentle and grace-filled God. There wasn't enough sophistication to recognize creeds and beatitudes, therefore, commandments and rules were required. The Old Testament people were nomads and tribal; apparently, they needed a more harsh God.

With the New Testament came a more enlightened people, those who were prepared to embrace love and pardon. The educational, cultural, and communal life was now ready to support Jesus and His teachings. The fact is that all of these explanations may be true, or they may be false. For the purposes of understanding the impact of the religious legacy, however, it doesn't matter.

The plain truth is that most people are downright confused about what they believe. Old Testament stories from Sunday School about a warrior God, mixed with New Testament stories about Jesus holding a lamb or healing a child, creates questions.

Elisha calling a "she bear" out of the woods to kill a bunch of kids because they made fun of his hair, and Jesus urging his followers to turn the other cheek and walk the second mile, presents a mixed message to children trying to understand the place of God in their lives.

Add to this hodge-podge of bewilderment a father who is a cop by profession and disciplinarian by role, along with a mother who balances her husband's strictness by overlooking every wrong the children do, and you have the makings of a marriage between the religious legacy and family legacy. Most children, in this situation and others like it, will be totally puzzled about God, to say nothing about how He speaks to them. Will He speak with the authority and rigidness of Dad, or with the compassion of an over giving mother who seems somewhat like the meek and mild Jesus, but not at all like the mighty Jehovah who created and controls the world?

Growing up in a culture like ours, it is very difficult to avoid being a product of the divine merger between family and religion. Even for those children who never attend church/synagogue, or whose parents avoid participation in religious activities, a sense of God is **still** installed in their legacy programming. School room experiences, street corner lessons, and television stories seem to put out a concept of God as ever-watchful and involved with humanity. Children learn about God from the culture, the living room, and the pew, and sometimes these lessons contradict one another. Other times, confirmation of family dinnertime conversation is found in the morning homily. A lot depends on the subject as well as the nature of the Sunday morning presenter. Since some studies have shown that people tend to seek out congregations and clergy who confirm their own legacy beliefs, the chances are that children will experience a "baptism" of their legacy in the corner church selected by their parents.

For the most part, the church and synagogue teach that the bad guys get caught, and the good guys do the catching. Hollywood, running with a good thing, plays this theme to movie-goers who buy tickets to watch their legacies take life. It may take some time, as it does in the Superman movies, but "good wins out," and it's curtains for the villains. "Crime doesn't pay" is not only the slogan of the courtroom, it is echoed by Dad as you leave the house for the evening and confirmed by Lot's wife, who turns into a salt lick when she is

189

caught looking back at Sodom.

Critical to this concept is the fact that you cannot grow up in this culture without a sense of God as a police officer. The notion that children do not have enough verbal skills and sophistication to separate out myth from literalism is seldom taken into consideration when God's stories are spit out in religion classes. Conversation about a God who sees your every movement may be fine for those who are seeking comfort and solace in loneliness, but for children who rarely do anything right anyway, it is a set-up for fear. And for children of critical-based legacies, God as police officer is on target and quite understandable.

Try, for example, to hear the story of David and Bathsheba from the point of view of a child. First of all, as David falls for a steamy Bathsheba and plots a way to place her husband in a dangerous position in the army, children instantly are aware that God is on to him. The writers make it clear almost immediately; God has spotted David's overactive glands. Not only does nothing escape God's ever-watchful eye, but He just happens to inform his trusty friend, Nathan, of David's shenanigans. To a child, this means that you don't have a chance at all when it comes to God's police force; they're everywhere. With the Top Informant watching, you're bound to get caught the first time you cross over that line to the side named "wrong." Of course, "right" and "wrong" are determined primarily in your Legacy Bible, and then stamped with the seal of approval from the pulpit or printed word.

Pointing his finger at David, Nathan thunders, "Thou art the man!" referring to David's passion for Bathsheba. In this case, the voice of God is one of accusation and indictment. All that remains is for Nathan to read David his rights.

When a child hears this story, he does not examine the culture of the day. There is no interest in the writer or his bias. Language is not explored nor is the mythology of the time questioned. Instead, the child hears with his or her heart these thoughts: God is just waiting for you to do something wrong. The minute that happens, He will not only catch you, but others will know of your indiscretion. "Your goose is cooked; you're mine. Gotcha!"

Children, then, who grow up in critical-based legacies, have a much greater tendency to see God as police officer than children from other legacies. I cannot emphasize enough, however, that NOT EVERY CHILD of a critical-based legacy will see the long arm of the law connected with God. Some children will find another way; they will search for grace, understanding and love. These children, in spite of being rooted in criticism and guilt, will seek out a better, more constructive path. They are, however, in the minority.

CHAPTER XIV

GOD AS JUDGE

"…She got even in a way that was almost cruel;
she forgave him."

Ralph McGill

"Take someone who doesn't even keep score,
who's not looking to be richer,
or afraid of losing,
who has not that slightest interest
in his own personality:
He's free!"

Rumi

GOD AS JUDGE

I recently watched a movie in which a small town police officer arrested a man for speeding. Protesting vigorously and demanding an immediate hearing, the man followed the officer to the town hall for a meeting with the local justice. There was more than a mild reaction when he discovered that the Justice and the arresting officer were both the same man. Even he knew that he was not going to get out of this one easily. He was found guilty before he got a chance to open his mouth in self-defense.

That's how it is when the judge and the cop are played by the same character.

For children, that's how it is when the same parent who says "Gotcha" also says, "Guilty as charged." But then, how could it be any different? Since being caught in the act is pretty much an admission of guilt, all that remains is the formality of the court hearing. Sometimes it takes place immediately; other times, the hearing is postponed until more family members are present.

"Wait until your father/mother comes home," is a familiar statement to a captured child. Implied in this statement is the belief that "court" will be more meaningful if the absent parent can be a part of the proceedings. In this way, perhaps the child will understand more seriously the nature of the charges and be less inclined to commit the same offense in the future. With luck this could save a little one from a life of crime or deceit.

Critical-, shame-, and fear-based legacies all use the concept of the judge to enforce the rules and regulations of the system. "Why did you do that?" and "What were you thinking of?" are common courtroom tactics to arrive at the truth, and at the same time, reinforce the teachings of the legacy. It bears repeating here to state that parents as judges are not about the business of being cruel, mean, or heartless. They are parenting, plain and simple, as they define the role. Concerned for the well-being of their children, and dedicated to the continuation of their own legacy, parents "ride herd" on their charges. As they see it, it is their job.

THE DIVINE COURTROOM

By now you're probably getting the idea that I make a lot of connections between the legacy and God. When your parents keep a critical eye on you, catching you time and time again with the evidence in your hands, you start to develop a philosophy of "being seen." After a time, even when you're all alone, that critical eye is present, or, the voice that warned you over and over about being good is heard in your inner ear. Sometimes, if you close your eyes, you can imagine a parent standing over you, shaking a finger, and saying, "And now what are you up to?"

So it is, or can be, with you and God. The Almighty, regardless of His grace-filled posture, gets all mixed up with the cops and judges in your life, and you're no longer sure of this business of pardon. It gets very difficult to switch horses in the middle of the stream as you ride to worship with parents criticizing you for your wardrobe or your manners, and then listen to a word of joy from the pulpit or classroom about your worth and value. When your father glances in the rear view mirror and catches you poking your sister, arrests you, and reads you your rights in a threatening tone, how can you possibly believe in this unconditional loving God proclaimed in the morning hymns?

Some people say that children make clear distinctions between Mom, Dad, and God, the same way they know that Wile E. Coyote doesn't really fall off a cliff. While that may be true for some children, it is my experience that most kids carry the cop and judge in their emotional registry, and it is extremely difficult to erase such programming, not only regarding other authority figures in their life, but also regarding God.

Children, for example, who have vast experience with a critical or shaming legacy, will expect the same treatment from their teachers, adult neighbors, and other authority figures. After all, don't they all work together? School conferences are held in order for one cop to talk to another about you. Every conversation between your parents and your neighbors can hold a potential disaster, especially if you feel you are hiding something. Granted, if you are doing well in school or are avoiding neighborhood problems, you may relax during these briefings. However, if you are fearful of getting caught in a secret crime, great anxiety can occur when authority figures talk about you.

Can it be any different with God? Our assumption is, of course, that as we age, become more sophisticated and informed, and arrive at theological maturity, we will automatically separate the *stuff* of God from that of our parents. While this makes a great deal of sense, each time I work with a client or family in great distress or crisis, there seems to be an immediate return to the religious legacies of childhood, including the cop, judge, and disciplinarian of their history.

For several years, I have been working closely with dying people as a part of the hospice movement. Visiting patients and families in their own homes, I am continually amazed at the consistency with which dying people return to their religious roots. Perhaps it is because during childhood you first hear of death, funerals, or heaven. Sometimes when a grandparent or pet dies, parents attempt to talk about "going to heaven" as a way of offering comfort. In worship services and congregational life, when mention is made of the death of a certain member, you listen with eager ears. When faced with your own impending death, then, or even with any major crisis, such as the loss of someone you love, the retreat into the religious legacy becomes automatic. For all of our sophistication and knowledge, the emotional registry kicks-in, the Legacy Bible is opened, and God becomes the reflection of the gods of childhood.

I am suggesting that there is a depth of belief that is rooted in the legacies of our childhood, and although it can be covered with education and knowledge, it still lives and breathes. Buried under pounds of adulthood and maturity, the childhood concepts of God leap out when we are faced with significant issues of fear and guilt. To proclaim the goodness and glory of God, when success and happiness is prowling in your home, is one thing. However, when the police arrive at your front door to announce the death of your daughter in an automobile accident, all sorts of confusion reigns. The clergy's fine attempt to talk about "things working together for good," doesn't quite do the trick. Well-meaning friends and neighbors who support Hallmark with cards of "she's home now" haven't any idea of your pain and suffering. The notion of God being good and glorious is now erased, usually to be replaced with the childhood thoughts of punishment and judgment, as though the loss of a child is the verdict of God. The books lining your shelves with words of theological wisdom are now meaningless; the thoughts themselves are hollow.

While much of this can be attributed to the grieving

process, the fact is that tragedy and crisis sends us scurrying back to our original programming. Childhood beliefs surge forward into the present and make themselves felt. Our minds play all sorts of tricks with us, most of them destructive and non-sensible. Consider, for example, that when your legacy taught you the powerful *if/then* concept as a child, it always seemed to come true. "If you hurt your brother, then you'll pay for it," came to pass when you were caught and punished for being mean to him. Does this mean that because your daughter was killed in an automobile crash, it was your fault, or that something you had done necessitated a punishment so severe that she was taken away from you in death?

While this may seem like a ridiculous idea, many people express it to me in pain and guilt. "If only I had insisted that she not drive tonight, this never would have happened." Or, "If I had found him another doctor, maybe the cancer would have been discovered in time." These are the legacy teachings of childhood being expressed in the minds and mouths of adults, who have been driven back, through pain and crisis, to their Legacy Bible. Being forty, fifty, or sixty years old has nothing to do with the emotional power of childhood beliefs, especially those housed in the Legacy Bible.

Seeing God, then, as cop or judge is not so far removed from reality in the minds of fearful, guilt-ridden, or shamed adults. As a matter of fact, that is exactly how most people of critical-, fear-, or shame-based legacies think of Him. When St. Paul talked of putting away childish things now that he was an adult, perhaps he was not considering the power of the family legacy. It certainly sounds like a fine goal, but nevertheless, is an extremely difficult one to accomplish.

Sitting with a group of men one evening, I heard a fascinating story of expectations, judgment, and disappointment shared by Drew, a thirty-seven year old school teacher. Raised in a family of active church members and the grandson of the minister, Drew was constantly being told that his behavior was a reflection not only on God, but also on his grandfather. "Sometimes, I got God and granddad so mixed up that I didn't know where one stopped and the other started. He was a big man with bushy white eyebrows, and a way of looking at me that made me feel like he could see right through me."

GOD AS JUDGE

"One Sunday morning," Drew told the group, "Granddad asked me and one of my friends to come up on the platform with him. I was so nervous because I didn't know what he wanted, and no one had told me this was going to happen. Anyway, he held up two things for everybody in the congregation to see: one was a little Bible, and the other a silver dollar. Then, he turned to the two of us and asked us each which one we wanted. Well, I knew right away that what I wanted was the silver dollar, but I also knew that wasn't what I was supposed to want. Meanwhile, my friend, who didn't have the worries and pressures that I did said, 'I'll take the dollar,' and everybody laughed.

"'How about you, Drew?' asked my Granddad, and as much as I wanted to say that I'd take the dollar, I said 'I'll take the Bible.' So my Granddad handed the dollar to my friend and the little Bible to me. Then he told us to go back to our seats, but just before I sat down, he called me back up to the front. 'Look in the front of your Bible, Drew,' he said to me, and when I opened it up, there was a silver dollar taped to the inside front cover."

"My granddad had this big smile on his face as he said something about 'accepting the kingdom and all these other things would be added unto you.' I didn't know what he meant by it, but I did know that I had made out the best in that deal. Besides that, my granddad was real proud of me, and when I sat down beside my dad, he squeezed my leg, just like I had done something wonderful."

Drew related a series of stories about a powerful grandfather figure who not only represented God to him, but filled Drew's Legacy Bible with verbal teaching, rules, and commandments that were a blend of Bible teachings and family morals. "By the time I started for college, I was all mixed up in terms of my religious beliefs. Every time I did something wrong, I imagined my grandfather's bushy eyebrows rising in disapproval. When I try to meditate or think about God, all that fills my mind is this image of granddad. How do you get around that?"

Before the group could respond, Drew said, "One time when I was about eight years old, I was sitting in Sunday School class and this kid, Billy Orr, sat down next to me. I used to hate that kid because he was a real jerk, always causing trouble, and he could barely read when the teacher asked him to. Anyway, he usually acted up in class, and this one day he was behaving like an ass. So, he started crawling back and forth under the table where we were seated. The first time he went by me, I ignored him, but I was getting more and more angry. In the first place, I didn't like him, and secondly, he was really bothering me.

"Mrs. Tuttle, the teacher, said something to him once or twice, but he just ignored her. And I guess all my rage at being stuck in that boring classroom, and feeling like I didn't have any choice, came boiling to the surface. So, the next time he crawled by me, I kicked him as hard as I could right in the side of his head." Drew looked at the group, laughing, "And in those days we used to wear those hard-soled shoes, you know, dress-up shoes, so that when I kicked him, it really hurt. I think I practically knocked him unconscious.

"Mrs. Tuttle didn't even bother to see if he was all right, she just grabbed me by the arm and pulled me outside the classroom door." Drew rubbed his arm as if she was still squeezing it, "She pushed me against the wall and got her face real close to mine. I can still remember that she smelled like bath powder; and she said, 'Drew, I don't expect anything of Billy Orr, but WE expect much more out of you. Don't you ever forget who you are!'"

With those words, Drew silenced. Offering some insights regarding expectations of adults, some of the men admitted to their own struggles of disappointing the important people in their lives, and the resulting confusion in personal decision-making or the expression of their own desires. How does a man make a choice for himself or reach for his own star if the gods in his life are not approving of his choices? Are there imaginary judges who daily arrive at decisions in a man's life, regardless of his own dreams? How can a man run himself and his own life when so many important and historic people are carried around in his mind and Legacy Bible?

The clarity of Drew's Legacy Bible was apparent to all in the blending together of his granddad's bushy eyebrows, Mrs. Tuttle's squeeze of disappointment, and his concept of God. To Drew, God was a mixture of the wisdom and watchful eye of his grandfather, the expecting and policing nature of Mrs. Tuttle, along with other cultural and religious views presented to him in his childhood years.

While Drew's experience is filled with his confusion between a clergy grandfather and his concept of God (with bushy eyebrows), many people struggle with a similar puzzle. It seems as though a common intersection is created between the authoritative people in our lives and our concepts of God. In Drew's case, because his grandfather preached religious ideas, it is relatively easy to see his merger of the legacy with his thoughts of God. However, in our own way, each of us has a comparable convergence of our learned Legacy Bible with our religious concepts. When it comes to God as judge, the legacy blends with the ideas of God as easily as ice cream and milk at the local Dairy Queen.

Almost daily, life presents us with challenges and opportunities. Sometimes we handle them well, other times, we don't. Every decision gets weighed against our own desires, our belief system, and potential consequences. Once we have moved from thought to action, all sorts of second-guessing can occur, as we judge and evaluate our most recent behavior. Of course, we tend to judge our own actions against the yardstick of the Legacy Bible. A young woman, who echoed her own legacy teachings in condemning the extra-marital affair of her girlfriend, suddenly finds herself drawn dangerously close to a similar relationship as her own marriage becomes stagnant. How can she allow herself to violate her marriage vows without the rigid and strict rules of her Legacy Bible coming into play as a measure of her morality? At this point, the very legacy itself becomes a judge, calling her to account and condemning her behavior.

In the same breath, her image of God visions Him sweeping into the court room, black robe flowing, and right hand clenched in a fist of justice. The trial which follows is swift and to the point. This is not a judge to trifle with, nor to be fooled. Displaying an uncanny ability to cut through the excuses to the truth, Judge God quickly adds His exclamation point to the Legacy Bible. Sending the jury out with explicit instructions, the judge sits and waits, expressionless, except for a brief look of disappointment which crosses His face from time to time.

THE VERDICT

Judges do a lot of things, but basically they listen to the evidence, weigh the facts, arrive at a decision, and announce a verdict. When it comes to the Internal Judge, housed in the pages of the Legacy Bible, the verdict is almost always the same: Guilty as charged! Shame on you! In an earlier chapter, I mentioned that I have not known many people to enter their internal courtroom without a preliminary reflection which claims they are already guilty. Since this is so true in critical- and shame-based legacies, the verdict is known before the court even convenes. Think, for example, of the number of times in your own life when you have done something beneficial or helpful for someone else. Do you call court into session to proclaim a verdict of "well done"? The chances are that your court only convenes when the legacy has done a quick spot check and found you to be lacking. An internal court hearing and a guilty verdict are almost synonymous.

There are three primary feelings which surface when a verdict is announced. Once found guilty, you experience the feeling that you have, once again, done something wrong. Secondly, being caught, prosecuted, and found guilty leads to enormous feelings of shame. You know that you have been found out; others realize that not only have you done something wrong, something is wrong with you. Closely following the guilt and shame, as night follows day, is the feeling of fear. Since you have been caught and judged, all that is left is your punishment; fear knows all about that. The next chapter will explore the impact of fear on your concepts of God and punishment.

Being guilty and feeling shame in the eyes of your Legacy Bible is one thing, but experiencing those same emotions in your relationship with God is quite another. And yet, it is virtually impossible to be pronounced guilty in your legacy without being equally seen that way by your concept of God. Since the Legacy Bible is carried within, and determines to a large extent the way you view and conceptualize God, how could they differ when it comes to a judgment of your latest life actions? If your father is disappointed in you for getting fired because your employment record was poor, can you imagine God not feeling that same disappointment? Or, if your child gets injured while in a day care center, and your mother reminds you that she never left you alone just to earn a few dollars, do you think you can escape that familiar feeling of guilt? And will God shake His head, also, because you didn't check out the day care workers with enough care?

Julie came in for her first therapy session at the age of thirty-three. Her anxiety was so great that she asked for several glasses of water during the first hour. Experiencing enormous shame because she was talking to a therapist, and frightened that her father and mother might find out about the session, she begged me to promise never to call her home for any reason at all.

"You still live at home?" I asked her.

Her eyes never left the floor as she said a very meek, "Yes."

"Have you ever lived somewhere else, like your own apartment?"

Again her eyes remained fixed on a spot on the carpet, "No."

I was silent for a moment, and then she said, "So, I suppose this means that I'm really sick. I knew I shouldn't have come here, I just knew it. My one friend told me that the first thing you would say is go move out of my parent's home."

"Is that what you want to do, Julie?" I asked her.

"I don't know what I want," she started to cry, "I just know that my life feels like it's more than half over, and I'm still living at home. I have two sisters, you know, and they both moved out when they were in their twenties. Here I am, like the last daughter in a fairy-tale, stuck at home until my parents die."

Julie shared a story of a very loving but closed family. Living in a rural area, she talked about her feelings of responsibility for her mother, a woman who had been sick for much of Julie's adult life. "When I was fourteen, my mother 'took to bed.' I wasn't sure what that meant, but later on I understood that she was having problems with depression. She's a little better now, but during my high school days it was really hard because I had to come right home from school to help take care of Mama. Since the other girls were younger and my dad had a factory job, most of the work fell to me. So, even though I hated it, I did what had to be done. I also missed out on a lot of high school fun. I never got to go to one football game during my senior year, and I guess I was plain lucky to go to the senior prom."

"What made you decide to come in for therapy, Julie?" I wondered.

There was a long silence, and then Julie said, "Because I'm no good."

"What does that mean when you say that?" I asked her.

"Just exactly that. I'm no good; and I don't think I've been good for a long time." At that point, Julie said that she had to go to the bathroom, and she didn't feel that she could talk anymore.

In subsequent appointments, Julie shared a story of a family system that was very enmeshed and fused. Her grandparents had lived with the family until their death, as well as one of her mother's brothers. Everyone was taught enormous responsibility to look after the family. Talking with the neighbors about anything was strictly forbidden. One time the next door neighbor asked Julie how her mother was feeling. Julie, not realizing she was saying something wrong, said, "She's a little better today, thank you."

"In my family," Julie said, "that was not allowed. First of all, I talked about my mother, and secondly, because I said she was a little better, that must have meant she had been worse. I guess I must have given away a family secret. Of course, I didn't understand it at the time, but my father and mother were furious with me."

"How old were you at that time?" I asked her.

"About ten, I think," Julie answered," and I learned quickly after that about the number one rule: don't tell the neighbors *anything*!"

Julie went on to relate a very sad story about her younger sister's pregnancy. Her parents were away for the weekend, leaving Julie in charge of her two younger sisters. Sometime, during those two days, her youngest sister found enough time to escape Julie's watchful eye and join her boyfriend, literally. A few months later, the story came out and Julie was blamed for her sister's plight. Because of Julie's irresponsibility, her sister was now going to be an embarrassment to the entire family. In order to avoid the neighborhood gossip, Julie and her sister went to visit her father's sister for an extended vacation. The baby was born, given up for adoption, and Julie never said a word to anyone before sharing this story in therapy.

"My sister's life was ruined, and it's all my fault," Julie cried, "And now she's had two miscarriages. She doesn't have any babies, and it's because of me. I'm just no good."

Julie's guilt and shame were enormous. Obviously, it doesn't matter if her feelings are logical or sensible; to Julie, they are real and valid. They will not be talked away easily, nor erased as though they didn't happen. Her pain has kept her stuck for nearly fifteen years in a difficult and unhappy environment. Feeling guilty, she has little sense of entitlement for her own life.

As we attempted to explore resources together, Julie told me that she was very active in her local church. "It's one of the few activities that I do," she said, "I play the piano during the Sunday School hour, and sometimes I sing in the church choir."

"You know," she confided in me, "once I wanted to be a minister. When I was a girl, we had a woman minister and I really admired her. But it wasn't possible."

"Why not?"

"Well, because God doesn't want mixed-up people as His ministers," she said, "And I certainly fit that description."

I looked at her, "How do you know that's what God thinks of you?"

"It's easy," Julie answered, "God saw everything I did, and He's terribly disappointed in me. I just know He is. I can feel it, you know. He looks inside me, and all He sees are dark things. You know, I let Him down all the time, just like I let my parents down."

"Maybe you have them mixed-up," I offered, "Do you think it's possible that God might be a bit more kind toward you than you seem to give Him credit for?"

Julie sat up angrily. "Don't you talk like that about God!" she was angry and loud. "He knows what's right and wrong, and what I did was wrong. I learned those things a long time ago, and no matter what you or anybody else says, right is right, and wrong is wrong.

"I did wrong! I know it, and God knows it, too. Sometimes I imagine God looking at me, shaking His head, and turning away from me."

Julie is a supreme example of a person who absolutely believes that she knows herself better than God knows her. Any attempts to cut through her self-condemnation will only be met with resistance and defiance. She is certain that God is unhappy and disappointed with her life and behavior. Her Legacy Bible is so filled with notations of guilt and shame that she cannot see herself any other way. At this time in her life, to look at herself through the eyes of love or understanding is an impossibility.

The tendency for most of us is to try to show Julie the errors in her thinking. For many people, the notion that God would hold her accountable for her sister's behavior is unacceptable. Her sister went sneaking into the barn, met her boyfriend, and conceived a child, while Julie was sitting on the back porch reading a book. Julie had no part in any of this; she was simply deceived. However, even these facts are meaningless to a "child" of thirty-three, who has deified her legacy and owned the teachings within the good book created by her parents.

Julie's concept of God as judge is a powerful extension of her mother and father's concept of justice. To find any room in her Legacy Bible for grace or forgiveness is extremely unlikely to occur. The crucial issue here is to understand that with the pronouncement of guilt by her parents, *IMMEDIATELY* God agreed with the verdict. Mother, father, the Legacy Bible, and Julie's concepts of God are in absolute harmony. Discord only occurs when she is challenged on any of these basic beliefs, and to challenge one belief, in her mind, is to challenge every belief. The result of opening herself for discussion in one area could lead to a total breakdown of her belief system, a dynamic Julie does not understand, but nevertheless senses.

Again, it is important to recall that Julie's beliefs, recorded in her Legacy Bible, are stored in her altar-heart. People who see the real Julie are likely to grieve her self-condemning nature. Trying to be helpful, they may point out to her all of her kind and helpful attributes. Hoping Julie may think more highly of herself, people offer her compliments on her unselfish and caring nature. Unfortunately, none of this matters, because Julie *KNOWS* better than anyone that she is a "bad" girl. Her concepts and judgments of herself are written on her heart; words and praise will do little to penetrate.

While her guilt seems to be heavy, her shame is even more so. Sensing that she could make up for things she has done wrong, Julie tries to be available for her youngest sister all the time. Going out of her way to help her clean, run errands, or even loaning her money, Julie seeks forgiveness for "ruining" her life. Although she has been told over and over that it is not her fault, Julie believes otherwise; she *KNOWS* it is her fault.

There are so many assumptions and fantasies surrounding Julie's thinking process that the temptation is to simply point out to her the insanity of her conclusions. However, because she believes that she does wrong things, it must follow that she is the thing that's wrong. Helpful words and kind comments are wasted energy on Julie, since she is aware of her inadequacy.

For Julie to embrace a loving and generous faith would be extremely difficult. She needs the judging and damning God to extend her Legacy Bible and fulfill the beliefs and lessons of her history. This is how God as *judge* is born. It doesn't matter whether He exists or not; in the minds of children from the critical and shame-based legacies, He is very real, very harsh, and quick to punish.

CHAPTER XV

GOD AS EXECUTIONER

*"You, dear friends, are about the business
of punishing yourselves
before God gets His hands on you."*

Emmanuel

*"It is now grotesque to talk of anything else,
especially suicide, which no real loser ever commits
because it would deny him the pain
he so richly deserves."*

Thomas Berger

"Punishment is lame, but it comes."

Herbert

GOD AS EXECUTIONER

Talk radio shows astound me. I suppose by now I should be used to them, but I'm not. Driving through the Pocono Mountains of Pennsylvania, I recently heard a fascinating dialogue. "I can't understand it. Am I crazy or what?" the announcer spoke to me through the radio speaker, "Prisoners are asking for cookies in their vending machines, made with healthy ingredients instead of artificial flavoring and preservatives. What's going on in our country? Since when do these people have rights like this? I didn't even know they had vending machines in prison, did you?"

He went on, "What do you think, out there? Should prisoners have the right to demand healthy cookies?" He picked up the telephone, "Marie, what do you think about this? Are you in favor of healthier cookies for these jerks?"

Marie nervously came over the radio, "Well, I don't think so," she said, "But what's the difference between prisoners receiving Social Security checks or library privileges? I mean, cookies are just one more thing they get."

"Is this crazy or what?" repeated the announcer.

"These people hurt other people," Marie went on, "They steal and rape, and so on. I mean, they take away other people's rights; why should they have any rights at all? Especially things like cookies and Social Security money."

"You're absolutely right, Marie, prison life is too soft these days." The announcer was obviously delighted in Marie's insights, "Prisoners are there because they can't make it in society. In my view, they ought to suffer, and not complain about unhealthy cookies. And people are taking them seriously!" His voice was incredulous.

I turned the radio off and started to wonder about the times I had been in "prison." The corner in the kitchen was the closest I had even come to steel bars, but one thing was for sure: my mother never served me any cookies. Instead, like thousands of other kids who had misbehaved, I waited there, cookie-less, for my father to come home. One time, I decided to put my thoughts of dread to paper, a way to fill time while waiting for the impending doom.

In through the door marched my dad,
shoulders hunched; eyes suddenly sad
as they caught me, crouched on the stool,

he knew one more time I'd played her the fool.
My mom, I mean, the gullible one
who never knew a lie from a pun,
trapped me in one, but sparing the rod
said, "Climb up on the stool, and wait there for God!"

Even if you did not grow up in a critical-, fear-, or shame-based legacy, in all likelihood you are very familiar with punishment. From the court room to the school room, the threat of punishment is omnipresent. Park on the wrong piece of concrete and receive a ticket. Pass a slow car at a fast speed and watch your punishment approach in the rear-view mirror, or take a peek at your neighbor's homework assignment, and be prepared for the watchful eyes of the classroom police officer to wander in your direction just in time to spot and note your indiscretion. Offend the IRS and risk your financial well-being. Fail to pay your VISA or American Express Card on time, and discover the consequences to your credit rating, courtesy of the same marketing folks who seduced your business in the first place.

Ours is a culture of consequences. But, then again, what society is not? To live together in harmony and sensibility requires certain rules and regulations for the entire community. Without the ability to police and enforce the law, the community may be at risk. For the most part, we all understand and accept this notion. Sadly, the very system which stands for justice sometimes gets in the way of it, but overall, the percentages are pretty good. Occasionally, there are those who "get away with it," while others get treated unfairly, but most everyone knows and understands the laws and the system which enforces them. Hopefully, society benefits from the rules and consequences of the community.

Families, however, are another story, since they are all so vastly different. When I was dating my first love, my parents were astounded that her family did not give her a curfew. Her decision-making ability was trustworthy to her parents; the choice of time to return home from a date was hers. There seemed to be no rule, but rather the dynamic of trust. On the other hand, my parents felt that young people needed guidance and structure. Since her parents were unwilling to present her with a curfew, they presented me with one. I remember being horrified as the one who had to be in at a certain time, nevertheless, the rule was made and enforced.

GOD AS EXECUTIONER

In talking with my classmates, I was surprised at the number who had no curfew. Others lived and floated on a tighter ship than mine, yet we were all from relatively the same educational, cultural, and economic base. While this was not an empirical study, it nevertheless was one of my earliest discoveries about the profound differences in the family legacy, and the ways in which rules and potential consequences are created.

Admittedly, I had learned as a child that families punished their children differently. My friend Bill was cozy with the hairbrush; Larry, on the other hand, was grounded before it became a word. Christine was sent to her room, and Gene was made to go outside to play. I suppose that parents attempted to use whatever seemed to work to impress their children with the necessity of obeying the rules.

Since each family legacy has its own priorities and issues, disobedience or disloyalty is met with the punishment that is most appropriate to the severity of the crime. In a critical-based legacy, for example, getting caught cheating in school might be viewed as a serious offense by the system. The potential for becoming a juvenile delinquent, or embarking on a life of crime could be added to the fears of the parents. Punishment, obviously, would be severe. However, the same issue in a legacy of denial, in all probability, might be brushed aside as "kid stuff." Comments such as "What kid didn't cheat when he was in school?" would not be unusual. Punishment, if at all, would be minor.

A mother rooted in a shame-based legacy who received a call from school that her child had been caught cheating, would immediately enter into shame. Important to her would be issues such as: Who called from the school? Was it someone the family knew? Would the caller tell others? What repercussions would be felt if other family members in the community found out about it? What about the neighbors? Would they find out? What other classmates were present when the teacher collared her child? Would they tell their parents? Will anyone in the church find out about this? Or the card club? Or the Band Parents? Punishment for this child, in all likelihood, would be severe; it might even border on child abuse. In the parent's mind, her child could have done nothing worse; the entire family has been placed on display for the community to see. All of the system's faults are now seen through the cheating behavior of her child. The sham has been exposed, the entire family is ashamed, and it is important that her child NEVER do this again! The punishment will, indeed, be formidable.

Contrast, for example, how a fear-based family might struggle with a teenage pregnant daughter. What punishment would be appropriate for this young girl in her very difficult position? Or would any punishment be necessary at all? It is important to recall that fear-based systems run away with "what ifs?" Always looking to the dreadful and awful possibilities that could occur, questions would come from every corner: "What are your plans about this? You have to make a decision, you know. Time is short, and if you are considering an abortion, don't you think you should decide right away? And what about the money? Have you thought about that? Where is it going to come from, and how much is it going to cost? What about going to your Aunt Mary's to have the baby? You could give it up for adoption there, and get back to your senior year without missing a beat. Have you thought about that? What about adoption agencies? Have you taken the time to call them? And the airlines? How much will it cost to fly out there? Do you have any idea where that money is going to come from?"

A family of this type is in such fear that paralysis could set in, allowing no decision to be made at all. Being stuck with the inability to decide might very well be the very punishment this young lady will have to endure. Sadly, an infant may have to pay the price for the power of the legacy of fear. On the other hand, the fear may be so great that any decision that can be made at all might be welcomed, even a decision which could be costly to the emotional and physical well-being of the girl herself. "You should have thought about that earlier," is not an uncommon statement to young people trying to work their way through difficult decisions. Many clients, in relating stories to me from their childhood, recall a parent saying, "You've made your bed, now lie in it." While this may appear as a motto to steer a child through life, in reality, it is a punishment which keeps children stuck in the results of their mistakes.

Each family system will determine its own punishment for infractions of the legacy. To uncover a common thread in such a diverse number of systems is impossible. Regarding punishment, the only consistent rule I have been able to see across legacy lines is: "The degree and severity of punishment is in direct proportion to the violation of the legacy teachings." In a sense, all disloyalty has a price, and you pay according to the price tag on the violation.

THE HANGMAN

Regardless of the ways in which family systems dole out punishment, there is a clear understanding of the direction in which the power flows. When you break the rules, Mom and Dad determine the punishment. Depending on your family's approach to legacy violation and the severity of the "crime," your parents, grandparents, older siblings, or baby sitter will provide the appropriate punishment. Like a stream flowing downhill, the punishment comes from the "big" people in life to the "little" people. Sometimes one big person catches you in the forbidden fruit tree and another will administer the necessary demerits. Other times, when you're caught by Dad, court immediately convenes, the verdict is announced, and sentencing is carried out by his hand.

Again, for children, it becomes virtually impossible NOT to confuse punishing parents with the concept of a punitive God. Instead of a "big" person correcting you, a "BIGGER" person waits in the wings, prepared to administer a discipline of His own. And because God is such a superb police officer, He will catch you in any and all wrongful acts, even those which manage to escape the watchful eyes of Mom and Dad. You will, of course, have to pay, and somehow, divine retribution seems potentially so much worse.

While we seldom realize it, life is a story. As we watch it unfold, our imagination plays with certain events and possibilities. Dreaming of making the last-second goal and winning the game or traveling with a beautiful person to a tropical paradise are thoughts which can send us off to sleep at night. The ability of our minds to create, dream, and fantasize is incredible. A recent study claims that it takes thirteen billion brain cells to create an image! We are all superb creators, filling our minds with all sorts of fascinating thoughts.

Into this fantasy world, unfortunately, we also "dream up" our punishments. What will God do to me for this last little act of evil? How will He punish me? It is true that I escaped the belt from Dad and the tongue lashing from Mom, but is there anywhere to run from the retribution of the Almighty? Because of the amazing ability of our minds to create imaginary punishments, it is possible to lie in bed at night seeing the righteous hand of Justice hammer down on our life. Depending on the messages we have received from the parenting gods in life, the "hammer" could be seen as one which strikes us off the baseball team; or, the finger of God could point into our life, causing us to stumble and fall in relationships.

Again, it is important to recall that logical thinking has nothing whatsoever to do with emotional conclusions. Spinning the wheel of the imagination as it gleams divine retribution from the pot is not a mental exercise. Instead, it is fear turned loose and given thought. It may be guilt, given imagination to run rampantly through the gauntlet of pain. Shame, blended with the felt disappointment of God, may force a retreat from life of monumental proportions. Regardless, when the concepts of God get added to the feelings of wrongdoing, the potential for powerful and all-encompassing punishment may exist. It is important, however, to notice that it is the *concepts* of God, as well as the *feelings* of wrongdoing, which lead to these conclusions. Both notions are learned through the legacy and then accepted as truth.

Sometimes, life will present a person with a terrible blow. It may be the death of a child, the loss of a marriage, or the diagnosis of a terminal illness. Physicians and counselors may be at a loss to determine exactly why these things happen. Biological or relational analysis doesn't provide the answer. A child is dead, but the cause is a mystery. Other times, with great study and time, an autopsy reveals the truth: the child died of a drug overdose, or of accidentally drinking a household chemical. Or in therapy, a discovery is made of the absence of intimacy in a marriage, which led it to dissolve. Perhaps a sad husband discovers too late that his unwillingness to be vulnerable sent his wife away.

The fact is that sometimes in life we know why things happen and sometimes we don't. Unfortunately, knowing why something happened doesn't change the fact that it did. A lost marriage is a lost marriage, regardless of the reasons. It is true that husband and wife can learn from the loss, and, hopefully, not repeat the mistakes in the next relationships. Nevertheless, there is a profound and tragic loss which has occurred.

GOD AS EXECUTIONER

In listening to clients and congregants over a quarter of a century, I still sit in amazement as I hear the countless number of statements in which God is "at fault" for the blows of life. "Either He caused it or He allowed it to happen" is the common complaint from angry or hurting people. Attributing ALL pain to the thinking and activity of God, many people feel like helpless bugs, scurrying through life with little chance for happiness. "If He decides to zap you, He zaps you," one woman told me recently, regarding the alienation between her two sons. "You just have to take it, you know; you take the good with the bad."

When God is viewed as executioner or hangman, it follows that life's trail of tears is His doing. Of course, the only way such a concept of God can be entertained is if His punishment is viewed as a result of our failures. Since pain is personalized by most of us, when something bad happens in life, it must be the result of our "bad" behavior, either present or past. Amazingly, even when something tragic happens to someone important to us, many people believe "God is punishing ME" through the pain and difficulties in another's life.

One woman sadly mentioned to me that her father was dying of cancer. "It's lung cancer," she told me, "and the doctor says he only has about three months to live. I feel so bad for him because his breathing is so difficult; it's so labored. It's such a terrible way to die." She sat quietly for a moment and then added, almost as an afterthought, "And it's my fault."

"Why do you say that?" I asked her.

"Well, it must be." she said, "Your sins find you out."

"Meaning?"

"Meaning I've been bad." she said. "Or else my father wouldn't be dying such a horrible death."

When I pressed her about her "badness," she had little response. Over time I came to realize that she was not talking about specific badness, but rather a generalized philosophy about herself. Believing that she was never good enough and that she, personally, had to pay for this lack, it followed that the loss of her father, and even HIS pain, was her fault. God was punishing her for being a bad person by causing pain in the life of the person she loved the most. In this way, it was a double-whammy: not only was she losing her father, a punishment of great severity, but she, through her "evil" life, was also responsible for his pain. This, of course, led to enormous guilt, with the potential for future punishment.

The power of this legacy belief is so enormous that it simply is not permissible to raise the question of the type of God who would inflict pain in a father in order to punish his daughter. To dare to question the Almighty would be paramount to inviting even greater pain and punishment. It is almost with awe that I listen to clients speak of their Legacy Bible's teachings regarding punishment. Containing a logic of its own, an entire thought system exists explaining the painful and suffering side of life.

Sharon was a thirty-seven year old mother of four children. Diagnosed with leukemia at thirty-three, she had fought a hard and remarkable battle against the disease. At the time I first met her, she had moved from remission to a re-occurrence of her illness; the prognosis from her physician was "less than eight weeks." Raised Baptist but having left the church at nineteen, Sharon had explored virtually every religious trail. At this particular time, she was landing at the edge of Scientology, wanting me to help her plan and arrange her funeral in that tradition.

In the beginning of our conversations, Sharon discussed her enormous fears for her husband and children. Wondering about their well-being and future, she had begged her husband to promise he would remarry. "Quickly," she told me, "because he doesn't have the slightest idea how to take care of these kids." She started weeping as she told me that she "never should have had children. God is punishing me by taking me away from them. They're going to suffer because of me."

"You see your children suffering because of God?" I asked her.

"Not because of God, but because of me," she said, almost angrily, "I'm the one that's been bad, not them." Sharon proceeded to share a story about a very difficult decision she had made early in her marriage. Following her first child, she found herself immediately pregnant. "It was just too soon," she told me, "We couldn't afford it, and I wasn't emotionally prepared for another one. So, I kept it a secret. I went and had an abortion, and I've never even told my husband." She started to cry again and wept for a long time. "I killed my baby and now God is killing me...He's punishing me."

GOD AS EXECUTIONER

Speaking bitterly about her religious history, Sharon talked of unbending rules and harsh punishments. Recalling a time when her minister publicly embarrassed one of her friends who was caught shoplifting, she expressed anger at the judgmental attitudes of the church. "Dancing, drinking, and card playing were all under attack," she told me, "and if you were in the movie theater on a Sunday night and Jesus decided to return to earth, the punishment would be unimaginable. My parents thought the same way as he did," Sharon said, referring to her pastor. "One time, when I had planned to attend the high school New Year's Eve dance, my dad made me break the date to attend the Youth Fellowship party at church. It was either that or stay home. For me, my parents and my minister showed me that religion was about the business of stopping you from having fun."

I wondered to myself about Sharon's fear of punishment. Did her fears come from the teachings in the church, or from her concepts of God, as presented to her by her parents? Did her pastor's treatment of those who had "wandered astray" influence her sense of God's treatment of "sinners?" Was her illness a punishment from God as retribution for her choice to abort her child?

Over the next few weeks, Sharon deteriorated rapidly. Her level of pain increased, but she steadfastly refused any pain medication. Even at her husband's pleading, she would not take Tylenol or aspirin. "I deserve this pain," she told me, "You and I and God all know it. This will be a horrible death, and maybe God will forgive me a little if I have enough pain." While I had often wondered about the refusal of patients to allow pain management in their lives, this was the first time I had ever heard my thoughts confirmed out loud. Sharon was punishing herself before God could get His hands on her. Also, she was hopeful that if she was in enough pain, perhaps God would be gracious and overlook any need to punish her children.

As the pain became almost unbearable, Sharon started to accept some minimal pain medication. However, it did little to relieve her physical symptoms and the pain remained. Even as the medication was increased to higher levels, and eventually to extremely potent doses, Sharon's pain was never touched. It was as if her will to suffer overrode any and all narcotics. During these times, she was in and out of consciousness, begging me to ask God to spare her children. Even the physician and nurses joined her husband in continually praying for her death. Everyone, it seemed, except Sharon, had felt enough suffering. Apparently, she needed her pain. As a result of her perceived sins, Sharon evidently allowed herself to hurt, a self-inflicted punishment on behalf of her concepts of Almighty Justice.

Eventually, Sharon died, and I remember being stunned at the incredible length of time that she remained in pain. While some may argue that this was beyond her power, I firmly disagree. The ability of patients to control the quality and amount of pain in their life is astounding. In many cases, it may be due to a belief that "as long as I can feel pain, I'm still alive." However, in Sharon's case, and in the lives of many others, especially those who hold to the concept of God as Executioner, pain serves a magnificent purpose: the doling out of self-punishment, since it is bound to come anyway.

Attending a conference recently, I heard Stephen Levine say that pain is a fact of life. To the degree that you resist that thought, he says, you suffer. I absolutely concur with his position. It is impossible to live and walk on this planet without pain; indeed, it is a fact of life. Loss is everywhere, even if it is only the leaves on the oak tree spinning down for one more season. Gorgeous sunsets disappear in five minutes, and pets live for five years. Some babies are born healthy; others are still-born. Regardless, life is filled with pain at every level.

Now, this doesn't mean that I am going to rush out and leap off the nearest bridge. I'm too afraid of physical pain, and I'm not sure about my feelings regarding suicide. So I'll hang in there and keep going. However, pain will be around my life as it is around the lives of everyone I know. This entire chapter is focusing on punishment and the way in which it is connected with our concepts of God. It is true, however, that if a family legacy presents a correlation between pain and punishment, then an entire system of thought will follow, as in Sharon's case. Hooking her impending death with the notion of God's punishment, Sharon had determined that God was doing this to her because she had an abortion fifteen years earlier. Her Legacy Bible, then, contained a philosophy that instead of understanding the struggle of a young mother, God gets even. If it were possible for medical science to inform Sharon that leukemia entered her body because of a rare viral infection, she would not entertain a different thought than the one she already carries. Twisting the logic to fit the situation, as all people do who see God as Executioner, Sharon would claim that God then *allowed* the viral infection into her body.

Those who believe in a concept of God as Punisher will take the ordinary, given pain of life and fit it to their own self-judging situation. Falling out of an apple tree and breaking an arm can be termed a punishment of God to a young boy who copied his best friend's homework. "You had it coming," is food for the Legacy Bible, when told to a scratched child who pulled the cat's tail. "What goes around comes around," says my cousin as he sits and waits for those who "sin" to get their just desserts. All of these thoughts are simply a reflection of legacies which present punishing parents as god and extend that philosophy to the concept of Jehovah.

Consider the possibility, for example, that God never existed. Because of pain, He would have to be invented. How else could we explain the bad things that happen to people in life? And if God does exist, then surely He doesn't mete out punishment for no good reason, or else He would not be God. It follows then, that since bad things and pain happen in life from time to time, and God can't make any mistakes, He must know what He's doing. Therefore, when something happens to me that is painful or tragic, I certainly have it coming. Only the bad are punished is a silly thought; nevertheless, it sits on a very sacred spot in the Legacy Bible. To wonder if the Almighty, Creator, King of Kings would have a need to cause His children, whom He loves, to suffer, is an unthinkable question for the Legacy Bible of punishment.

God as Executioner is held dearly by many. Sadly, the pain which follows is intensified by such a belief. The issue of the existence of pain is never under discussion; it is the cause of such pain that children, who view God as Executioner, embrace. Believing that He operates out of absolute righteousness, they have only themselves left to blame. This tragic thinking and belief is widespread, and, in my opinion, the cause for great unhappiness and hopelessness. It is, as the next chapter explores, the root of all spiritual pain.

CHAPTER XVI

SPIRITUAL PAIN

*"We're all on the same side,
we're out to get me."*

Bob Schneider

*"Amazing Grace, how sweet the sound,
that saved a wretch like me."*

John Newton

*"And Cain went away from the Lord's presence,
and lived alone in a land called Wandering."*

Genesis

SPIRITUAL PAIN

Several years ago, I started working as a chaplain in a hospice program. In this multi-disciplined service to terminally ill persons, I represented the "spiritual dimension." Attending my first team meeting, I was shocked when the director turned to me and said, "Do you think this patient is in spiritual pain?"

First of all, I was hardly aware of the patient's name or the nature of his disease. Secondly, even if I had known the full particulars on this man's illness, I didn't have the slightest idea what "spiritual pain" was. Oh, I had my suspicions, which trickled down from the notion that the patient had trouble praying, all the way to the possibility that he was upset with his priest. Not wanting to appear unsophisticated nor unaware, I answered with a phrase with which I had already become familiar through listening to the reports of the nurses. "I'm not sure," I said, and I remember trying to look serious, as though I knew what I was talking about, "But let me go out and do an assessment." I knew that "assessment" was big in health care, so why not?

The problem was, obviously, that I had no concept of what I was assessing. To tell the truth, I had not even given the term "spiritual pain" much thought, and to the best of my ability, I could not recall any discussions with my professional peers on the subject. Certainly, I had attended more clergy breakfasts and seminars than I could count. Spiritual pain had never been addressed, or even alluded to.

Over the course of the past decade, however, spiritual pain has been a central focus of my life. The hospice program, dedicated to the easing of all pain—physical, mental, emotional, and spiritual—led me into this path. Once wandering down the road, however, it became a part of my own personal, spiritual journey. To understand and resource spiritual pain is of critical importance to me, not only to provide help to patients and clients, but also to nudge me along the road of life with more inner peace and joy.

All the previous chapters have led to this issue. The powerful concept of the family legacy and the creation of a Legacy Bible lead each of us to the threshold of a type of spiritual pain. It begins to appear as we place the teachings or beliefs of our parents and grandparents in our own altar-heart, and deify the legacy. Blending this holy curriculum with our childhood tendencies to view our parents as gods, we arrive at a belief system we call our own. Seeking a religious tradition, church, or synagogue which sympathizes with our own Legacy Bible, we reach our final destination, namely, our own personal theology which contains our concepts of God. Absolute Truth, if there is such a thing, apparently gets lost along the way, as the beliefs of Grandpa and Grandma combine with the guilt, shame, or punishment of our system, and become the Way, the Truth, and the Life. Our concepts of God, then, are "culturized," familiarized, and "churchized."

Assuming the above scenario is the case, when life presents us with the inevitable punches of loss, disappointment, and tragedy, is it any wonder that our accumulated concepts of God seldom lift and carry us through to the other side of comfort and hope? When this occurs, the common feeling is one of aloneness and isolation. Apparently let down by our beliefs or Legacy Bible teachings, and feeling abandoned by God, we stand alone in the midst of struggle and heaviness. This condition is one type of spiritual pain. It can be heard in the writings of the Psalmist, and the cry of Jesus, as spiritual pain is given voice, "My God, My God, why hast thou forsaken me?" It is the felt absence of God.

RELIGIOUS PAIN

Before an adequate discussion can be made regarding spiritual pain, it must be clearly differentiated from religious pain. For purposes of understanding, it is important to view the distinctions between the two terms. Religion, on the one hand, generally refers to a communal system of belief regarding God and the sacred. Normally taught and transmitted from a priest to the people, religion essentially reproduces itself by educating the young. For most people, religion contains certain dogmas, creeds, and beliefs which express the content required for a holy life. It is an organized means to discover, worship, and express the concepts of God.

Spiritual, on the other hand, refers to the personal, in contrast to the communal. Focusing on the *relationship* with the Source (God) that is within and beyond the self, spiritual always points to connections and union. Whereas religion mainly addresses a system of beliefs, the spiritual path highlights the felt merging with God. Surrounding itself with careful perimeters, religion teaches morality, ethics, or rules, as communally gleaned from the written and spoken word of the tradition. In contrast, the spiritual path is one in which the person determines direction and behavior through unity with God.

It is true that most religions maintain the goal of aiding individuals in their discovery of God. Sadly, the mud and mortar of organization tends to work in the exact opposite direction. Choosing appropriate leadership, maintaining buildings and shrines, and a systematic program to proselytize the young often drains the energy and resources of the community, drawing away from the spiritual thrust that created the religion in the first place.

On one occasion I had been visiting a dying congregant, a forty-seven year old man, father of four children. Relaying to me, through much physical and emotional pain, a story of the dreaded loss of his children, he wept in helplessness and fear. For over an hour we discussed the struggle of trusting in the wisdom and guidance of God. Overriding our conversation was a profound sense of the unfairness of cancer, which strikes both the young and old alike. Nevertheless, he believed he was dying before his time. With both parents still living, and much unfinished fathering yet to be given to his children, he felt betrayed and abandoned by God. In some ways, this is another type of spiritual pain.

As I left this sad conversation to attend a meeting of the Building Committee at the church, I was struck with the feeling of my limitations. Feeling somewhat helpless myself, and unable to provide this man with the necessary resources to help him move toward peace, I pulled into the church parking lot. Walking into the meeting room, I heard loud voices in obvious disagreement. As I pulled up a chair to join the group, one man said, "I'm sure the pastor, here, agrees with me." He looked to me for support, "Don't you think it's wrong for the nursery school teachers to use the tables that belong to the Sunday School?"

It was at that precise moment that I realized instead of being a spiritual leader to people attempting to connect with God in their lives, I was the political figurehead of an organized religious community. When I left the room that evening, I left the church.

While I am well aware of critics who will point to the

countless meaningful tasks which I performed, nevertheless, there has been a subtle shift in the church over the past 2000 years. Beginning as a spiritual path toward union with God and the discovery of peace within, it has become an unrecognizable business today. I have no desire to single out my own tradition in a negative way. It is critical to understand that virtually all religions risk the same fate as the church. Founded by spiritual giants, religions grow as guided by the spurts and jumps of normal human beings. Sometimes the need to be right supersedes the spiritual teachings, or the fear of economic or population loss leads the community to retrenchment and stagnation. Either way, well-meaning and caring people, regardless of their commitment to the spiritual path, continually encounter detours in their attempts to organize and institutionalize spirituality.

It is fascinating to note that family legacies, when presented with powerful authority, can sound dangerously like religion. Beliefs are held sacred by children in the same manner as they are by congregants. God, as Ever-Watching, All-Powerful, and Just, can be tossed back and forth, in confusion, between the church and the family legacy much like a ping-pong ball. Charged to teach their children, parents faithfully labor, quite creatively, to present the teachings of the legacy, praying their offspring will incorporate the daily lesson into the Legacy Bible. Similarly, religions fiercely train the young in order to guarantee the continuation of the faith, as well as to assure the adherence to the doctrines and creeds. In both cases, failure to learn is seen as risky to both the religion and its youth.

Sometimes, in a most amazing way, family legacies can clash with the very religions in which they are involved. As religions struggle to survive and, at the same time, respond to the changes of society, new thoughts and beliefs surface. Even though such change may be necessary for growth and community ministry, family legacies, rooted in old legacy beliefs, will immediately rise up to clash with new leadership and ideas. "We always did it that way," is not just a longing for old days in the tradition; it generally reflects a loyalty to the legacy line. In the Baptist tradition, for example, the Civil War and family legacy does more to divide the denominations than any theological principles.

So it is that many children are raised in a marriage between the beliefs of their family Legacy Bible and the doctrines of their religious tradition. Often, to violate one is to violate the other. Regardless, all violation or disloyalty to both religion and family legacy is considered unacceptable by God, either the heavenly One, or the earthly two, namely the parents. The emotional result of this violation is religious pain.

Feeling guilty or ashamed for breaking the rules (called sinning, in most religious traditions), children immediately are aware of their "badness." Religious pain, then, is the feelings of fear, shame, and guilt that surface because of a violation of the dogmas, creeds, or rules of the tradition. The same can be said for similar offenses within the family legacy. Transgressing against the teachings or beliefs of the Legacy Bible and sinning against God's rules, as expressed through religion, lead the individual to the same predicament—the disapproval of God, with the potential for punishment and consequences.

In my work with dying persons, I have discovered a wealth of information surrounding religious pain. As might be imagined, a great deal of reflection takes place in a person's life when he or she recognizes life is drawing to an end. All sorts of questions are raised such as: "What did I do with my life? Is this what it is all about? What would have happened if I had married my first love? What about that job that I wanted to take, but didn't? What difference would it have made in my life?" These and other thoughts continually surface in the minds of the dying.

Unfortunately, there are other reflective thoughts which are far more prejudicial against the self. With regret, and sometimes shame, some people look back on things they did in their youth. They remember times when they misbehaved or made very selfish decisions. Recalling events which went "against their upbringing," patients will chastise themselves for unacceptable behavior. "I remember, one time," a patient told me, "when I was with my mother over at my Uncle John's house. They went into the kitchen to talk and I went into the bedroom. I couldn't believe it, but there was a two dollar bill sitting on my aunt's night stand, and I took it." Reaching over on the other side of the bed, he picked up his Bible. Opening it, he took out an old, frayed two dollar bill. "I've always kept this to remind me what a sinner I am." He started to cry, and his oxygen hose fell away from his face, "God is so ashamed of me, and all those years I sat in Mass and took Communion."

This patient is speaking of his religious pain. Experiencing guilt, shame, and judgment, he is illustrating a common theme in religious pain. His religion taught the rules against stealing. It was not only a desire of God, as expressed in the Ten Commandments; this sin was denounced by both his priest and parents. And, as in all religions, as well as family legacies, violation of the rules is costly. In this particular case, this man had spend decades judging himself for his theft. Assuming that God saw him with the same disapproving eyes as he saw himself, he only could assume punishment fitting to the crime. As we explored in previous chapters, that punishment, in all likelihood, will match the parental punishments doled out by his earthly police officers and judges.

You are in religious pain anytime you feel guilt, shame, or fear as a result of breaking the rules of your religious tradition. In my case, I entered into religious pain the first time I walked into a restaurant which served wine. Reading the monthly church covenant which expressly forbid the use of alcoholic beverages, I almost collapsed under the weight of my guilt. As silly as this may sound to many of you, it illustrated the power of religious teachings, and the naiveté of young children.

Religious pain is experienced in different ways according to the rules and creeds of your religion. In some cases, abortion is open for examination; in others, it is a sin of the worst magnitude. Divorce leads to religious pain in some people, while the inability to have children can be viewed as punishment by others. By the time you are in your early teens, between the teachings in your Legacy Bible and the pronouncements of your religion, you know very well when you have committed an unacceptable act. Those feelings which follow fall under the classification of religious pain.

In some cases, the emotional fall-out of violating a religious dogma can be so severe as to cripple an individual. It is not unusual to experience physical symptoms as a result of the guilt and shame of religious pain. High blood pressure, rapid heart beat, upset stomach, or bowel problems can often be linked to emotional upheavals. And while this knowledge is common within the psychiatric and medical community, it is my contention that religious pain is seldom examined as contributing to the root cause of the physical ailment. Most mental health workers and psychiatrists steer away from any religious issues at all, preferring instead to remain within the confinement of the therapeutic/psychoanalytical model. Sadly, even many of today's clergy persons have parentified the psychiatric world to the point of abdicating their own resources for the alleviation of religious pain.

Religious pain is an almost universal phenomena, especially for those of us raised within the Western world. Regardless of your religious tradition, and even if you feel you do not have any tradition, it is very difficult to be raised in this culture and not cart off some religious rules and dogmas. Even the political arena of welfare is an extension of the Golden Rule. Prisons and rehabilitation programs claim they are about the business of helping people get their lives in order. This fine humanitarian goal is only several thousand years old, as expressed through the earliest religions. Because of our cultural/ethical roots, it is very possible for even non-religious people to experience religious pain and never be aware of the source of the pain.

Obviously, not every emotional difficulty is rooted in religious pain; however, there are many people who suffer great guilt and shame that goes untreated, since religious roots and teachings generally go unexamined by health care professionals.

FACING OUR RELIGIOUS PAIN

Unlike many family legacies, most religions have doctrines of forgiveness. If you make a mistake, there usually is a formula for redemption or mercy. Unforgivable sins seldom exist in religious communities and teachings, even though congregants may believe or wish it were otherwise. Apparently, God was far enough ahead of His creation to understand the great tendencies of His children to wander far off the narrow way. Since this has tended to be the case, a plan for "wiggling off the hook" has, indeed, been necessary.

In the Judeo/Christian tradition, sin is a fact of life: it is an expression of our humanity. Likewise, both faiths have their own system of atonement, a symbol of repairing the relationship between creation and Creator. In ancient Hinduism, forgiveness occurred through the sacrifice of Purusha, the Great Hindu Universal Ideal Man. Early Judaism corrected the broken Law through the offering of sacrifices and ceremonies, whereas, in Christianity, atonement is seen as received through the sacrifice of Christ on the cross. Buddhism offers the six perfections to which beings are committed, but since help is needed along the way, various savior gods and goddesses offer suffering and sacrificial love. In the early Vedic religion, sacrifice was seen as the way to gain the favor of the gods.

To ease religious pain, then, requires the employment of the formula for forgiveness, or attaining the grace of the Divine. In Judaism, for example, Yom Kippur, or the Day of Atonement, provides a time for private and public prayer for forgiveness. In a religious-therapeutic fashion, Yom Kippur extends an excellent opportunity for the easing of religious pain. Christianity, on the other hand, offers the forgiveness of sins and the resulting feelings of religious pain, by embracing the sacrificial offering of Christ.

Ruth was a seventy-seven year old woman, and an active member of the local Methodist church until she was diagnosed with ovarian cancer. When I received a telephone call from her husband asking me to visit with her, I was somewhat surprised, since I had known of the close relationship between Ruth and her pastor. Sitting down beside her bed, she reached over and patted my hand, "I'm so glad you've come to see me," she smiled at me, "and you probably wonder why I'm not talking to Rev. Phillips."

"I just thought you might want the prayers of a Baptist, too," I tried my attempt at humor.

"Well, I'll take anybody's prayers," she said, "but to tell you the truth, I was too ashamed to talk with Rev. Phillips about this. He thinks I'm so faithful and strong, you know, but I'm afraid there's a lot he doesn't know about me."

Having learned to keep still at certain times, it seemed to me this was one of those moments, so I said nothing. "I'm so ashamed to tell you this, but I'm not sure if I'm going to heaven," she said, lowering her eyes to stare at her sheets. "And I know that everybody over at church would be so upset if they knew I felt like this, but it's true. I'm not sure if God will have me; and if I told anybody this, they wouldn't believe it. I mean, I taught Sunday School for over forty years, and sang in the choir for nearly fifty. Wouldn't you think that I'd get a free ticket into heaven just because of all the hours I've spent in church?"

"It sounds to me like you're really struggling," I told her.

"It's more than that," she said. "I'm afraid to die because

I'm not sure what happens afterwards."

Ruth continued to talk, sharing with me the story of a very unhappy marriage. Describing her husband as cold and inattentive, she admitted to a brief love affair when she was in her early thirties. "I knew it was wrong," she said to me, "but I was so lonely and just found myself swept away with the tide. Before that I used to judge other people who went running off with their emotions. I couldn't imagine how a woman could go off to a hotel with a man, until I found myself doing it. Now, I know better; I keep my mouth shut and my opinions to myself. Nobody has any idea why people do what they do."

Expressing her religious pain, Ruth spoke of her fear of condemnation for adultery. Flipping through the pages of her Bible, she showed me the dog-eared passages referring to the sins of the flesh. "I let God and my children down," she said, "and now I'm going to pay the price."

Ruth said, "You're only the second person I ever told about this, and the first one was an evangelist who came to our church to conduct a series of meetings. He told me that I was in grave danger of hellfire, and I never forgot the look in his eyes when he said those words. He sort of breathed the word 'hellfire,' like it was some kind of whisper from someplace deep inside his chest. I just remember crying myself to sleep that night, and wondering if God would ever forgive me since."

In Ruth's case, her religious pain was intensified by the lack of sensitivity and harsh judgment of the visiting evangelist. Sadly, misinformation and manipulation often are used as ways of keeping people in religious pain. In all probability, the evangelist simply wanted to be sure Ruth stayed on the straight and narrow. Believing firmly in the danger of straying, he used dramatics to control her future behavior. Certainly, given Ruth's sense of fear and guilt, the ploy worked. She walked the straight and narrow path, but there was little peace or joy on the journey. A "religious" woman, Ruth spent much of her life suffering because of a zealous religious leader and her own naiveté. Teaching Sunday school, attending worship, or singing in the choir did little to erase her fears or comfort her anxieties. She was dying in religious pain.

Providing ease for religious pain is a matter of granting release from guilt, shame, or fear. In some cases this occurs by teaching people the *truth* from their religious tradition. For example, Ruth desperately needed to hear the other side of hellfire—the gift of grace. She longs to hear, from her Methodist roots, the doctrine of forgiveness, grace, and atonement. It needs to be personalized and given to her with gentle love. On occasion, prayer and certain grace-filled readings can be helpful in releasing guilt and shame. Regardless, religious pain is a profoundly frightening experience for those who struggle in it. Rooted in the violation of their religious doctrines, and experienced in guilt, shame, and fear, it is eased only through the gift of forgiveness as presented in their own personal religious tradition.

THE TRUE CRISIS

The guilt and shame experienced by those in religious pain carries its own power and difficulties. It is, however, relatively defined by the personal religious tradition of each person. Spiritual pain, on the other hand, is not nearly so kind nor so clear; instead it is much more cruel, with little sense of hope or escape. It is not determined by religion but rather defined by the legacy with all of its consequences.

A few pages ago I implied that spiritual pain is a universal condition, commonly shared by all, yet seldom considered. In my research, I found no writings about it. Rarely did anyone allude to its existence. However, as I have grown to understand and respect spiritual pain, I have learned that it carries enormous power and influence in all of our lives.

Spiritual pain is a condition in which people feel isolated and forgotten by God. Understanding that it is a FEELING is critical; logic or intellect has little to say to it. In religious pain, individuals tend to feel guilty or ashamed, generally because they have broken the religious rules of their tradition. Spiritual pain, on the other hand, is not interested in the EXTERNAL rules proclaimed by any religious body; instead it is only aware of the INTERNAL rules placed in the altar-heart by the family legacy. Existing entirely inside your heart and mind, the rules of your family system teach you the rights and wrongs of life. As I wrote in the first part of this book, the legacy defines you, and, as you grow through childhood, more and more parts of yourself come under the guidance and judgment of your legacy.

Spiritual pain is developing any time you violate the rules

and teachings of your Legacy Bible. It is a condition which occurs through the accumulative effect of self-judgment and sentencing. A young boy, for example, raised in a system which teaches the evils of smoking, wants to try it since his peers are all involved in the same thing. It may even be that his religious tradition also speaks against it, since in all likelihood, his parents will seek out a system which reinforces their own. Any time, then, that the boy tries a cigarette, he will suffer feelings of guilt, to both his religion and to his legacy. In this simple illustration, it is easy to see this boy will be in religious pain, since he has broken the rules of his tradition, the EXTERNAL rules. His church may offer a way out of his sinful act. Through confession and assurances to Jesus that it won't happen again, he may receive some type of pardon. However, what type of forgiveness is available from his legacy? What conclusions will he arrive at regarding the violation of his INTERNAL rules?

These are the questions which lead to spiritual pain, since each one holds the promise of a negative self-definition. Forgiveness by God, through this boy's religion, is one thing. ACCEPTING that forgiveness is quite another. This is the core of spiritual pain.

Since most people grow up with a limited and unimpressive view of themselves, feelings of positive self-worth are scarce. It is almost impossible, as we have seen, to escape childhood intact. Most of us have defined ourselves in a negative fashion, at least many parts of our being are seen as lacking. Carrying these beliefs of our Legacy Bible into adulthood, how can we simply ACCEPT a religious statement that we are a forgiven people? It is neither that easy, nor believable, for most of us.

Spiritual pain, then, is the felt condition of a person who is forgiven by God, but unacceptable to himself. The peace and joy, promised by God to all, is unavailable to anyone who decides he/she is unworthy. Since even God, Himself, doesn't force His love and peace on His people, folks wander around in spiritual pain, the *felt absence of the ever-present God.*

To better understand this concept, sometimes I try to imagine the love of God flowing through the space around me. This invisible *energy of love* touches me both inside and outside my body. Since entire volumes have been written on the omnipresence of God, I choose to simply imagine that He's everywhere. Assuming this is the case, the only remaining question for me is: Why don't I feel this love energy which flows all around me? The answer, it seems to me, rests with the fact that we have made a choice NOT to experience the presence of God because we feel unworthy. Caught, judged, and sentenced by our Legacy Bibles, we find ourselves in a land of little peace or joy, and no room to consider inviting any in. Obviously, if I see myself as a bad person, forgiven by God or not, I cannot allow myself to enjoy the peace which comes from my pardon.

Since God is only known emotionally, or through our feelings, then it stands that all other movement towards God is mental. You can know *about* God through discussion and books, but you only KNOW God experientially, through your feelings. Therefore, it is truly a personal choice as to the degree of God's love which gets allowed into your heart. It is quite possible to know that God has forgiven you; certainly you have heard it proclaimed from a multitude of religious leaders. This knowing, however, is mental, one more fact for your mind. Only when you know, in the Hebrew sense of the word—as Abraham *knew* Sarah—can you experience the presence of God in your life.

It is true, however, that all emotion is preceded by thought. When you have a feeling, even one that seems instantaneous, there is a brief second in which your mind "fills you in" on what's going on. Feelings, then, will follow. In the spiritual area, in particular, it is important to realize that if your mind tells you of your unworthiness, your heart will quickly receive the message and close up. God, who is present everywhere, anyway, will still be present; you, however, won't feel that presence since you have decided against it. Recalling that spiritual pain is the felt absence of the ever-present God, at the moment you close down your heart because of self-judgment, you enter this pain.

Reading these words, you might think that it would be easy to simply decide to open your heart to God. However, since most people believe they are quite unlovable, and since they truly believe they know themselves BETTER then God does, how can they open up to Him? Forgiveness by the church, the priest, or God won't impact a closed heart shut down by self-sentencing due to feelings of unworthiness and shame. Notice how many of these judgments rest in the Legacy Bible teachings and reside in the altar-heart. In a true sense, until the Legacy Bible opens its pages for a new look, people will remain in spiritual pain.

Whereas the feelings of religious pain are guilt, shame, and fear, the emotions of spiritual pain are feelings of aloneness, isolation, and separation. How could anyone feel differently if they have decided that even God, if He truly knew them as they know themselves, would abandon them? The beliefs of the Legacy Bible, along with the definitions of the self, override all religious and intellectual arguments to the contrary. Have you ever tried to assure someone that he or she was a good person? The resistance is enormous. While they may admit that what you say could apply to others, it obviously is not for them, scum that they are.

The belief that you know yourself best is an untrue one. Nevertheless, most of us accept our self-definitions as truth. Who else knows my secrets, my passions, my bad thoughts, my unworthiness, my failures, and my sins? I know, and, of course, God knows. But even God doesn't know how damaged and flawed I am, because I, and only I, *feel* it. While some people may trust that God knows their innermost thoughts, few believe that anyone else, God included, feels what they feel. What goes unexamined is the notion that my feelings are the direct results of my thoughts, which in turn were programmed in my early years. Who would ever think, for example, that perhaps my legacy gods knew less than I did? And yet, I have allowed their opinions and the beliefs of the generations, to become my own.

Spiritual pain exists only because people are unwilling to let go of their own self-judgments. The isolation and aloneness, then, are self-imposed conditions. A friend of mine who pastors a large suburban church recently asked me to meet him for lunch. Over a turkey sandwich, he told me that he and his wife were separating. He also indicated that he had turned in his resignation to the church council a week ago. I asked him why he felt he had to resign.

"I can't stay there," he said. "I've let them down too much. I mean, if the pastor can't keep his own house in order, what right does he have to stand up there and preach to others about love and relationships?"

"Maybe you have more to say now then you ever did," I offered.

He thought about that for a minute, "You might be right,

but I don't have any right to lead these people anymore."

"Did they ask you for your resignation?" I asked him.

"No," he shook his head. "In fact, most of them asked me to reconsider. But a few didn't say anything, and I suspect they were giving me a message that I did the right thing by resigning. I feel I lost the right to remain as their pastor."

"It sounds to me like you're feeling a lot of shame," I said to him.

"Absolutely," his eyes filled up with tears. "I let everybody down: my wife, my kids, my parents, and the church. I should have known better than to think I could nurture the church while ignoring my family. Now, I've lost both."

Sharing with me that he was moving to another state, he said, "I suppose, in some ways, it's fitting. I don't deserve much love right now in my life."

My pastor friend was doing something that I have noticed so many people do when they judge themselves as inadequate or as a failure. He held court and sentenced himself to isolation and aloneness. In a true sense, because he found himself so lacking, he even abandoned himself. Moving to another state would be an appropriate punishment for his "sins." Away from all the supports and love of his life, he could then suffer properly.

This is the exact process of spiritual pain. Accepting the teachings of the Legacy Bible as accurate and truthful, people sentence themselves to isolation and separateness. As they are found guilty in their inner courts, they make absolutely sure there is no space for the acceptance of pardon. God may offer it and surround them with His love and spirit, but there is a "no vacancy" sign on their hearts. With a closed heart comes the felt absence of God.

Feeling alone and abandoned by God brings enormous fear into our lives. It doesn't matter if we are the ones who closed the door to the heart, the fear is still present. Therefore, the primary emotion of spiritual pain is fear. Do you ever recall times in your life when you felt all alone and frightened? It may have been when you were a small child, shut in your room at night, frightened by unusual sounds. Perhaps it was when someone played a trick on you, leaving you stranded in a strange place. Regardless, the fear, in all probability, was overwhelming. Unfortunately, no matter how hard you try to comfort yourself, to assure yourself that you are safe or that your fear is simply an overactive imagination, it tends to have great power, sometimes feeling as though it paralyzes you. In the same manner, scripture, theological arguments, or religious words will never budge a stuck door to the heart. Spiritual pain will not disappear because of a quiet conversation with yourself. It is too powerful and too historic.

The final chapters of this book will address themselves to the movement beyond self-sentencing, isolation, and separateness. Spiritual pain is a common struggle for everyone; it keeps people separate from one another and straight-arms God. Deserving attention because of the enormous weight it brings into life, spiritual pain is perhaps the most difficult obstacle any of us will have to face this side of dying. Moving from separation to unity is the greatest gift you can give to yourself; it is also the most profound.

CHAPTER XVII

POINT OR LINE?

*"What wound did ever heal
but by degrees?"*

Shakespeare

*"With time and patience,
the mulberry leaf becomes silk."*

Chinese Proverb

"I want what I wants when I want it!"

Popeye the Sailor

POINT OR LINE?

I was ten years old the first time I ever sent away for something through the mail. After years of humiliation for being skinny and countless confrontations with bigger kids, it was time for Charles Atlas and me to show the neighborhood toughs a surprise. It was after a particularly difficult afternoon in which the "king" threw me down off his "mountain" at least ten times, that the back cover of my comic book introduced me to Mr. Atlas. Identifying with the poor jerk who was having sand kicked all over his face by beach bullies, I decided to send in my money.

Each day I stood around near the front door, waiting for the mailman to bring me my instant muscle magazine. My mind soared into endless thoughts of rippling muscles causing a new respect among the neighborhood kids. At the ballfield, it would be a different story. No longer would I avoid sliding into third base for fear of being injured; my muscles would take care of me. There would be no more extra holes in my belt; my pants would stay up just fine, thanks to Mr. Atlas. I smiled when I thought of my mother's face, covered in amazement, as she recognized that my shirt was staying tucked in. What a different world was on the horizon for me!

When it finally arrived, I was horrified to discover that Mr. Atlas had neglected to tell me one little detail. To get those bulging muscles shown on the back of my comic book, I had to WORK for them. Exercise was required, and plenty of it. There weren't any pictures on the back page of the skinny guy doing exercises before he turned into Mr. Muscle. He was a wimp in one drawing and belting a bully in the jaw in another. Charles, my savior from skinny arms, was rapidly teaching me something about life and marketing. Not only did I spend my money on a dream, I had to spend a lot of other things, too, such as energy, time, and discipline. In other words, I really had to desire muscles enough to work toward developing them.

Complaining to my grandfather about Mr. Atlas, he gave me my first lesson in *real* life. "To get to where you want to go," he said, "you keep following the line. You'll get there, one step at a time." This, obviously, was not what I wanted to hear. I wanted muscles, not a course in muscle-building.

The past several chapters have painted a rather difficult dilemma for those of you, as well as for myself, who are searching for a sense of spirituality in your life. As you understand the impact of your family legacy on the way in which you envision and relate to God, these insights can be both frightening and overwhelming. For many of you, this may be the first time you ever gave this issue serious consideration. Others may find themselves horrified at the possibility that their religious beliefs are a hodgepodge of family legacy teachings, church school curriculum, and the culture.

Adding to the blending of legacy and religious teachings are the many ways in which your family type has helped you define yourself. In turn, this often determines your willingness to accept or deny any spiritual love and forgiveness, since your evaluation of yourself is always seen as more personal and accurate than the grace of God. Believing yourself to be smarter than God can cause numerous problems in your spiritual and personal life.

For several years now, I have been working on the thoughts for this book, knowing full well that I would arrive at this inevitable question: What to do about it all? What good does it do to understand that your legacy and spirituality are somehow linked unless that understanding moves you to growth and fulfillment? So what if you believe you understand yourself better than God, and, therefore, deny yourself any peace or joy, if you don't do anything about it? Or, if you can't *feel* the forgiveness and grace of God, where do you turn? There needs to be a direction to address these and the countless other questions raised by the previous chapters—a way to move from a blended spirituality of legacy, church, and culture, to one of inner peace and joy, experienced in the world and in your relationships.

Wondering about this final section, and how to best help people make positive spiritual movements in their lives, I did what most writers do—I read a lot of books. Plowing through hundreds of books and tapes to determine how other authors arrive at solutions, I found over and over again similar approaches. There were formulas for solving problems, three and four step plans for changing your relationships, and various exercises to improve your life circumstances. Some books had accompanying journals for writing your objectives and strategies, others had boxes for self- inventory tests. Almost all had answers to the problems they posed in the first half of the book.

POINT OR LINE?

Unfortunately, my answers are neither formulas nor strategies. You won't find any boxes or self-help tests in these chapters. In fact, my answers will look suspiciously like suggestions, since I do not believe the problems I have outlined in the first sixteen chapters of this book can be simply answered. The confusion between family legacy, self-identity, the concept of God, and your spirituality cannot become clear with a few short paragraphs of recovery or a spiritual inventory. If you're looking for the Charles Atlas Quick Muscle-building course, you need to try another book. There are no pat answers to the muddy waters of family legacy and spirituality. If there were, this book wouldn't be necessary, and you wouldn't be reading it.

Perhaps we all long to live in a Charles Atlas world, where the bad bullies of life are easily disposed of—where life's struggles are erased with a mail order booklet. Sadly, that's not the kind of world where I find myself. The easy answers of television never seem to hold in real life; I have yet to see even a minor family problem resolved in thirty minutes. Homilies and sermons tell a good story, but I clearly recognize their shortcomings, particularly when it comes to assisting people onto the narrow way. Preaching seldom works, nor does flowery poetry. Similarly, telling the truth, working hard, and operating with integrity do not guarantee you a world without hills and curves. Difficult issues demand time and energy to work through, regardless of what your legacy teachings may say.

If anything that I have written to this point makes sense, it seems to me that we all walk a demanding road. Each one of you is working with his or her own stuff to try to make sense out of life, and to reach for some joy and peace along the way. Most of us do not live in towers where butterflies drip gold along flowery pathways; instead we travel in a world where both good and bad occurs. Butterflies flit to and fro in meadows, but they also get splattered on car windshields, and some have their wings pulled off by ants or spiders. In your own life, some days you're happy; at other times you may wish to pull the covers over your head and not move. Sometimes relationships are wonderful, exciting, and passionate, but the next day you may wish to disappear forever from everyone you ever knew.

We do not live in a simple world with simple answers. The family legacy merely adds to the complexity of life. Combined with the various institutions of life such as schools, communities, and religious traditions, is it any wonder that your life is confusing and uncertain? To think that an answer to all of this could be placed in a neat formula at the end of this or any book, to me, would be an insult to the intelligence and struggle of anyone reading it.

The only sensible approach, it seems to me, lies in the realization and acceptance that none of us arrived at our place in life instantaneously. Numerous theories have outlined, instead, that human beings develop in stages, from infancy to old age. Consistent with each stage is the fact that life is a process, a movement from one day to another. Years lead into other years, all filled with both wounding and healing. It is not as if one morning you wake up and say, "Today I am wounded." Rather it is an accumulation of struggles, disappointments, and injuries that lead to the felt experience of pain. Feeling wounded is the result of a hurtful process over decades of living. Similarly, most healing occurs over time. Since most of us are not easily prone to forgiveness, however, allowing the process to flow grants new visions and insights from the past.

I have always been amazed when a couple chooses to enter marriage therapy, sharing a horror story of pain and abuse in their first session, only to ask me at the end of the session, "How long do you think it's going to take to straighten us out?" Sometimes talking to me about limited finances and time, couples then ask, "Do you think three or four sessions will be enough?" Admittedly, I understand the financial and time demands on everyone; however, it never fails to surprise me when I realize that people actually believe that years of wounding and abuse can be resolved or healed in less than two-hundred minutes. A quarter of a century of stored anger, abuse, or silence does not get addressed on three consecutive Tuesday nights. Often I discover that marriage partners have carried their childhood wounds into the relationship, looking to the other person to heal their past and blaming them when it doesn't work. How can anyone believe that this type of injury can be healed without the process of time and discovery?

So it is with spiritual pain. In many people, the self-exclusion from the grace of God, the confusion of the legacy, and the blending of religion, often leads to enormous feelings of aloneness and isolation. Questioning your worthiness, many of you truly believe that you know yourself better than God. He may offer you healing and hope, but you understand that

POINT OR LINE?

if He really knew who you were, with all of your filth and shame, He would announce an exception to His grace. Most willingly, then, you would step to the rear of the room and face the wall. Admittedly, God is in the same room; it's just that you cannot allow yourself to feel His peace and love. You are simply too unworthy.

This kind of aloneness and separation presents a pain all of its own. Because it is self-imposed, and reinforced by the legacy teachings regarding *goodness* and *self-worth,* the resulting fear and despair is enormous. People in spiritual pain desperately desire connection and union, even though their self-judgments have determined that such longings are not for them. Believing it is only a brief time before God discovers the deception, with His abandonment sure to follow, many choose to isolate themselves from His love, not knowing what else to do. In a sort of beating-God-to the-punch routine, they end up frantic without any design for self-redemption and acceptance. While this may summarize the struggle of the person in spiritual pain, it in no way addresses a blueprint for movement beyond the fear and aloneness.

Since the *felt* absence of the ever-present God does not disappear through the reading of a book or the mumbling of some words, religious though they may be, a different approach must be embraced for change from spiritual pain to spiritual wholeness. Just as in the case of the couple entering marital therapy, there are no fast or quick answers to the experienced pain prompted by an "absent" God. For most of us, it took years to reach the point of dismissing ourselves from the unconditional love of God. Similarly, it will take no less time to transform your pain of isolation and separateness to one of love, joy, and union. Spiritual and relational movement toward wholeness is always a process of discovery and awareness; it does not occur in the twinkling of an eye or by a washing-away process in an act of baptism or confession.

BUT WHAT ABOUT CONVERSION?

When I made the decision to write this book, I realized almost immediately that I might end up alienating some members of various religious institutions—the church, in particular. However, I also feel that many supporters of the church are equally aware of their own spiritual pain or lack of emotional connections with God. Regardless of the outcome, my hope is that the struggle toward spiritual wholeness can be one of bridge-building within the church, rather than a construction of walls by frightened or retrenching people. Unfortunately, some of the thoughts presented regarding spiritual pain and the intersection of legacy with religious teaching may be viewed as a threat to the church. Instead, it has always been my intention to support those persons in their spiritual journey who have felt the aloneness that comes from the felt absence of God.

In order to do this, it is important to understand that spiritual pain has nothing to do with salvation. This is not a book about being saved; there are enough of those around. As far as salvation goes, I choose to leave that up to the plan and activity of God in His world. Concerning itself with the struggle toward wholeness in daily life, and separate from the concerns of salvation, spiritual pain has to do with the experiencing of God in my relationships and worship, not with whether or not my soul is in danger. From my perspective, that is never the question.

Most religions speak of an event in life, a special moment when *truth* is envisioned. More pointedly, this is seen in Christianity, which speaks of a time when individuals *turn around* toward Christ, in an act of choice. Called "conversion," it is viewed as an abrupt shift in nature, a change of mind and behavior. In a unique example of pain caused by unhelpful choices, the Prodigal Son story illustrates this change of direction. Recalling this parable of Jesus, Luke suggests that the younger son, after wandering down the wrong road for a period of time, "came to himself," choosing to return home to a waiting and forgiving father. Christianity would claim this as a conversion experience for the Prodigal, brought on by his awareness through struggle. Returning home to a celebration and full acceptance into sonship, I often wondered how things went for this boy two or three months after his homecoming party. Did he question his decision, speculating on what would have happened if he had stuck it out with the pigs? Was it possible that he slipped back into his old feelings of dissatisfaction with his life? Conversion, however, does not refer to the process, preferring instead to focus totally on the life-changing *event.*

Regardless of what happened to the prodigal son after his

return home, it was clearly a PROCESS that followed his conversion EVENT. And it is at this point that spiritual pain has a great possibility to be experienced. Coming to your senses that working with pigs is poor employment, and returning home to a loving father is one thing; living day after day down on the farm is quite another. Conversions are moments in time, markable on the calendar and clock. They can be traced on timelines, with fancy dots to signify the instant they occurred.

Evangelical Christianity has always focused on conversion events. Spiritual pain experiences, instead, focus on the searching for God in the broad and lengthy times between these milestones. Unlike conversion in Christianity, or liberation in Buddhism and Hinduism, spiritual pain is a daily experience, a process during which you feel alone and isolated. Seldom is it touched by events or moments in time, but rather responds to an ongoing process of healing that is more in tune with daily awareness.

The first time I met Dan, I was working in a small inner city parish. A computer programmer by vocation and musician by avocation, Dan had attended worship for years, but never felt like joining the church. Perhaps because we both liked golf and shared a similar sense of perverse humor, Dan and I formed an immediate friendship. We enjoyed laughing together as well as philosophizing over coffee. "I want to join the church," he told me one evening on the way back from the bowling league.

"Why?" I asked him, never thinking about the inappropriateness of the question.

"Because it's time," he said.

On Easter Sunday Dan joined the church. I suspect it was not a theological statement, nor a position of faith, but an affirmation of our friendship. Nevertheless, he was a new member, adding to the church numbers, sending another message to the denomination as to my astonishing capabilities. His baptism, as an adult requirement for church membership, was attended by his entire family, as well as aunts, uncles, and cousins who had given him up for "lost," at least his soul, anyway. For Dan, this was his event, his moment of conversion, a change of direction.

During the next two years, Dan attended worship periodically, played golf regularly, and remained a good friend.

One day as we sat on his front porch, I asked him, "When you were baptized, did you experience anything special? Was it a sort of mystical experience for you?"

"I guess so," Dan said. "At least I remember feeling goose bumps, the kind that tell you this is an important thing taking place. My feeling was that this was something special I was supposed to do."

"What happened to that feeling?"

He thought for a few seconds, rubbing his head as if he was searching for the right words, "I don't know. It just came and went, sort of all in the same breath." Looking at me, he said, "Isn't that what happens to everybody?"

Looking back on that time, I'm not sure how to answer Dan's question. I'm sure that holy moments come and go in a person's life; I'm not sure how long they last, nor exactly what kind of impact they have toward growth and change. Dan certainly had his event; it's recorded in the business minutes of the church, and was witnessed by a church full of family members. On his timeline, he could mark a dot, write the date, and call it a special event. And while many would question if it was a conversion, he saw those moments as special and God-filled.

Like Dan, many of my clients speak of a momentary shift in their perspectives. Occurring in a flash, it appears to be an instantaneous insight, bringing healing to hurtful memories. However, there are two important distinctions to make regarding these "miraculous events." First, most changes which occur in people's lives do so after months or years of struggle. Working to heal memories of the past, you may find yourself wrestling with the history of your father and mother, or with learning to see *their* side of things differently. While this may take several months and great desire, eventually, there may be a moment when everything falls into place. This is your point of discovery and insight. Marked on your timeline, it is dated, for example, at the moment you saw your father's pain from a new perspective. It did, however, take you an enormous amount of energy and time to attain this point. Months of drawing a line led you to this moment, a point of discovery.

Secondly, because you have made a shift in your life, marked by a point in time, does not mean that you will maintain your new position. Rather, now the process begins—a time of living your life with your new insights fully in sight. In all probability you will slip and slide all over the place, as the old insights clash with your shift of perspective. It is never easy; the process is demanding, and the need for self-forgiveness and understanding is critical. From your point on your timeline, your line of new vision may wander all over the place. One day you might be particularly rooted in your recent discoveries, the next, you may find yourself filled with the old rage and feelings of victimization.

For many people rooted in religious teachings, this is a very difficult concept. Much of the struggle originates in a widely held belief that God will take over from the point of your conversion. It is a way of saying that when the prodigal son finally "bumped into himself," experienced his point in time, and returned home, God took over and his life was rosy from his homecoming party into the future. Spending a great deal of time in my first four decades with church people, I know the words by memory; they are a part of my catechism. "If you truly have a God experience, you are home free and His child; peace and joy will be yours." Without ever saying so, the reverse argument rings loudly, "If peace and joy are not yours, then you obviously did not have a God experience."

Nothing could be more distant from the truth. Experiences with God do not necessarily lead to joy and peace. To the contrary, they most often are disturbing or disruptive, leading instead to a process of struggle. While you may have a momentary sense of joy and peace as you touch the Spirit beyond yourself, this point is short-lived, leading instead to great soul-searching—your line of transformation.

All of this is a way of saying that spiritual pain is not erased by a religious experience. While it is true that it may be eased briefly, the process of healing is ongoing. Your movement from spiritual pain to spiritual wholeness is a continual tussle with your legacy, religion, and sense of self. Jesus will not come to you in a cloud and make things better. Along the way there may be moments of grace—those times when you sense that you are not alone. They may come in a sunset or a symphony. In my understanding, these points are the oases of life, the places where cool water is found and rest is taken before beginning the continuing journey toward wholeness.

However, since God apparently expects us to wrestle with

the things that belong to us, the expedition is ours. Your legacy, religion, and sense of self are clearly personal; they apply to your life. Having little to do with your religious experiences, the process from spiritual pain to spiritual wholeness becomes a matter of changing your inner conclusions about yourself, God, and your beliefs. Easier said than done, however, the next chapter begins to outline the blueprint for this journey.

CHAPTER XVIII

THE GOD OF YOUR LIFE

"She probably laboured under the common delusion that you made things better by talking about them."

Rose Macaulay

"Where it is a duty to worship the sun, it is pretty sure to be a crime to examine the laws of heat."

John Morley

"Nothing's easy."

Grandma

THE GOD OF YOUR LIFE

The term "dysfunctional" has been bantered about a lot these days. Used to describe families that tend to be abnormal or peculiar, it often is pointed in the direction of addictive and abusive behavior. However, as the term has become better understood, it seems that almost every family has some degree of dysfunction in it. We all struggle, question, wonder, and hide throughout large hunks of life, mainly due to a certain amount of craziness in childhood. The very humanity of parents means we're in for both a glorious and rough road. All in all, I suppose, we may be lucky to arrive at adulthood even vaguely intact.

Dysfunctional parenting has been around since the beginning of time. Perhaps tribal living helped compensate for some occasional meandering by troubled parents, as the community stepped in to protect the children from too many suffering events. Nevertheless, children have always paid a price from intergenerational legacies which were rooted in imbalance or abuse. It becomes impossible for concepts of the self, the community, and the world not to be enormously impacted by the power of the family legacy.

As indicated in the past few chapters, the legacy leads to certain conclusions about the self, which in turn, profoundly influence all relationships. Seldom without any awareness at all, people make decisions of colossal importance based on legacy deductions. Feelings about husbands or wives, children and employers, or priests and God all bob to the surface from the deep waters of the legacy.

In particular, I have attempted to share my sense of the ways in which the legacy impacts your own judgments about yourself, which in turn determines any willingness you may have to relate with God, in even a limited degree of peace or contentment. Knowing yourself better than God knows you is not only a personal belief, it pertains to everyone reading this book. Spiritual pain is the universal condition of internal numbness—a freezing of the emotions—as the only way most of us know to keep God at arm's length. Admittedly, we may all long for the felt presence of God, with the corresponding feelings of love and safety promised from some far away memory. Regardless, since we know ourselves so very much better than the Almighty, a sentence to emotional exile is so much more appropriate.

Consider for a moment a very old story. Recorded in the

book of Judges in the Old Testament is a story of Jephthah, a rather brave soldier, husband, and father. There seems to be no question as to his dysfunctional background, the son of a prostitute and unwelcome in his own family. Sibling rivalry ran rampant back then, as well as today, and Jephthah was tossed out of the house, since his stepmother and stepbrothers felt he was not one of them. There is no record of his father's standing up for him in any manner, thus sending him out into the world without any inheritance at all. Behaving like any person who had been dismissed from his own family, Jephthah found himself a bunch of friends who all felt about as unlovable as did he. It's unclear at this point if they became his followers or not, but within a few years, he is pictured as a leader and soldier. The first time I read this story, it reminded me of one of my legacy teachings which said, "Join the service; it will make you or break you." I assume, from the blend of the story, that Jephthah responded positively.

There is a fascinating twist to Jephthah's story that occurs as he is going off to war against the Ammonites. Feeling that he needs to cut a deal with the Lord in order to win a victory, he offers to provide a human sacrifice as a way of expressing his thanks. "If you will give me victory over the Ammonites, I will burn as an offering the first person that comes out of my house to meet me when I come back from the victory."

Two things happen next to Jephthah. First, he wins big against the Ammonites. Second, when he returns home, his daughter, and only child, rushes out of the house to greet him. There is great joy in her greeting of her father and only sorrow in his embrace of her. One thing, however, is in Jephthah's defense: he certainly is a man of his word. Perhaps his legacy said something like, "If you make your bed, then you have to lie in it." So it was that within two months, Jephthah offered his daughter to God as a human sacrifice.

Many things can be said about this story, and I clearly understand it can be read from various perspectives. It can be seen as myth, parable, or literal, but that doesn't really matter for the sake of this discussion. For me, the one colossal fact that leaps out of the story is that God was silent throughout the entire event. You will notice that the sacrificial suggestion belonged to Jephthah; God didn't ask for it, nor demand that it be carried out. Striking a bargain with God was Jephthah's notion of a good idea.

THE GOD OF YOUR LIFE

This story tells us a lot about Jephthah, the culture, and the writer(s) of Judges. It doesn't, however, tell us anything about God. To assume that God wanted any sacrifice at all was rooted in Jephthah's legacy beliefs, blended in with his sense of theology. Still further, to carry out his promise in the light of his faithfulness had nothing to do with God, but everything to do with Jephthah's *concepts* of God.

This story illustrates perfectly the ways in which we assume that we know what God wants, that possibly we know even better than He does what His expectations are. For example, do you really think, for a moment, that any "God" would want a living sacrifice to prove a point? Can you conceive that the Creator Being, who carved out the universe, could be bought off with the promise of burning an unsuspected victim in exchange for military favors? Certainly, cutting deals or being oblivious to the death of an innocent girl sounds far more human than divine.

Believing that you know yourself better than God is equally ridiculous; nevertheless, such thinking constantly occurs. Unlike Jephthah, however, most of us prefer to sacrifice ourselves instead of some poor unsuspecting child. Actually, self-punishment and self-dismissal feel far better since we have concluded that we *deserve* it so much. Beliefs such as these permeate our world, regardless of all of our talk about self-worth and accomplishment. Sentencing ourselves to a life outside the peace and joy of God, we suffer in spiritual pain. Because we believe we have earned His *dis*favor, we assume God wants us to get out of His way. Like Jephthah's daughter then, we wander out into the mountains, feeling alone, isolated, separate, and afraid—the emotions of spiritual pain. Unlike her, however, it doesn't end in two months, but continues through decades with the fear of death always around the corner, bringing us face to face with the Almighty, who will finally get to see us as the dark lump of coal that we truly are. Perhaps believing our body has protected us from His all-seeing eyes, like lead reflecting Superman's X-ray vision, we fear dying, when only our soul will stand before Him, with destruction waiting around the corner.

I know that many of you will be nodding your head in agreement with the above thoughts. However, others will be struggling to make sense out of such "irrational" thinking. Recalling that spiritual pain roots in emotions and feelings may be helpful in understanding the incredible sense of isolation and self-condemnation which surfaces in these times of inner-judgment. Logic or intellect has little to do with the conclusions leading to spiritual pain. Rather, the inner feelings of "badness" and unworthiness carried in the emotional body powerfully impact any negative conclusions about God's courtroom verdict. As I stated in an earlier chapter, the Legacy Bible may begin in the mind, but it steadily finds its way to your heart. Placed on your *altar,* it feeds your feelings about yourself, the world, and your concepts of God. Not everything in this world makes logical sense; certainly spiritual pain, with all of its fears and aloneness, does not. Nevertheless, it exists, has powerful ramifications, and impacts virtually every area of your life.

THE "GOD" OF YOUR LIFE!

By now, the authority and strength of the legacy can be clearly seen. Programmed by the beliefs of generations, it now belongs to you. As though some brilliant wizard placed you under a spell in which your memory was gradually erased, the legacy suddenly is seen as YOURS. How you arrived at various thoughts and beliefs doesn't matter, rather, you only know THEY ARE YOUR BELIEFS! Questioning them can lead to great discomfort; when they are challenged, you find yourself defensive or angry. The hard truth of the matter is that your legacy has become *sacred* territory.

In order, therefore, to address any of the issues raised by the blending of family legacy with religious teachings, it is vital to understand that *YOUR BELIEFS HAVE BECOME YOUR GOD!* This statement is both a key and crucial element in the movement toward the experiencing of peace and contentment in your life. Since your parents are viewed early on as gods and their teachings as sacred, within a short time the LEGACY BELIEFS have turned into your CONCEPTS OF GOD. Defining yourself, in the light of the Legacy God, as unworthy, bad, or hurtful, you are left with little choice except to sentence yourself to spiritual pain. Believing that you let down your legacy is absolutely no different than believing you have let down God. Since legacy and God are seen as one, the conclusions of both will be the same.

Assuming it is true that YOUR LEGACY BELIEFS HAVE BECOME YOUR GOD, how can you possibly allow yourself to be open to any thoughts, beliefs, or suggestions that run contrary to yours? Is it any wonder that there are no easy answers or formulas to address this dilemma? Messing around with your beliefs is akin to messing around with God; it's just not done.

To me, this leads to a major conclusion: since your legacy beliefs are your God, and since these beliefs are all contained inside your mind and heart, it only stands to reason that in your life, YOU ARE GOD! It is important to realize this is a statement that I do not lightly conclude. Nor is this a type of New Age thought in which you and God are one, since you're all made out of the same divine stuff. Believing that you know yourself better than God, while at the same time seeing your parents as gods and their teachings as sacred, building your own Legacy Bible within your mind and heart, YOU INDEED HAVE BECOME YOUR OWN GOD! Since you know yourself best, and you understand your beliefs to be the *truth,* what better concept of God could you possibly find than *yourself?*

Lest you find yourself growing wildly upset over the above notion, let me hasten to explain that there is a vast difference between GOD AS GOD, and YOU AS GOD. I am speaking here of the powerful, ruling arm of the family legacy that gradually leads us all to a point where we feel we surpass God. Embracing our self-judgments and beliefs, we assume we are carrying the truth within us. The fullest sense of what I am saying is that YOU ARE THE GOD OF YOUR LIFE! It simply means that you have placed YOUR beliefs, legacy, and conclusions ahead of the God of the Universe, since you are certain that your truth is accurate and absolute. My suspicion is that all the talk of idols seldom gets around to the greatest idolatry of our time: our beliefs are our God.

The tragedy in all of this thinking is that, self-proclaimed God or not, we are very aware there is a major foul-up here. Intellectually, we understand we are not the God of the Universe, but emotionally we live our lives, arrive at our conclusions, and protect our beliefs as though we are. Standing in front of God, we have decided in favor of our own conclusions; nevertheless, there is an incredible longing for things to be in the right order. Certainly, we know that we cannot give ourselves the peace and inner contentment that we are seeking. At the same time, making our beliefs sacred and our conclusions about ourselves absolute, we have no alternative but to arrive at the felt absence of the ever-present God in our lives. Aching for inner joy and peace, we never find it, since we are standing in the way of the Source from which it permeates.

It is a fascinating notion that God stands silently while we play around with our own sacred beliefs. Like Jephthah, we busy ourselves with our various deals and sacrifices, assuming that our own conclusions about God and His expectations are accurate. Equally, since we have put ourselves above God in both wisdom and judgment, self-dismissal becomes so very easy to do. Because most of us emerged from fear-, shame-, and critically-based families, what other conclusion could we reach? When God offers grace or forgiveness to you, how can you accept it since YOU, AS YOUR OWN GOD, have determined your unworthiness? Bumping into each other, the two Gods of life collide, the one Universal God offering peace, the other Self-Proclaimed God offering judgment and pain. God, as Spirit, hands you grace; YOU, AS YOUR OWN GOD, hand it back. After all, remember, YOU know about your own blackness and dark spots.

THE TRAIL BACK

Many of you reading this will be saying, "That's exactly how I feel. Perhaps I never put it in those words, but I have been struggling with spiritual pain for years. Now, what?" As I said in the previous chapter, all that happens from now on is a process toward accepting the love and peace that is yours. Scripture won't turn this dilemma around, nor will formulas. Like me, you arrived at this place through trusting in the sacred teachings of your legacy. Allowing them to determine your own worthiness, these teachings became your own sacred beliefs about yourself, life, and God. In turn, you gradually started to own them, as though they came from a sacred spot deep within your body. Over time, YOU BECAME YOUR OWN GOD, ruler of life, determiner of worth, judge, and executioner. In short, you separated yourself from others as though you were different, and from God because you pronounced yourself unworthy.

As I see this issue, the only way out of this self-judgment and dismissal is by using the very system which has previously been working against you. Spiritual pain can only be turned into spiritual wholeness through the acceptance of grace and love in your own life. Obviously, without any success at all, these have both been offered to you for decades. It is impossible to live in this culture, listening to the various pop psychologies and self-help guru's, without knowing that grace and love are good for you. You know, as do I, that learning to embrace them in your life would give you a more harmonious and peaceful life. But it doesn't happen, nor—in my view—will it ever happen, until you turn your attention away from the words or affirmations of others and shift your eyes totally to yourself.

As I wrestled with this issue, I tried a multitude of approaches that might help me release my hold on the sacred legacy beliefs of my life, many of which kept me in spiritual pain and separation. My books shelves are loaded with literally tons of reading, most of which was interesting and informative, but did little to help me stand aside from my position in front of God. I learned to say affirmations and, indeed, they have power to help with self-esteem or self-rejection. Most of the time, however, I forgot the affirmation when I found myself in a position where I needed it the most. I said nice words to myself, touched myself, placed myself in the company of people who were supportive, but still refused to let go of my own self-condemning thoughts.

Believing that different therapies would help, I embraced many. My head was opened up, allowing history and pain to spill out on the table, but well-meaning and loving therapists couldn't lead me to love myself. I dazzled myself in attempting the many new "body therapies." I "breathed" for hours in re-birthing, cried for days in therapeutic touch, screamed and pounded the floor in anger work, and danced around in psycho-drama. Carrying a teddy bear around for months didn't help, even when I pretended he was me. It did get me a lot of attention.

I listened to dying people give me clues about life, particularly seeking out the wisdom of the elderly. To my dismay, they were wrestling with the same familiar demons of spiritual pain that kept throwing me to the floor. I went through a broken marriage, new relationships, job changes, and re-working of issues with my parents, but love and grace still stood outside someplace, straight-armed by my own judgments and self-condemnations. Male groups became the in-thing; I immediately joined, only to find that most of the men were far away from the kind of struggles that I was having. Buying tapes, I played so many that my car cassette player wore out, but still no inner peace found its way into my heart. In short, I lived in spiritual pain no matter how hard I tried to alleviate it. Some friends suggested Jesus could help, but He and I go back a long way, and I knew that before I could do anything with the God of the Universe, I had to find a way to crack open my Legacy Bible and release the judgments of myself, along with the accompanying self-punishments.

I suppose that a critical insight came one day when I was listening to a Fairy Tale. Since I've always been a storyteller, whenever I get the chance, I seek out new stories which I can add to my repertoire. Also, I love to hear others tell stories, especially if I can steal some of their techniques or tricks. On this particular day, I was listening, with fascination, to an old story entitled "The Nubian Woman." An ancient tale, it tells of a woman who is tricked into casting her necklace into the river. In her sadness, she wanders along the river bank until a voice urges her to "plunge in." Diving into the water, she sees a terrible creature covered with seaweed, mud, and sores. The creature looks at her, and says in both a pleading and demanding way, "Lick my sores!" In a bold act of courage and compassion, the Nubian Woman takes the hand of this ugly river goddess and licks her sores. The story continues with all sorts of good things happening to this woman who is willing to tend to the pain and bruises of an ugly creature.

Having been a student of fairy tales, I realized that this was not just a nice story of a woman who was willing to take a risk. Licking somebody's sores is not necessarily a good idea. When I repeated this story to a group of hospice nurses, all I heard was horrid sounds as they imagined the Nubian Woman placing her tongue on the ugly sores of the underwater old woman. Fairy tales, however, never happen *out there* someplace; rather they occur inside a person. In "Sleeping Beauty," for example, when the Prince and Princess find one another, get married, and live happily ever after, the storytellers are not speaking of a grand, exquisite wedding in some far-away palace; instead they are speaking of the wedding that takes place *inside* a person, as various parts come together making the individual more whole and happy. Fairy tales are "up close and personal."

For a moment, consider the Nubian Woman in this light. Since Fairy tales occur inside a person, the ugly river goddess was actually an unacceptable and repulsive part of herself. This is a critically important concept to understand, since most of us have a tendency to place all events external to ourselves. Much of what I have been trying to claim in this book is that, contrary to what we normally think, while the legacy may have begun *out there* someplace, with your parents, aunts, uncles and cousins, somewhere along the trail, it became *internalized,* a part of you. It now lives inside you, an internal teacher, judge, and God, guiding and watching you each step of your life. It belongs to you.

In a sense, the Nubian Woman was tending to her own wounds; they were a part of her. Located deep within her being, she "plunged in" to lick them. From these types of deep dives into the heart of yourself, tremendous healing can occur. To be honest, I debated a long time before using this example of the Nubian Woman. Because I didn't want you to get stuck on a limited interpretation of a fairy tale, I almost didn't include it. However, it was this story which truly gave me a sense of direction and movement from spiritual pain toward spiritual wholeness. Regardless of what interpretation or analysis you may choose to give to the Nubian Woman story, she did "plunge in" and gently licked the sores of the unacceptable part of herself, from which enormous personal healing occurred. The important issue is that she is the ONLY one who can do this for herself. Her friends, family, priest, teacher, or neighborhood paper boy can't do it for her. Since it is her pain, her ugliness, and her sores, it is up to her to begin the process of healing. Without "plunging in," there would be no meeting of her "ugly" side, no opportunity to heal the hurts of her life.

It was during this story that I began to understand that if my view of spiritual pain is accurate, it can only be tended to by me. Rooted in my past, taught through intergenerational teachers, and finally owned by me, I carry around my own Legacy Bible. Filled with sacred beliefs, I have made myself the God of my own life. Believing that I know myself better than the God of the Universe, I find myself feeling empty and numb, with little inner peace or joy. Since much of the feelings of separation and isolation from God occurs through self-judgment, it became apparent to me that the only way to change all of this was to become God to myself. If the process of life has led me to a place where I have become my own God, then why not care for myself in the manner in which the God of the Universe cares for His world? If I am going to "play God," then why not get serious about it?

Is it possible to become God to yourself? In a true sense, you already are doing it each time you deny yourself peace and joy. Whenever you determine that you don't deserve forgiveness or gentle treatment, you are playing God to yourself. The times that you harshly judge yourself for certain behavior or punish yourself for making mistakes, you are extending the legacy to the position of God and making it sacred. For anyone in spiritual pain who does not truly believe in his or her worthiness, it would be impossible to feel otherwise.

One evening I was speaking with a friend about this concept of becoming God to yourself. His agitation quickly became apparent, and I recognized that I had triggered something very important in his tradition and legacy. As I had been developing this thought, I also had been extremely wary of it being misunderstood. It is critical to understand the difference between *receiving* the love and forgiveness of the God of the Universe, and *feeling* that love. The following story may help:

ONE GOLD COIN

Once upon a time, when wishes still came true and animals could talk, there was a young boy who lived with his father and grandfather. They were very poor, and in order to get enough money to buy some meager food, all three men had to work hard each day. Living on a small farm, they managed to survive by selling a few of their vegetables to people who passed by. Sometimes, a hungry person wouldn't have any money to buy vegetables, but the boy's father was a kind man, giving them some carrots or tomatoes anyway.

Each night when they would sit inside their small cottage, they would carefully count the few pennies they had earned during the day. Keeping only one or two pennies for expenses, the boy's father would carefully place the remaining coins in a small box he kept under his bed. "Do we have enough, yet?" the boy would ask his father each night before they would go to sleep. "Not quite enough," his father would always answer, and they each would sigh.

He couldn't even remember the first time he had known about the Gold Coin, but the boy understood that his grandfather needed one Gold Coin in order to pay the Master of the Ferry Boat when it was his turn to cross the river. "Without the Gold, there's no trip to the other side," his grandfather had told him, "and the Ferry Master can let you off on any island at all, even the island where the Demons with the small teeth live."

"Isn't the Ferry Master kind, like papa?" the boy once asked his grandfather.

Shaking his head, the old man said, "It's not that he's not kind; he has a job to do. The fare is one Gold Coin, and that's that. You can never bargain with a Ferry Master." And the old man would wearily sigh and shuffle off to bed.

One day when he was working with his father, the boy asked, "How many pennies do we have to save to get one Gold Coin for grandfather? Do we have enough yet?"

Pulling some weeds from the earth, his father stood up, "Not quite enough," he told him. "And I'm not exactly sure how many we need, but grandfather knows."

"Have you ever seen a Gold Coin?" the boy asked his father.

"Never," his father smiled at him, "but I understand the King has them for sale." He looked at his son, "Now, don't you worry, we'll have enough for the Ferry Master when it becomes time for your grandfather to cross over to the other side."

But the boy wasn't sure, because his grandfather seemed to grow older every day. The old man's hearing was not like it used to be, and from time to time, he would forget the names of the customers who stopped along the road. The boy also noticed that his grandfather seemed to be walking a lot slower, and his balance was very unsteady.

"Do we have enough, yet?" he asked his father that night.

"Not quite enough," his father answered, as always, pushing the box of pennies under his bed.

Then one day something quite extraordinary happened. An announcement was made that all the citizens of the King's Country should appear at the palace for a special appearance by the King. The boy was so excited, and he noticed that even his father and grandfather seemed to be wide-eyed and wondering. It felt like ages passed before the appointed day arrived when they would all go to the palace. Putting on his best pants and blouse, the boy started off with his father and grandfather toward the spot where the sun set. While he had never been there, the boy knew the King lived near the place the sun went to sleep each night.

When they arrived, everyone from the surrounding

countryside was standing there. Never had the boy seen so many people gathered in one place. While he recognized some of their neighbors and customers, many of the people he had never seen before. The excitement in the crowd was contagious as everyone stood impatiently waiting for the King to appear. Suddenly, on the balcony of one of the palace windows, the King stepped out into the evening sunlight.

"Citizens of our great land," the King started to speak, "I have a most wondrous and joyful announcement to make to all of you tonight." Immediately the boy found himself liking the King. His voice was so kind and loving, and he seemed to be surrounded in a light of power. Of course, everyone knew the King was a compassionate and generous person, but, as the boy said to himself, "it always helps to find these things out yourself."

Continuing with his announcement, the King said, "There are two important gifts I have to give to you all." A murmur of excitement went through the crowd. "After speaking with my Advisors and Officers, I am delighted to announce to you all that beginning tomorrow morning, and every morning after that, one of my ministers will come to each of your homes to give you each ten pennies." The murmur in the crowd grew to a roar of excitement. Ten pennies to each home every day was unbelievable! Even the boy couldn't believe his ears; ten pennies was more than they sometimes saved in a week. If the King meant what he was saying, and he was known as a person of truth, they would receive seventy pennies each week from the royal treasurer!

As the King raised his hand, the crowd grew silent. "And secondly," he shouted, in order to truly be heard by everyone, "as of this night, I have ordered the Ferry Master to freely carry everyone to the other side; you no longer need to have one Gold Coin to cross over the river!"

At that moment, the entire Kingdom erupted in joyous applause. Looking around, the boy saw his grandfather's face shining with delight. No longer would they have to work hard to save their pennies since the King had removed all of their problems in one moment of time. Everyone in the crowd was buzzing with excitement and disbelief. They kept cheering the King with words of thanksgiving and praise; the boy felt that he couldn't find enough words to tell the King how grateful he was, not just for himself, but for everyone.

That evening, as they got ready for bed, his father pulled

the small box out from under the bed. Counting the pennies, he sighed again. "What's the matter, papa?" asked the boy. "Why are you sighing?"

"Not quite enough," his father answered him.

"What do you mean, papa?" the boy said, "The King said that each day he is going to give us ten pennies, and besides that, the Ferry Master has to take everyone to the other side freely. The King said so."

His father shook his head, "Well, you never know about these things."

"What things, papa?"

But the boy's father didn't say anymore. He just sighed again, and went to bed. The boy stared into the dark for a long time trying to understand why his father seemed so sad. Hadn't the King just given them the most wondrous of gifts? Didn't they now have everything they would ever need? He fell asleep, but instead of happy dreams, he dreamed of an evil Ferry Master.

The next morning, as they were working in the garden, one of the King's ministers stopped by their house. "Good morning, men," he said with a smile, and handed the boy's father ten pennies. "Have a good day, and I'll see you all tomorrow morning." Quickly, the boy's father ran inside and put the coins in his small box. And so it was that each day, the King's minister stopped by to give them ten pennies, and each day the boy's father rushed inside to put the coins in the box.

When customers came for fruits and vegetables, the boy noticed that his father had increased his prices. Before the King's announcement, his father would sell potatoes, carrots, and beets for one-half of a penny; now the charge was one penny each. When he was paid, his father would immediately take the penny into the house and place it in the box. Soon the boy noticed his father building a bigger box, since the smaller one was now filled.

On the other hand, his grandfather had started to relax a little, leaving the gardening and selling of vegetables to the boy and his father. Sadly, however, the boy noticed his grandfather growing weaker; his breathing seemed more difficult at night. And then, one morning when he woke up, the boy discovered his grandfather was gone. His father was sitting at the table, drinking a cup of morning tea, and weeping. "Where is grandfather?" the boy asked him.

"He's gone to the other side," his father said, "and you know that the Ferry Master only travels one way. Your grandfather will never come back."

The boy started to cry, also, but after a time said to his father, "Isn't it wonderful, though, that grandfather didn't need one Gold Coin to pay the Ferry Master to cross over? We don't have to worry about him stopping at the Island where the Demons with the small teeth live. Grandfather will be safely on the other side.

His father sighed. "I hope you're right, son," he looked at him.

"But the King said so, and he is a good King," said the boy. "Hasn't he given us ten pennies just like he said he would? It is his gift to us, and the Ferry Master gets his pay, now, from the King."

Sighing again, his father said, "I hope you're right, son."

All day long, the boy was troubled by the conversation with his father. He missed his grandfather so much, and he felt great sadness, yet he could not understand why his father didn't trust the words and gifts of the King. He certainly took the coins quickly and hid them in the house. Why would the King lie about the Ferry Master?

So it was that each day the King's minister continued to stop by the house, giving ten pennies to the boy's father. And each day, he rushed into the house to place them in his much larger box. Watching all of this, the boy grew very uncertain about what to believe. He could not understand the need to save and hoard all of this money when the King had promised to give them enough to live on every day. Nor did they need to buy one Gold Coin to get to the other side of the river. And yet, his father was living as though none of this was true, and that they might become poor again tomorrow. Or worse yet, that the King's decree to the Ferry Master would somehow be changed. Perhaps, thought the boy, my father knows more than he is telling me because he seems so fearful and uncertain, and after all, he is my father. It may be that we truly are not safe, and that we will still need one Gold Coin to cross over the river. And I suppose, he thought, that my father must know something beyond the words of the King, and, after all, he is my father.

So it was that the boy grew as fearful as his father. Watching him hide the pennies each day, the boy realized that something bad could happen at any time. Certainly, the King *was a good man, and clearly they received their ten pennies every day, but you just never know. Soon, he was helping his father build an addition to their house to hold the several boxes of pennies that they had saved. The prices on their vegetables and fruits grew higher and higher, just in case the Ferry Master decided that he once again would collect one Gold Coin.*

The two of them lived together, working hard, and saving their pennies all the days of their life. Worrying about whether the King meant what he said, while at the same time receiving their daily gifts from him, they lived unhappily ever after.

This story illustrates the contagious power of fear when parents model such behavior for their children. While this very generous and kind King (God) offers daily gifts to the citizens of his Kingdom, some of the people wonder if he can be trusted. Even when receiving daily gifts from him (abundance and joy), the father questions how long it will continue before the treasury runs dry. Therefore, living in the center of the Kingdom, and in the midst of generous and constant care, the father and son retrench even further, believing their own assessment of the situation is more accurate and dependable than the King's promises.

As the King announces his decree that the Ferry Master has received new instructions, the people cheer and shout. Crossing over to the other side is a universal promise and gift (salvation). You will notice, however, that *receiving* the gift, and *trusting* in it, depends on the belief system of the individual. In the context of this book, spiritual pain is the emotional feelings that are experienced when the promises of the King (God) are not *trusted.* Living in fear and hoarding pennies in case something bad may happen, the father and son live unhappily. Fascinatingly enough, they, themselves, are responsible for their sad and distressing feelings. The King can do no more than he has already done; the rest is up to them.

In this case, the father and son grow to believe they know life's situations and possibilities better than the King. While he may mean well, you just never know about the Ferry Master's devious mind, which may decide at any moment to re-institute the passage fee of one Gold Coin. Just as the father feels he knows more than the King, we conclude we know more than God. After all, life does toss curve balls from time to time, and you just never know. When this type of thinking occurs, usually rooted in our legacy conclusions, we stand in front of the God of the Universe, receiving His daily gifts while at the same time, out of fear, guilt, or shame, straight-arming the joy that accompanies them.

The trail back, then, is clear. To trust in the generosity and kindness of the King in such a manner that we can experience inner peace and joy is to move from spiritual pain toward spiritual wholeness. Since many of us have become God to ourselves, the key is to unlock the doors of mistrust, guilt, shame, and fear, in order to discover the delight found in each room. To do this, we need to learn how to become God to ourselves so that we can truly experience the God of the Universe. The following chapter will move us down that trail toward wholeness.

CHAPTER XIX

MOVING TOWARD SACRED LOVE

*"Kabir says: Listen, my friend,
there is one thing in the world that satisfies,
and that is a meeting with the Guest."*

Kabir

*"Don't honor your ego,
even with your guilt."*

Hugh and Gail Prather

*"Out beyond ideas of wrongdoing and rightdoing,
there is a field,
I'll meet you there."*

Rumi

MOVING TOWARD SACRED LOVE

Joe and Barbara had been married for ten years when they quite suddenly found their relationship in trouble. Meeting an old high school classmate, Joe became involved in a brief affair. Always priding himself on his honesty, Joe confessed his attraction toward his former girlfriend to Barbara. Finding the daily situation too painful to cope with, she moved into her own apartment. Deciding that the children would be better off remaining in the family home, she decided to leave them with Joe.

While the affair lasted only a few short weeks, it was several months before Barbara and Joe began working on their relationship. With a goal toward reconciliation, they entered therapy. Since both of them felt they had neglected the relationship during the past decade, they started spending time talking and sharing feelings with one another. One evening, Barbara decided to take Joe to a restaurant that she enjoyed. Wanting to share a special evening with him, she was disappointed, when they drove into the parking lot, to see several people standing inside the lobby of the restaurant. As they walked inside together, Barbara pushed her way toward the hostess, only to see a note pad with a long list of names written on it. Turning around, she looked at Joe and "knew" that he didn't want to wait.

In a quick and angry motion, Barbara left the restaurant, jumped in her car, and drove off, leaving Joe standing inside the lobby. Within a few minutes, she returned to pick up Joe. Looking in the window, he said to her, "I'm willing to wait. Why don't you park the car and we'll wait at the bar?" Returning to the lobby, Barbara asked the hostess how long they would have to wait for a table. She was told it would be about a thirty minute wait.

"I'm not waiting thirty minutes," she said to Joe, and the two of them left the restaurant together. A few minutes later, Barbara was speeding down the highway toward their home. "Where are you going?" asked Joe.

"I'm going home. I don't deserve to eat." Barbara answered him, stepping more fiercely on the gas pedal. After a few minutes of silent driving, Barbara calmed down. Soon they found another restaurant and enjoyed dinner together.

It may seem to you that Barbara was acting somewhat silly and immature, and it certainly is true that she assumed a great deal just by looking at Joe's face. However, it is far more interesting to notice her words as she sped away from the restaurant. Since she had behaved so badly, apparently she felt she didn't deserve to eat. To his credit, Joe remained silent during her tantrum. Later in the evening he said to her, "I wasn't sure what was bothering you, but I felt at that moment it would be better for me to keep my mouth shut." Able to laugh about it, Barbara began to realize that she was the one unwilling to wait. Projecting her feelings onto Joe, Barbara had blamed him, initially, for "his" impatience, even though he gave her no indication that he was in a hurry. As she thought it through, however, she found herself "guilty" for petty behavior and inaccurate assumptions, leading to her need to "go without dinner, since she had been a bad girl."

Barbara's thought process led her to a conclusion that she was guilty of being immature. Immediately following this judgment was the need for punishment, perhaps an old childhood repeat of "going to bed without supper." Since Joe appeared unwilling to "punish" her, she would go home without eating, thus denying herself the pleasure of a good meal, as well as the joy of an intimate time with her husband. Fortunately, as she was driving toward home, she became aware of the inappropriateness of her decision.

At the relational level, Barbara's actions parallel those of a person in spiritual pain. From time to time, assuming that we are bad, inadequate, or damaged goods, we may deny ourselves the intimate connections with God. "Going to bed without supper" may simply be our resistance to accepting the peace and joy that God has to offer. The grace, love, and acceptance of God is always present; our receptivity of those gifts is not. Since we are unwilling to enjoy the peace God has to offer, we punish ourselves by our *refusal* to emotionally join with Him, thus finding ourselves feeling isolated, separate, and alone.

AWARENESS

As I indicated in Chapter 17, there is no easy way out of this struggle. Rooted in the humanity of our parents, and the power of the Legacy Bible, linked with the judgmental teachings of religion, spiritual pain is a universal problem. It belongs to us all. It seems to me, therefore, that since it has taken decades to arrive at the place where most of us walk around feeling disconnected and separate, it will equally take enormous energy and time to reconnect and join the hallmarks of spiritual wholeness. The movement from spiritual pain toward spiritual wholeness is exactly that, a process in self-healing and self-love. Sometimes, in therapy, the expression "working on yourself" is used. Denoting the *push* necessary on the part of the client to make progress in his or her life, it is an appropriate phrase. Similarly, the process of motion from spiritual pain toward spiritual wholeness can aptly be called "godly" work.

Before any journey can be undertaken, there needs to be **Awareness.** Coming from the Old English word meaning "wary" or "watchful," it appears that this is a vital ingredient for change in anyone's life. In a sense, this entire book is designed to bring you to awareness in your life. Many people, for example, have shared with me their longings to feel the peace of God in their lives. They assume that something is wrong with them, since, obviously, God must know what He's doing. Concluding that it is because of their own badness, guilt, or past that God withholds His peace, they remain in spiritual pain. Reading this book can allow you to become aware that perhaps the only one withholding anything is YOU.

Before you can begin the process of movement toward spiritual wholeness, you first need to become deeply aware of the nature and style of your own family legacy. Hopefully, as you were reading the earlier chapters in part I, you were thinking of your family of origin. There are many issues that need to be explored as you unravel the threads of your own legacy. What type of family did you live in? What were the beliefs given to you by your parents? How were they taught? These three questions alone can start you on a process of awareness as you activate your memory of childhood. Other issues to examine include questions regarding your sense of "self" such as, how do you define your *self* today? How powerful was your legacy in leading you to any conclusions about your self, community, and God? Have you been aware of any ways in which you were programmed as a child? To which of those teachings do you find yourself still loyal, as an adult? Are they beneficial or unhelpful? How have you been able to let go of negative or distressing legacy teachings?

Secondly, you need to examine the impact of your religious legacies on your life. Regardless of how educated or sophisticated you may be, childhood religious teachings still carry enormous weight. The guilt and judgment of religion may be pushed into the background for decades, only to surface during times of deep crisis or loss. It is stunning to discover that old teachings you felt had been buried long ago can suddenly become resurrected when life presents you with a devastating blow. What are your childhood religious teachings? Have you ever examined them? If not, how *aware* can you truly be of the impact they currently have on your life? For years, I sang with great gusto the hymn "Amazing Grace." Speaking of the grace of God which saved a "wretch" like me, I never gave a moment's thought to the meaning of the words I was singing. Later in life, I found myself quarreling with the notion that I was a "wretch." But, then again, that simply amplified the religious teachings which labeled me as a sinner, selfish and filled with lust. Coming from a critical- and shame- based legacy, I was ripe for hearing the judgmental and condemning teachings. Unfortunately, I was not so open to the forgiving and merciful lessons, which were sadly lacking in content and consistency.

How many of your religious or legacy beliefs have you bothered to explore? It does not take an expert to become aware of your own beliefs; after all, they belong to you.

I recall being amazed one evening when I sat down at my typewriter to list my beliefs. Starting slowly, I picked up speed, and within an hour had listed over 110 "important" beliefs of my religious and family legacy. As I read them slowly to myself, I could barely believe that I was still holding on to so much old stuff. When I allowed them to flow, beliefs that had no place or merit in my life still came spilling out of my mind. That evening I made a crucial discovery for my life: if I didn't even know what my beliefs were, and they were the fuel for my life, then I was running on automatic pilot, trusting the legacy to steer me on a happy and pleasant highway.

There was one belief, for example, that fueled my life at least two or three times each week. On my list, it was number seventeen: "Never order from the left side of the menu." I love to eat out, and try to do so as often as I can. Admittedly, however, I always decided what to eat based on the cost of the item, instead of what I truly wanted to order. While part of this belief is an economic reality, another part does not fit my life today. Why should I order meat loaf if my desired choice is veal? Because one item is two dollars less than the other seems to be the only rationale. Usually the tip is more than that. In reality, the reason I order the lesser priced item is because of my belief system, not my wallet. It may also have something to do with another one of my beliefs, which states that I'm not worth being pampered with veal. It's okay to be fed with hamburger, but going too far over the line might be considered extravagant.

You will notice that any **awareness** that I was able to glean out of looking at my religious or family beliefs came only in the *process* of exploring them. There is no one placed in this world whose primary business is to go around and make you aware of your beliefs. How they positively or negatively affect your life is a primary task of responsible exploring that belongs only to you.

The problem with *process* in our Western World seems to be that we are so incredibly busy and pre-occupied with everything, there is no time left to think about, or notice, much of anything. Perhaps it would be helpful if we began by teaching the children in their early education to *think* a few minutes about what the teacher is saying. When I used to teach college classes, I felt it would be wonderful if we required one hour of "think time" for each hour of lecture. Instead, students wrote notes furiously and then attempted to feed back to the instructor everything that he or she already knew. Called "education," they learned a lot of facts, but not much about fitting the pieces together in life.

Between television, earning money, and the demands of daily life, where does the average person find time to think? Perhaps, as the studies have shown, we have become a nation of spectators and followers. How can anyone march to the "beat of a different drummer" if he or she is too busy to listen? How much time do we actually spend in thinking about our beliefs and programming, even when we realize that our very lives are determined by them? Sadly, **awareness** seems to surface only when we find ourselves in deep trouble or pain. A man who never thought a thing about the way he behaved in relationships suddenly became **aware** when his wife left him and refused to return. At that moment, his education began. With a curriculum based on his belief system and family legacy, he started to understand himself and the ways in which he had been programmed to behave in relationships.

Awareness is critical for movement and change in your

life. Without it, you will remain in the same place you have been standing for decades before. It is the first baby step towards a life that belongs to you, instead of your legacy or beliefs. Awareness leads you to an identity based on *your own* insights, choices, and perceptions. It is the beginning of a path toward true peace and spiritual wholeness.

DESIRE

Seldom does change occur in life without desire. Coming from the Latin word meaning "to consider," desire appears to be a matter of consciousness. It seems to emerge from a sense of longing within a person—a yearning for something to happen. Perhaps all of us are born into a world of desire. We long for happiness, achievement, love, and security. Even as infants, we desire the attention and adoration of our parents. Crying to be held, seen, and given our favorite food, we let them know our own desires.

Realizing that much has been written by the experts and professionals regarding instincts, drives, or our own natural predispositions, in this case I am referring to desire as a conscious consideration, a choice you make regarding anything that you want. Separate from instinct, it is a conscious wish for something. Experienced as an aspiration or an ache, desire is a deliberate and necessary ingredient for change.

In order for any of us to move from spiritual pain toward spiritual wholeness, not only is awareness an essential component, but conscious desire is also a basic element for the beginning of the process. Without it, there will be no thrust toward movement of any kind. Desire is crucial for lifting your life out of stagnation towards more helpful or healthful living.

While we live in a world of enormous desires, longing for more money, sex, and excitement, there seems to be a vast absence of yearning for life change. Certainly it is true we all long to hit the lottery, to find the perfect mate, or to drive an expensive sports car. These "wants", however, are quite different from the desire to change our lives or to move toward spiritual wholeness.

I am writing, here, of the little desire necessary to change your life, the longing to start your engine for a new journey toward peace and wholeness. As much as you would think that most of us would hunger for such a change, the truth is far removed from that thought. True, we all want wonderful things in our life, but do we desire peace and joy enough to begin the process of awareness and change? My observations and suspicions say something quite different.

Many of us would certainly enjoy good things happening in our lives, but to examine our legacy or religious beliefs and the impact they have on our lives calls for a particular amount of energy and work. It doesn't just happen. For the most part, no one grows into peace, joy, or happiness by sitting around wishing for it. Instead, desire claims that you are making a conscious choice to *want* awareness in your life, and that you are willing to invest yourself in it enough to strive toward awareness and the process of change.

THE BOOST

My guess is that most of us would not spend a great deal of our time trying to change our lives simply because someone suggests that it might be a good idea. Change is hard work; it demands enormous energy and ambition. For the most part, you truly need to be motivated to desire change in your life. When things are running relatively smoothly, why would you bother to investigate your legacy or explore your belief system? If you are living in some degree of comfort, why would you disturb the "status quo" by opening up a can called "change?" If spiritual pain is a given in life, and you have learned to live with it without too much struggle, why begin the process toward spiritual wholeness? Certainly books, tapes, and speeches will not inspire you to begin this process, especially when you sense the labor and effort involved.

The unfortunate truth is that only pain and discomfort tend to motivate us to action in life. Regardless of how often most of us claim to be eager to improve our lot in life, the energy and motivation to do so does not seem to come from good intentions. How many times from the early days of Charles Atlas to the present time have I declared my resolve to exercise and eat properly? Yet, it is only when my physician warns me of high blood pressure that I decide to truly get motivated and desire to improve my physical condition. It may be a sad fact of life, but we all seem to need a *boost* to begin the process of change, whatever the issue may be.

Some people, for example, refuse to invest any energy or initiative into their marriage relationship until their spouse announces a visit to an attorney to begin divorce proceedings. Suddenly, the fear of loss *boosts* the inactive person into action. No longer does he or she sit passively on the sidelines of the relationship. All of a sudden the need to learn communication skills becomes essential. The importance of understanding the relationship is seen as crucial in order to bring about healing and growth. Awareness and desire receive a *boost* from fear and uncertainty; the process of change begins.

I was first introduced to Kyle by the hospital dietitian. Apparently in an act of both anger and desperation, he had tossed his pancakes "frisbee" style from his hospital bed into the hallway. "I pushed that button for fifteen minutes and no one even bothered to come into my room," he said to me as I sat down on his bed, "Thank God I wasn't dying, and all that I wanted was some syrup. Tell me, Chaplain, do you think it's right that they serve you pancakes without syrup? Or for that matter, pancakes that are cold?"

Riding down in the elevator, I chuckled to myself as I imagined this angry man flinging his pancakes out of the door of his room. Looking at his chart, I discovered that Kyle had been hospitalized with chest pains. Tests had shown a series of small "heart attacks," followed by a massive attack in the emergency room. While he had survived this "scare," Kyle's prognosis was poor. "The specialist says I need a new heart," he told me one day. "I guess he's going to put me on the waiting list."

Kyle was in and out of the hospital several times during the next few months, each time growing considerably weaker. As we talked together, he began to share his story with me. The oldest of five children, he had always been seen as the family hero, looking after his younger brothers and sisters while his mother worked to support the family. His father was absent most of the time while Kyle was growing up, and drunk the times he was home. Assuming the role of the man of the house, Kyle grew into an over-responsible and somewhat domineering person. He expressed great anger at his mother for her continual willingness to accept his father back into the home, even when he showed up at the front door, obviously drunk.

"I loved my mother, but to tell you the truth I never

respected her much," Kyle told me. Whenever his wife, Sharon, visited, he tended to treat her with the same disrespect he attributed to his mother. "Women are all wimps," he complained, "they talk a good game, but when push comes to shove, they go into hiding every time."

As Kyle's heart disease started to take a great toll, he began to openly express his fear. For the first time, he became aware of the delightful smell of fresh air coming in through his open window. He asked Sharon to pick some daffodils and bring them to his room. Life began to take on greater and greater meaning for Kyle, as he felt himself losing more and more strength. "I never knew how much beauty and love surrounded me," he said, motioning to the family picture of Sharon and their three children. "You know, if I ever get out of this, I'm going to really embrace life. We've never taken a vacation before, but the first thing I'm going to do when I recover from my surgery is take Sharon to Hawaii. She deserves it for putting up with me."

Kyle was beginning to see life differently, to become *aware* of so many aspects of living that he had never perceived before. His sense of relationship was changing as he started to see the part he played in Sharon's flight from conflict. Through this very frightening and serious illness, Kyle received a *boost* toward change and growth. Without a rotting heart, Kyle could have lived years in a stagnant relationship without any sense of meaning or joy. His desire for change came from a very real threat of loss of his own life, as well as losing everything and everyone meaningful to him.

Unfortunately, Kyle died before a donor heart could be located. He did, however, bring great healing to himself and his family as he learned to see things differently. He was boosted into new vision and insights through his illness. Both his awareness and desire blossomed through his crisis. Like most of us, Kyle needed struggle to propel him toward movement and growth in his life, and, as I have learned in my hospice work, there are some things more important than physical healing. When a dying man learns about love, or how to give to others, there is a healing of the spirit that occurs. Learning to see through new eyes is a gift which emerges out of most pain and illness; it is yet another form of healing.

DIVINE NUDGINGS

I have consciously tried, throughout this book, to keep responsibility where it belongs. When, for example, you struggle with a legacy of shame or guilt, instead of blaming your parents for your difficulties, I have suggested that the need to accept your own responsibility for bringing about healing change is critical. To rush around through life blaming others for your unhappiness is not only unproductive, it is simply not true. While others, such as parents or siblings, may have had a profound effect on your belief system and life, it is now up to you, as an adult, through awareness and desire, to change things.

Sadly, there are many people who prefer the role of victim, looking to charge others with causing life's unhappiness. In all probability, *victims* will remain so until thrust into new awareness through either pain or hurt. Even those who feel victimized will, eventually, have had enough. At that point, the process of change begins.

There is a risk in trying to talk about the activity of God in all of this. However, at this point, it becomes imperative—in my view—to not avoid a discussion of the place of God in change and growth. At the outset, I want to be very clear in stating that God is not at fault for life's struggles and difficulties. While I realize that such a view sounds as if I know what God is up to, I am only stating my thoughts surrounding tragedy. Unfortunately, there are many people who blame God for every curve ball thrown in life. Just as I mentioned before regarding victimization and blame, there is great danger in embracing your own "helplessness", as the quarry in the great hunt of life. Viewing God as some type of gigantic tyrant wandering around looking to squash people on a whim only serves to confirm a lifeview of powerlessness.

It is true that life is filled with both surprises and ambushes. There are sudden deaths and painful diagnoses. Husbands and wives are unfaithful and abusive to each other; children often pay enormous prices. Sometimes fathers sexually abuse daughters and men in alleys rape old women. Fortunes are made and lost in a single conversation in a board room. An old woman, living into her nineties, begs to die, while a thirty-two year old AIDS patient pleads for life. The World Series is interrupted with an earthquake, and the SuperBowl is overshadowed by the Gulf Conflict. Continuing on and on, there is a list of events, both personal and corporate, which can both devastate and elevate life.

Where is God in all of this? Is He active in earthquakes and wars? Does He mind it if you have cancer? What about His watchful eye when a teenager pulls a gun in the hallways of the high school? If the judge rules against you in the divorce hearings, does God get upset? Is it His fault that the Intensive Care nurse was on the telephone talking with her boyfriend when your mother went into a coma? Who's in charge here, anyway?

For decades I have struggled with the question of the involvement of God in the things of life. There were countless nights when I tried to strike a deal with God—a bargain of mutual benefit. If He would show up in my bedroom one night for only a ten minute conversation, I would belong to Him for life...even for five minutes I would travel to the mountains of Burma to tell others about Him. Sadly, He never showed up and for years I figured it was His loss—although, to tell you the truth, I like comfort and convenience too much to consider being much of a world ambassador for God. So, I never found the answer to my questions about God's place in all of the struggles and successes of life. Eventually, I realized that it was up to me to make sense out of all of the crazy stuff of daily life.

Today, I am a bit further along the road toward understanding. The one thing I have learned is that I don't know much of anything and probably never will when it comes to the stuff of God. Too many unexplained things occurred in my life that I had been absolutely sure were not helpful, only to discover a few months or years later that they were the most significant events ever to have happened to me. Apparently wrong decisions that I have watched other people make, in time, have spun around to be the most magnificent choices I could imagine. Job losses which seemed devastating have led to new and exciting careers. Financial ruin has twisted into relational gain. Chronic illness has led people to inner peace and contentment. On and on the list of surprises goes, and you certainly could add your own discoveries to it. The fact is that all we can understand of God is that we can't understand much of anything.

For me, I have arrived at a spot where I accept

responsibility for the things that happen in my life, both the seemingly good and bad. By *responsibility,* I am not speaking of self-blame, which so easily occurs, but rather the *ability* to *respond,* to answer back to life's blows and blessings. When, for example, you find yourself called into the boss's office to be told your position is being eliminated, you have several options before you. In anger, you can lash out at your supervisor, the company, or God; or, you can get even by selling company secrets to a competitor. Blaming yourself, you can engage in self-destructive behavior, or turn on your spouse to blow up the relationship. If, however, you choose to be responsible in this event, you consciously—with your best interest in mind—answer back in wisdom, awareness, desire, and self-love.

Such a drastic course of action releases the need to retaliate or self-destruct. Instead, coming from a *higher place* within, the *answer back* can only lead to a new and exciting road in life. However, a decision of this higher type seldom comes easily when we are in pain or fear. Usually, we find ourselves doing what we have always done when faced with the unknown or hurtful—we strike out.

It is precisely at this point that I believe God acts in our life. In a true sense, there seems to be a "Divine Nudging" which takes place each time we are faced with a conscious choice as to how to respond to life's presentations. Being fired, hearing from your spouse that the marriage is over, or listening to your child explain why he or she stole a gold bracelet all present you with the opportunity to *respond* from either a place of fear or trust. If you rant, rave, scream, blame, hit, accuse, or retaliate, it means you are coming from a place of fear in your life. In all likelihood, instead of *responding,* you are *reacting;* the difference between the two is monumental.

When you *react,* for the most part, there is little conscious choice. Instead, there is simply a self-protective instinct which is called into play, a way of taking care of you. Unfortunately, reaction is seldom the most helpful method of good self-care. *Responding,* on the other hand, is a conscious decision to answer back to the issues at hand. It is also a way of taking care of yourself, but in opposition to reaction, responding always pushes toward positive growth and movement in your life.

"Divine Nudging" does not occur in reaction; you are too busy or fearful to feel anything at all except the need for self-protection. However, when you are responsible, since it is a conscious choice to answer back, awareness is always present. In the awareness, as I understand it, comes the Divine Nudging of God. Events themselves are not the issues, nor is blame the key factor, rather, it is the conscious awareness of the Nudging of God which is central. Choosing to blame God or others when life throws you a curve ball usually leads to reaction and stuckness. Listening to the Divine Nudgings of God in the midst of struggle means that you are living in awareness with the greatest potential for positive change and growth.

As I understand it, God is constantly whispering into our heart and mind. Awareness and desire are the necessary ingredients to assist us in the listening process. On the other hand, fear, mistrust, and blame play such a loud tune that many times we cannot hear the Nudging, thus leading to reactions and stonewalling. The question is not: why does God cause difficulties in life, or, when is God going to make everything better? Instead, the more appropriate consideration is: in my awareness, what is the higher way being whispered in my ear?

I first met Eric when he came to my office with a generous offer to donate a new sound system for the hospital chapel. A tall, friendly man, Eric said that he had not been a good "church-goer," a fact of which he was ashamed. Recently, however, he told me, "I've had a change of heart regarding my relationship with God; I want to do something with my life." Several times during the next two or three months, Eric came to the hospital accompanied by sound engineers. Together they worked diligently to install a new sound system, a gift for which I was most grateful.

Approximately six months later, I was astonished to discover Eric's name on our hospice census sheet. Diagnosed with lung cancer, he had been given approximately three to six months to live. The next day I visited him in his hospital room. Although he greeted me kindly, he seemed to be distant and somewhat angry. Dismissing his shift in personality as typical of any man facing death, I asked him to tell me about his illness.

"What's to tell?" he said to me spreading his hands apart and shrugging his shoulders. "I've got lung cancer and the friendly doc gives me less than half a year." He studied me for awhile; I decided to keep still. "You know how it is, Chaplain, you play the hand you're dealt. I'm fifty-seven years old; my kids are married and living on their own, so I guess it's my turn. It doesn't matter if I've got other plans or not, the Big Guy upstairs has other ideas, I guess." He pointed toward the sky, and then shook his fist upward.

"It doesn't seem very fair," I told him.

"Come on now, Chaplain. You know better than that. Who ever said life was fair? Some people get richer and live longer; some of us get screwed."

During the next few weeks, I visited Eric several times, both in the hospital and in his home. On one visit to his home, we sat together at the kitchen table. "You know the crazy thing about all of this," he said to me, holding his oxygen tube away from his nose, "is that this thing should have been caught a long time ago."

"You mean your cancer?" I asked him.

Nodding he said, "Exactly." He paused a few seconds to take some deep breaths. "I'd been a smoker my whole life, you know. Started when I was fifteen; I quit just last year." He laughed with sarcasm, "Two months later I get diagnosed with the Big C."

"Were you having any symptoms before you quit?"

"Well, just a little bleeding," he said.

I suppose I looked somewhat incredulous. "A little bleeding?" I repeated.

"Yeah," he nodded his head. "Well, to tell you the truth, I have been coughing up a little blood now and then for the past couple of years, but it was dark colored blood. You know, the kind you don't have to worry about."

"I thought you always had to worry about coughing blood," I told him. "I didn't know that color had anything to do with it."

"Sure," he said, "as long as it's dark colored, it just means you have an infection or something." He paused again while he struggled to gain some breath. "But then one day a few months ago, I was doing some painting down in my friend's shore house when I started to cough pretty bad. This time, the blood was bright red. That's when I knew I had to get to the doctor."

"Was that about the time you installed the new sound system in the chapel?" I wondered to him.

"Just about then," he grinned at me a little, " I guess I tried to tell God that I would do a lot of good for Him if He would take away this damned disease." His face grew serious, "I can't understand it. I mean, here I am ready to really get involved in my religion and God decides to pull the plug on me. I don't understand why God is doing this to me."

As I left his house and was driving back to the hospital, I couldn't help but be astonished at Eric's thinking and belief system. It seemed to be beyond my wildest thoughts to think that any man who smoked heavily for more than forty years, and had been coughing blood for at least twenty months, could have the audaciousness to question why God "did" this to him?

Eric died a few weeks later, feeling betrayed and victimized by God. Furious that his attempt at bargaining had failed, and unwilling to accept any responsibility for his failure to attend to his own body, Eric blamed God for the development and process of his disease. When I tried to gently help him to see another side to his sense of victimization, he told me that if God didn't "give" him the cancer, He, at least, "allowed" it to proceed, even after his serious willingness to embrace religion with enthusiasm.

Shortly before he died, Eric asked me to baptize him. "I've been a bastard most of my life," he admitted, "so I suppose I had this coming. After all, the piper always gets paid."

"How do you know that?" I asked him.

"Well, first of all, I know it because my old man told me, and so did his old man. Beyond that, it's always been true. I don't think I've ever gotten away with a damned thing in my life."

As Eric shared with me the story of his upbringing, I could see the impact of a critical-based family legacy spilling out everywhere. He was disciplined severely each time he broke even the most minor of rules. Several times he was tied to an old water pump in the backyard of their farmhouse. "They treated me like a damn dog," Eric cried, gasping for breath all the time. It was clear that Eric's notion of his parents as police officers, judge, and jury had totally been projected onto God, the ultimate authority and disciplinarian.

MOVING TOWARD SACRED LOVE

Never truly feeling "in the good graces of God," Eric lived most of his life in spiritual pain. Feeling separated or isolated from all goodness, he was unable to allow any spiritual comfort or peace into his life, even during his final days. As strange as it may seem, his entire life had been one of reaction, almost totally devoid of responding to life's presentations or curve balls. Instead of trying to consciously listen to any Divine Nudgings, Eric erupted in reactionary anger and blame. Rather than allow desire or longing for connection to enter in, he remained convinced that he deserved exactly what he was getting, even though he shook his fist at heaven from time to time.

It has become increasingly apparent to me that the process of awareness, in which Divine Nudging can be felt or heard, is a very narrow path. Perhaps when Jesus was talking about the difficulty of the narrow way, he was not referring so much to morality or behavior, as he was to getting *in tune* with God. Listening to the God-part of yourself calls for willingness and commitment. In contrast, it is so easy to wander into the detours of the world. Television, making money, sex, and boredom—none of which are wrong—are only a few of the slides off the narrow track. Like most of the things we bump into in life, they distract us from awareness or desire.

Like it or not, the Eastern World has much to teach us regarding the conscious, mindful movement toward connecting with God. Recalling that I am not discussing religion at this point, but rather spirituality, there are so many diversions in life that steer us away from hearing the Divine Nudgings, we constantly find ourselves back in spiritual pain.

Even beyond the normal seductions of life, there is one more major obstacle which keeps us from the movement from spiritual pain toward spiritual wholeness. Unfortunately, it is our own sense of self which holds us in separateness and isolation. The struggle with self-hatred and self-deprivation works to keep us feeling alone and unworthy in a world that cries out for connection. Simply believing that you are not worthy of Divine Nudgings can close up your mind and heart. Again, as one who is smarter than God, you obviously know that you are merely too inadequate for His guidance, peace, or inner presence.

The next, and final chapter, will continue the sacred journey from spiritual pain toward spiritual wholeness by looking at the incredible place of self-forgiveness and self-acceptance in this entire process. Without the willingness to embrace yourself, awareness and desire will provide only half the resources you need to experience and connect with God. The constant and consistent Divine Nudgings in your life, even as you are reading these words, will go unheeded and unfelt if you hold on to your self-condemning conclusions. Rooted in your legacy and affirmed by your religion, the sacred journey to connection can only begin with the connection between you and *You*.

CHAPTER XX

A NEW VISION

"What weapons has the lion but himself?"

John Keats

"Let the other side also have a hearing."

Seneca

"There is that in me...
I do not know what it is...
But I know it is in me."

Walt Whitman

Judy wrestled with the bag of charcoal briquettes, dragging them out of the garage and onto the patio. She was feeling particularly elated about the meal she was planning on serving to her husband, Charlie. It was thirteen years ago this night that they had met. She still remembered with fondness their chance meeting on the boardwalk, bumping into each other with their ice creams cones colliding. His vanilla and her chocolate had merged, symbolic of what was to come for the two of them.

Pouring the charcoal into the bottom of the grill, Judy squirted the lighter fluid onto the briquettes. Striking a match, she smiled to herself thinking of what Charlie would say about having his steaks done with real charcoal flavor, instead of the gas grill taste he was always complaining about. Glancing at her watch, she was delighted to see she had enough time to relax with her new book. Dinner time was still an hour away and she had everything ready except the steaks. Tonight would be a special night for them, she thought, as she folded her body down into the backyard hammock.

Thirty minutes later Judy stood staring down at the slightly smoking charcoal; her hand told her that there was little, if any, heat rising from the grill. She glanced at her watch as she squirted more lighter fluid on the coals. Feeling some panic, since Charlie always liked to eat on time, Judy dropped another match into the middle of the briquettes; a flame leaped in the air. Ten minutes later, however, it was clear that this special dinner would not be on time. She was fanning the briquettes with a magazine as Charlie drove up the driveway. Judy's heart sank.

Charlie sat patiently on the patio, reading the paper and watching Judy cook the steaks. As she poked a fork into the meat, Judy started to feel hopeful again; they could still have their celebration. As she was busily getting the salads out of the refrigerator, Charlie went into the bedroom, only to emerge almost instantly with his softball shirt on. "I'm going to have to go now," he said to her. "Keep my steak wrapped for me and I'll have it when I get home."

Judy was astonished, "I didn't know you had a game tonight," she said to Charlie.

"Oh come off it, Judy," he picked up his glove from the kitchen shelf, "I told you last Monday that I was subbing for Bill tonight. Maybe if you'd get your nose out of a book long enough to hear what's going on, you wouldn't get so many surprises." Putting his ball cap on, Charlie left the house.

Eating her steak, alone, Judy struggled to blink back her tears. She stared at the charcoal, burning brilliantly now, and cursed her own stupidity and poor planning. Her delightful evening of special time for her and Charlie had crashed around her head. By the time Charlie arrived home, she was in bed watching television.

"Aren't you coming down?" Charlie asked her as he peeled off his ball shirt.

"Well, to tell you the truth," Judy ventured, "I'm feeling hurt about what happened earlier with the steaks. I didn't know you had a ball game, and you sat there for thirty minutes without saying anything. If you'd said something, maybe I could have fixed the steaks on the gas grill. It's just that you hurt my feelings."

Charlie waved his hand at her and with a voice dripping with disgust said, "Oh, for God's sake Judy, grow up. I want a wife, not a child." With that, he left the room and went downstairs.

Two days later in her therapy session, Judy spoke angrily of her feelings of her husband's insensitivity. "I wanted so much for it to be a special evening," she said. "And now I realize that it's all my fault that it got messed up. I never seem to do anything right; Charlie always says that too, you know. 'Judy, you always start things without thinking them through, and then you end up upset because everything blows apart.'"

"Is that true?" I asked her.

She nodded her head, "Most of the time it is. It seems like I have time enough to do something, and then, somehow or other, the time creeps up on me and I end up rushing like crazy to finish. Just like this time, it always ends up wrong, and it's my fault. I don't know when I'll ever learn."

"So you're angry at yourself, not Charlie," I said.

"Why would I be mad at him?" Judy asked me. "He's not the one who messed up the meal. It's just like he said last night, 'Why would you be hurt? I'm the one who paid for the steak and I'm the one who didn't get to eat it!'"

When I pressed Judy about Charlie's part in not sharing his schedule for the evening, she said, "I should have known, and if I had listened to him earlier in the week, this never would have happened."

In many ways, Judy is an example of the countless numbers of people who rush around through life blaming and condemning themselves for things that don't turn out right. Even discounting Charlie's part in the barbecue fiasco, Judy is unable to allow herself the space to make a mistake. Her sense of total accountability for the cold charcoal and uncooked steaks simply illustrates an unwillingness to see life through any other eyes than those of self-blame and judgment. When I suggested that perhaps she was being a bit hard on herself, she snapped, "That's easy for you to say; you weren't the one who ruined the evening!"

Hating herself with enormous energy, Judy could not bring herself to consider another way of looking at the evening. To talk with her about the desire to gain a new awareness toward her self-condemning view only fell on deaf ears. Sadly, like Judy, there are many people who are so filled with loathing and self-hatred that only by remaining in pain can they arrive at the necessary and proper punishments. For Judy, to think of embracing herself as a way of self-nurturing would be unthinkable; she is unable to believe she deserves something as valuable and redemptive as self-love. Instead, suffering seems to be the far better way to go; punishment, the more familiar road.

A disastrous evening, such as the one Judy described, is an illustration of that which I called Divine Nudgings in the previous chapter. In the uncooked steak event was the possibility for an entire shift of perspective, the potential for movement from self-condemnation to self-love. Judy sees the evening as a nightmarish example of her inability to plan, a true illustration of her ineffective brain. Her self-hating judgments are the very thoughts which separate her from God, keeping her in spiritual pain and punishment. In choosing to see the evening as one more example of her flawed abilities, Judy misses the Divine Nudging toward attitudinal and relational healing. Unfortunately, she also sets herself up for another round of disasters sometime in the future. Simply put, God keeps nudging us until we begin the process of movement toward spiritual wholeness. And, as difficult as it is to believe, the events themselves are meaningless; only the responses toward or against growth have any value. For Judy, the next opportunity for growth may occur when she accidentally backs into a shopping cart in the supermarket parking lot. If that happens, one more time she has the chance to embrace her humanity with love and understanding. If not, another opportunity will occur as surely as the moon spins around the earth.

REALITY OR ACTUALITY?

Moving toward spiritual wholeness is a sacred journey, but that does not mean the path is smooth. For anyone who has tried to listen to the whispers of love, a major voice of the Divine Nudgings, the ruts and speed bumps in the road are quickly felt. The highway from spiritual pain toward spiritual wholeness is windy, hilly, and uncertain. Time and time again, you may want to go back to the old ways and beliefs. Self-hatred and condemnation seem always easier than self-love and acceptance. After all, for most of us, the old way is so familiar, and we are so good at it.

As I have personally struggled with this process toward spiritual wholeness, it seems to me there is no recourse to the removal of the road blocks of self-condemnation short of conscious desire to *see things differently*. Until you are willing, or have the desire, to take another look at your decisions and judgments about yourself, others, and the world, you will remain absolutely stuck in the old ways of fear, pain, and punishment. This means you need to discover the tiny spark of self-care, deep down inside all of us, that will allow you to open your eyes and mind for the possibilities of *another way of looking at yourself*. Without that one little ounce of self-care that gives you permission for a different vision, you will stay in the rut of self-condemnation and judgment. It is because of this need for permission to see differently that desire is so important to change and inner growth toward self-acceptance.

Attempting to find a way to see life differently, several years ago I sat down to watch a video tape of a presentation on forgiveness. Although the quality of the tape was horrendous, and the picture virtually non-recognizable, I heard the speaker talking about reality and actuality in terms which were unfamiliar to me. In that brief half hour, a great deal of my life was changed, and I am grateful to Dr. Michael Ryce for opening my eyes to a new vision. My suspicion is that Divine Nudging took place in my life on that particular afternoon. Perhaps I listened more carefully because the picture was so poor or because my life was in such absolute chaos and pain; nevertheless, I started to see differently on that day. In some way it pushed me over a monumental speed bump along the journey toward spiritual wholeness.

Since that time, I have worked hard to put this awareness into my life. In many ways, it was another impetus for this book: a need to share important discoveries with others as a way of helping them to *see with vision* instead of ordinary sight. Marion's story may help illustrate the trap of seeing life in the old way, and the incredible freedom found in seeing things differently.

Marion pulled into the church parking lot shortly before the 11:00 A.M. service. She had deliberately chosen the eleven o'clock service since Connie and Bob might be there. The two previous weeks she had missed them and had hopes of seeing her daughter and son-in-law today. Her face lit up as she saw Connie's van parked across the lot. Walking through the rear doors of the church, Marion was delighted to see Connie and Bob standing inside; they had not yet entered the sanctuary. Connie came over to her mother.

"Hi Mom, it's so good to see you," she said, embracing her mother and kissing her cheek.

"Hi Mom," Bob said. Marion noticed that he was not smiling. Well, she wasn't going to let him spoil her time with Connie; she gave him a hug.

"We're going out for brunch after Mass," Connie said. "Would you like to come with us?"

Marion noticed that Bob had moved nearer the entrance to the sanctuary. "Oh, I'd love to, if it's all right with Bob," she told Connie.

Connie smiled at her and took her arm, "I'm sure it is. Now come on, let's get inside or Father Sullivan will start without us." As they knelt down, Marion glanced over at Bob.

His face was staring ahead with no clue as to his mood or feelings. "It was," she said to herself, "downright cold."

This brief scene begins to illustrate the contrast between sight and vision; it also is an example of the difference between *reality* and *actuality*. When Marion looked at Bob, even though he had greeted her, he was not smiling. If others had been observing this scene, they too would have noticed his face was expressionless. It was an observable fact; indeed, Bob was not smiling. This physical fact is an **Actuality;** it can be seen, observed, and agreed upon. It **actually** happened that Bob did not smile.

If you were able to crawl inside Marion's head, you would hear a small voice telling her that the reason Bob did not smile was because he did not like her. Perhaps he was unhappy that she had arrived at the eleven o'clock service or maybe he simply was displeased at seeing her. This voice whispering inside Marion's head is very familiar to most of us since we all have one. It is the voice of conclusions, judgments, and history which tells us all sorts of interesting things. In this instance, it told Marion that her son-in-law was unhappy to see her. There is, of course, no way for Marion to know if her conclusion was the truth; she simply accepts it as if it is. In effect, Marion is judging Bob's **Actuality** and arriving at her own conclusions.

With this judgment of Bob's unsmiling face, Marion's inner voice talks to her of his dislike of her. This conversation invariably leads to several assumptions on her part, some based on her previous relationship with Bob, and others rooted in her own fears and self-doubts. These thoughts, then, become Marion's **Reality.** They are not necessarily accurate or reliable, and since her thoughts have not been checked out with Bob, they strictly belong to Marion. And for the most part, Marion believes her conclusions are accurate.

A **Reality,** then, is a judgment of an **Actuality.** It is personal, subjective, and normally rooted in the past. Most of us walk around all the time with our heads filled with **Reality** thoughts. A friend says that he will call me, but then doesn't. The **Actuality** is that my friend did not call. My **Reality** may be that he is angry at me. If I am from a fear-based legacy, my **Reality** may be that he has broken off the friendship, or worse, that something terrible or awful has happened to him.

A NEW VISION

If there are twelve people in a room and someone enters and tips over the waste paper basket, there will be twelve **Realities.** Everyone in the room observed the basket being tipped over; it was an **Actuality.** Why the basket was spilled becomes everyone's **Reality.** Someone may think it was deliberate; another might believe it was an accident. There may be a person present who feels the one who tipped the basket is an escapee from the nearby state mental hospital. Each person will listen to his or her inner whispers and arrive at a **Reality** conclusion.

Kneeling beside the pew, Marion notices Bob's "stone face." Again, her conclusion is that he is unhappy with her presence. Since, for most of us, the business of life is the **Confirmation of Realities**, Marion now has two **Actualities** from which to draw her conclusions. He did not smile in the outer room, and his face is "stone" in the sanctuary. Perhaps, she thinks, he does not want her to go to breakfast with them. He may think that she is intruding on their privacy. Marion, like all of us, builds one **Reality** on top of another. During the Mass, she notices that Bob does not sing any of the hymns, something he normally does with some gusto. Also, he does not bother to open the Mass book to any of the readings. Both of these **Actualities** simply lead Marion to more confirmation of her **Reality:** namely, Bob is unhappy that she is there, and this is his way of showing it.

Bob, on the other hand, is having a struggle of his own. On Friday evening he was called in to the boss's office and informed that his position was being terminated. Besides being a tremendous shock, since he had not seen anything of this sort coming toward the direction of his department, he was also suffering with shame. As of yet, he had not told Connie because he was too afraid of her reaction. Only the other evening they had been talking about the time being right to begin their family. Now, he found himself in a terrible position of telling Connie the baby would have to be postponed. Having been raised in a legacy in which the male was the chief provider and problem solver, Bob felt paralyzed; he did not know what to do. In one brief conversation with his boss, he suddenly found himself feeling like a failure both to his wife and to his legacy. If he couldn't even tell his wife, how would he be able to tell his father, who boasted of his son's success to his cronies on the golf course? At that moment, Bob would have preferred to sit at home rather than attend Mass. He had, however, promised Connie Mass and brunch. Perhaps, he had thought, he could gather enough courage to tell Connie at brunch. With her mother here, however, he realized it would have to wait. Bob was deeply troubled and afraid, and his entire being reflected his fear.

As the worship serviced ended and they walked outside, Bob said to Connie, "You know, I'm not feeling so well. I think that you and your mom should go out to brunch, and I'll go home and rest a while."

At that precise moment as she listened to her **Reality**, Marion **knew** that Bob was unhappy with her. She believed that he was lying because he did not want her to go to lunch with them. "Don't be silly," she said to both of them, "We'll do it another time. I'm sorry you're not feeling well, Bob. Is it stomach trouble?" He didn't answer. "Now Connie, I want you to take your husband home and tend to him. He is the chief bread winner, you know, and we've got to keep him healthy." With that, Marion gave Connie a big hug and patted Bob on his arm. As she walked back toward her car, Marion's **Reality** was given an exclamation point: she **knew** Bob did not want her with them. She thought about following them to see if they really were going home or if they would go out to brunch without her. Instead, she went to the drug store in the plaza to pick up a Sunday paper.

As she was driving home, Marion happened to glance over toward the parking lot of the local pancake house. There was Connie's van, parked there as big as life! In an instant Marion was both outraged and heartbroken. She continued on home and went to bed. Lying in her shade-pulled bedroom, Marion sobbed and wondered what she had done to deserve such an uncaring and cold son-in-law? Hadn't she tried to include him in everything, as well as to avoid any interference in their lives? Having experienced a dreadful time with her own mother-in-law, she had promised herself to give her children whatever space and distance they needed. And yet, here she was, alone and feeling hurt on a Sunday afternoon, when other families were together enjoying themselves.

Later on in the afternoon, Bob found himself driving toward his mother-in-law's home. He had finally found the courage to tell Connie the bad news about his job and was quite surprised at the supportive way she had handled things. Although she was naturally upset, she hadn't carried on in the way that he had feared. Now he needed to do something physical to release some of the tension and anger he was feeling inside. For Bob, chopping wood was one of the best releases for his physical stress. Unfortunately, his ax was over at Marion's house where he had left it a few weeks ago when he had chopped some firewood for her.

Driving up the driveway, he spotted Marion's car in the garage. He sighed deeply because he did not want to deal with his mother-in-law today; he felt too weary. However, he knocked on her door since he knew that Marion would be upset if he simply took his ax and left without saying a word to her. Upstairs in her darkened room, Marion had drifted into a deep sleep and didn't hear Bob's knock. After a few minutes Bob assumed that Marion was either sleeping or in the bathroom, so he went into the shed, retrieved his ax, and left.

Marion sat up in bed as she realized that she had heard a noise. Looking out the window, she saw Bob putting the ax in the back seat of his car. She knocked on the window and waved, but he was getting into the front seat; seconds later, he drove off. Wandering downstairs, Marion felt devastated. She couldn't believe that Bob had come over to retrieve his ax without saying a word to her. It was not that the ax was a problem for Marion; she knew that it belonged to Bob. The pain came in the realization that he had not even been polite enough to tell her he was taking it back. "Why," Marion said to herself, "even a neighbor would at least be civil enough to speak to me." One more time, Marion's **Reality** came into focus as she determined the poor manners and lack of consideration of her son-in-law.

For much of the week, Marion struggled with her pain and disappointment. Feeling slighted and ignored by her children, she began to slip into a depression. Each day seemed more difficult than the one before. On a whim, Marion picked up the telephone and called Father Sullivan to ask for an appointment.

The next day she sat in Father Sullivan's study telling him about Bob and his treatment of her. She described his cold greeting when she came to Mass on Sunday. Relating Bob's "stone face," she started to cry when she told the priest about

Bob's lie about brunch. Sobbing, she told him of her depression and feelings of being unloved. "I couldn't believe that he just drove out of the driveway without so much as a word to me," she said as she described Bob's **Actuality.**

When she finished her story, Father Sullivan sat quietly for a moment and then said, "You know, Marion, it sounds to me like you need to do some work on forgiveness. Your feelings of anger and hurt toward Bob are injuring you; they're making you depressed, and if you're not careful, they'll make you sick. I think you need to forgive Bob."

Marion was horrified. The last thing she expected was that **she** would have to be the one to do any bending; throughout their entire relationship she had been giving and looking the other way. After all, Bob was the one who did the ignoring, gave the cold looks, and drove off without speaking. Why, then, should she be the one to have to forgive? Besides that, she realized, she really didn't want to forgive Bob. What had he done to deserve forgiveness? If anything, Bob should be *asking* for forgiveness because of the way that he had treated her. This was asking too much.

"I don't think I'm that generous or kind to overlook the terrible things he's done to me," Marion told Father Sullivan. "Bob certainly hasn't given me any indication that he's sorry for the way he treated me."

Father Sullivan smiled, "Well then," he said as he put his hands together, "maybe we need to get some help from above for this one. Prayer does make a difference, you know." He closed his eyes; Marion bowed her head. "Almighty God, Father of us all, and Grantor of much wisdom," Father Sullivan prayed, "your daughter, Marion, has been injured by the insensitivities and coldness of her son-in-law. Help her, I beseech you, to find a quiet place in her heart to forgive him for his foolish ways. Open her heart that she might show the same grace to this young sinner that your Son gave to the world. And, I pray that you will touch the heart of this troubled man that his eyes might be opened to the higher way, Your path to truth and light. In the name of the Father, and of the Son, and of the Holy Spirit. Amen."

As Father Sullivan ushered her out of the door of his office, Marion was vaguely aware that she was supposed to thank him for helping her to feel better. The problem was, however, that she somehow or other felt more angry than before. Just like in the past, she had been the one asked to do the giving, the one to show the compassionate heart, whatever that meant. Driving home, she resolved, however, that the only way through this terrible situation was to try harder not to let Bob's immature behavior bother her. She would simply numb herself against his unkindness, a sort of inoculation against the pain of disappointment.

TRUE FORGIVENESS

Marion's problem is not unique. At one time or another, all of us have struggled with feeling injured or overlooked by another. We have felt the pain of being misunderstood or ignored. There have been times when the injury has been deliberate; other times we have not been certain. Husbands and wives betray one another, children are abused by parents who themselves were victimized, and people rob one another in countless ways. Employers manipulate employees, who in turn pass on their frustration in the treatment of co-workers or family members. Both men and women lie, sometimes for personal gain, other times for safety. Words and actions can quickly become untrustworthy as we try to maneuver our way through this unpredictable world.

There are thousands of Bob and Marion episodes with just as many frustrated and angry outcomes. Eventually people may find themselves simply trying to Novocain themselves against relationships and the possibility of further pain. Any hope of forgiveness seems to get dashed the moment the injury is addressed. Instead of discovering relief and inner peace, many of us find ourselves more enraged or depressed at our experienced injuries. And, if we are not very careful, at best, the injuries continue, and at worst, relationships decay, stagnate, and die.

Central to all of this, and resting at the heart of the pain, is our concept of forgiveness. For most people, forgiving another sounds something like this: "I will try to be big enough, and kind enough, and mature enough to overlook the terrible and dastardly things you did to me. Of course, it would help if you would admit to me just exactly how awful and horrid you have been to me. And if you would beg me for my forgiveness, with sincerity and pain in your voice, I will attempt to find a place inside myself to forgive you for being such a bad person."

Unfortunately, this common concept of forgiveness assumes that we completely understand what happened in the "sin" which was committed against us. It implies that we have all the knowledge necessary to make the judgment against the other, and that our information is accurate and complete. In Marion's case, it simply means that she believes her **Reality** is the *truth*. Without having any understanding of Bob's situation, she **knows** that her conclusions are accurate. Standing in her pain, and believing she has the truth, she fully accepts the role of victim. Forgiveness, then, will have to wait until Bob dons the robe of villain and pleads for her mercy.

Sadly, we know more than Marion in this particular case. Just exactly what is it that she needs to forgive in her relationship with her son-in-law? Is it his coldness? His stone face? His driving off without speaking to her? The truth is that as long as Marion stands in the belief that her **Reality** is **The Truth**, she will never be able to have an open and loving relationship with Bob.

Instead of needing to forgive Bob, the unclouded fact is that Marion needs to forgive her **Reality.** It is her judgments, conclusions, and interpretations against Bob that need to be released. Then, and only then, will she be able to look at the relationship with any clarity and hope of healing. To do this, of course, means that she must have the *desire* to see the situation differently. Instead of standing in the role of victim, Marion needs to find that small place in her heart to see another way, to look through *vision* instead of judgmental sight. With the awareness that she does not know everything, nor carry around **The Truth**, perhaps Marion can give herself permission to seek the necessary desire to embrace a new vision.

Out of this new vision emerge all sorts of new possibilities. Marion may find that she can give Bob a chance in their relationship. Realizing that she *doesn't know everything,* Marion can begin "going to school" on the relationship with her son-in-law. Trying to hear his side of things, and encouraging him to share with her his hopes and fears, Marion can begin to build an appreciation for Bob. The awareness of his struggles will begin to shift her **Reality,** leading to a new, and hopefully, loving relationship with him. Instead of remaining in relational stagnation, Marion and Bob will find themselves in process.

Since **Realities** constantly shift as more and more information is gathered and assimilated, we will always be in the process of understanding others. The acknowledgment that *we do not know everything* leaves all relationships open to the possibility of grace and understanding. Most of us realize that we struggle a great deal more with the *intent* of people who injure us than with the actual injury itself. And assuming, for even a moment, that we know and understand the intent of others is a monumental assumption. It was not Bob's driving off without speaking that hurt Marion so much, rather it was the fact that he apparently didn't care enough about her to stop. She interpreted his behavior as deliberate and intentional. Opening to the possibility that she did not know everything released the judgment of intentionality against Bob.

TURNING TOWARD OURSELVES

If everybody went away,
leaving me alone one day.
The tragic fact of this would be
that now I'm stuck with only me!

And so it finally comes down to the self. As some wise sage said long ago, "You are the center of your own universe." Everything in this book has pointed to the power of the legacy in your life, as well as its effect on your definition of yourself. Indeed, you are a programmed person, filled with the teachings of the generations of your family. Added to this is the impact of our culture, our school teachers, priests and ministers, and the television set. Regardless of how hard you may work to clear away the thread of your childhood teachings, no one arrives at adulthood uncontaminated.

Since our society places such importance on relationships, most of us tend to notice the power of our legacy in marriage, work, and parenting. Seldom do we investigate the nature of the most important relationship we have: the relationship with ourselves. If you worry about the relationship with your spouse or boss, you can rush to the neighborhood bookstore and find hundreds of books telling you how to improve communication or discover video and audio tapes on conflict management. For the most part, however, *the central relationship* you have gets dismissed or ignored. The relationship between *you and you* is absolutely central to your peace, happiness, and contentment in life. As a matter of fact, without addressing the nature of the *you/you* relationship, all other relationships in your life will suffer, continually failing to reach anywhere near their full potential.

I have attempted, throughout this book, to show the countless number of ways the legacy has led all of us to certain definitions of the self. Self-hatred or loathing, self-abuse or injury, and self-judgment and condemnation all stem from the embracing of negative legacy teachings. Not only do these indictments of the self keep us from functioning with any degree of success in relationships with others, they also constantly keep us in spiritual pain and distant from God.

It is because of this dilemma that self-forgiveness is crucial. Before you can give yourself permission to enjoy the loving arms of God, you need to let go of all self-judgments which lead to the need for punishment and pain. Moving from spiritual pain toward spiritual wholeness begins with self-acceptance and forgiveness. Sadly, no one else can do this for us. It is not the forgiveness of others that you are seeking since, at your deepest part, you know that others do *not* truly know you. Nor is it the forgiveness of God that you are desperately craving, since He has already forgiven you. Rather, it is only the loving forgiveness of yourself that remains.

Although self-forgiveness seems difficult and illusive, it is neither. Instead, it occurs in the same fashion as forgiveness moves in external relationships. Just as Marion had her own **Reality** experiences in her relationship with Bob, we all have our personal **Reality** in our relationship with ourselves. Daily, and sometimes hourly, you judge yourself in a variety of ways. Looking at your behaviors and actions, which are your **Actualities,** you arrive at your own **Realities,** your conclusions and interpretations regarding yourself. Similarly to Marion's judgments, yours are equally mistaken and cruel to you.

There are, as Robert Bly points out in the Grimm's Fairy Tale, "The Gnome," "parts of you which do not wish you well." Each one of you carts around a judgmental and condemning self, only too happy to find you guilty. Keeping you in pain and distress, the relationship with yourself feeds your need for self-hatred. You and you are on a merry-go-round of actions (**Actualities**), judgments (**Realities**), and punishment (**Spiritual Pain**). It is an endless cycle of distress and unhappiness.

Self-forgiveness is not rooted in attempting to be gracious enough to overlook the stuff you do. No matter how motivated you may be to show kindness to yourself, that will never work. There is too much self-hatred and loathing within. Rather, the hope for movement rests in the little desire necessary for you to forgive your own **Realities.** Just as it is true that you do not know what makes others act or think the way they do, neither do you know much more about yourself, certainly not enough to arrive at a place of accurate judgment. Your **Realities** surrounding your own behavior are as confused and ignorant as those pointed in the directions of others. The road to self-forgiveness is paved with the willingness to see yourself differently by releasing your **Realities.**

Seldom do I listen to clients who dare to say they "did the best they could." Instead, I hear tortured stories of selfish behavior, cowardly actions, or intentional sins. To suggest to others that they consider these **Realities** by trying to see themselves differently seems almost unthinkable. The need for self-punishment and self-abuse is powerful, keeping them in distress and judgment.

The forgiveness of yourself does not come from God; it appears in your life when you are willing to see yourself *with a new vision.*

AND GOD'S PART?

Whenever I attempt to write or discuss God's part in anything, I get nervous. Realizing there are always those readers who are crying out for an absolute statement about the Almighty, I sympathize. Nevertheless, the truth is that the only thing I can be sure of about God is that I can't be sure of anything. My beliefs tell me that He is always surrounding and nudging me, whispering in my ear, and busy doing good. I haven't the slightest idea how or why, nor will I ever understand. And that's okay with me.

There is this part of me that says that whatever I can be at my finest, God is far beyond. Whenever I find myself doing good things, I am aware that I am only an extension of Him. If I manage to put my ego aside and do something loving, it may be a part of God, nevertheless it doesn't hold a candle to Him. When I write a powerful poem, or am filled with a vision of awe, I know that it doesn't come from me. And that's okay, too. Whatever I am, at my finest, is simply an expression of the love of a grace-filled God.

I don't worry about heaven or hell, nor do I fret about salvation. There are some friends, however, who suggest I should. Instead, I try to point myself and others toward a higher way, whatever that may be for them. The rest is in the hands of God; for me, that seems to be enough.

Self-forgiveness is your work with you. Divine forgiveness is God's work with His world; it's also His business and I try to keep out of it. If, however, you can attempt to look at yourself through the eyes of God, you can be sure that your **Reality** about yourself will change. While I understand that no one can truly see things as God sees them, if you allow your imagination to soar anywhere near your sense of the way God views His children, that will be good enough for enormous change. Self-love and acceptance will rush in whenever you see yourself with the vision you imagine God to have.

It is my belief and hope that God surrounds the world with His love and Spirit. Ours for the taking, we only have to breathe It in. Self-judgment keeps us holding our collective breaths in fear and separation; spiritual pain is the result. As Kabir wrote, "I laugh when I hear that the fish in the ocean is thirsty." Tragically, we swim around in the womb of God wondering where we are and why we feel so alone. On the other hand, self-love and forgiveness allow for giant gulps of spiritual air in the movement toward spiritual wholeness. The result is inner peace and joy.

The path toward spiritual wholeness is one of constant motion. It is my sense that the movements are of several kinds, and discussion of those is for another time. However, the movement toward spiritual wholeness is one from a life of *control* to one of *trust*. It is a motion from fear toward love, and from judgment toward grace. Spiritual wholeness is a process of leave-taking: from separation to union, and from conflict to peace.

May your journey be constant, your love ablaze, and your joy afire with His Light.

REFERENCES

I am extremely grateful to the following authors for their incredible leadership in the areas of spirituality, death and dying, and relationships:

BEATTIE, MELODY, *Codependent No More: How to Stop Controlling Others and Start Caring for Yourself*. Harper/Hazelden, 1987.

BERTMAN, SANDRA, *Facing Death*: Images, Insights, and Interventions, 1991, Hemisphere Publishing Co., New York City.

FOSSUM, MERLE A., & MASON, MARILYN J., *Facing Shame*, W. W. Norton & Company, New York and London, 1986.

FOX, MATTHEW, *Original Blessing: A Primer in Creation Spirituality*, Bear & Company, Sante Fe, New Mexico, 1983.

FRANZ, MARIE LOUISE VON, *Interpretation of Fairytales*, Spring Publications, Inc., Dallas, Texas, 1970.

FRANZ, MARIE LOUISE VON, *Shadow and Evil in Fairytales*, Spring Publications, Inc., Dallas, Texas, 1987.

KAUFMAN, GERSHEN, *Shame, The Power of Caring*, Schenkman Publishing Company, Inc., Cambridge, Massachusetts, 1980.

HOOPER, JUDITH, & TERESI, DICK, *The 3—Pound Universe: The Brain*, Dell Publishing Co., Inc., New York, New York, 1986.

JAMPOLSKY, GERALD G., *Love Is Letting Go Of Fear*, Bantam Books, New York City, 1981.

LERNER, HARRIET GOLDHOR, *The Dance of Intimacy*, Harper and Row Publishers, New York, New York, 1989.

LEVINE, STEPHEN, *Who Dies?*, Anchor Books/Doubleday, Garden City, New York, 1982.

LEVINE, STEPHEN, *Healing Into Life and Death*, Anchor Books/Doubleday, Garden City;, New York, 1987.

LUKEMAN, BRENDA, *Embarkations: A Guide to Dealing with Death and Parting*, Prentice Hall, Inc., Englewood Cliffs, N.J., 1982.

MANDEL, BOB, *Open Heart Surgery*, Celestial Arts Publishing Co., Berkeley, California, 1984.

NISKER, WES, *Crazy Wisdom*, Ten Speed Press, Berkeley, California, 1990.

VITRAY-MEYEROVITCH, EVAN DE, *Rumi and Sufism*, Post-Appolo Press, Sausalito, California, 1987 (printed in English)

WEGSCHEIDER-CRUISE, SHARON, *Learning To Love Yourself*, Health Communications, Inc., Deerfield Beach, Floria, 1987.

YANCEY, PHILIP, *Where is God When It Hurts?*, Zondervan Publishing House, Grand Rapids, Michigan, 1977.

ALSO

A Course In Miracles, Foundation for Inner Peace, Tiburon, California, 1970.